Essays

on

Gospel Topics

Essays

on
Gospel Topics

by
Whitney N. Horning

With God,
All Things are Possible.
By Faith,
All Things are Accomplished.

Contents

Essay 1

Becoming a Subject Matter Expert on the Lord

Whitney N. Horning

©January 19, 2023[1]

Borrowing from the 13th century poet, Rumi, and St. John the Beloved:

> Our lamps are different, but the Light is the same.
> The Light flows toward us from all people and all things.
> Our Lamps are different, but the Light is the same.
> One matter, one energy, one Light.
> Jesus Christ is the true Light.
> In Him was the power of life
> And this power was conveyed into the cosmos
> As the Light in mankind and everything.
> His Light shines in the chaos,
> But those in darkness have not been able to grasp it.
> Our Lamps are different, but the Light is the same.[2]

---

[1] This talk was given at the premiere of "Who Killed Joseph Smith, Part 2: Redemption" by Justin Griffin on January 19, 2023, held at the megaplex theater, Thanksgiving Point, Lehi, Utah.

[2] I combined portions of a poem titled "The Lamps are Different, but the Light is the Same" by Rumi with words from The Testimony of St. John 1:1 retrieved from https://scriptures.info/scriptures/tc/toj/1.1#1 and https://medicine.hsc.wvu.edu/News/Story?headline=the-lamps-are-different-butlight-issame#:~:text=%E2%80%9CThe%20lamps%20are%20different%2C%20but,%2C%20states%2C%20countries%20and%20continents. All scriptural references in the talk are from the Restoration Edition of the scriptures

Every person born on this earth has sacrificed some level of progression, risking all they had previously attained, to come to a fallen world in an attempt to gain more light and truth and to further progress. Situated as we are, it is up to us, and no one else, to choose whether we will progress or regress. The nature of this fallen world affords each of us ample opportunities to taste the bitter that we may come to know to prize the good, to learn to discern for ourselves between the Light of truth and the darkness of error.[3]

> The glory of God is intelligence, or in other words, light and truth. Light and truth forsake that evil one. Every spirit of man was innocent in the beginning, and God having redeemed man from the Fall, man became again, in their infant state, innocent before God. And that wicked one comes and takes away light and truth, through disobedience, from the children of men, and because of the tradition of their fathers.[4]

The "tradition of their fathers" includes religious traditions, which can often pose the most challenging obstacles to overcome in our search for light and truth.

The Lord has issued this warning:

> They that will harden their hearts, to them is given the lesser portion of the word until they know nothing concerning his mysteries; and then they are taken

---

which can be read for free online at scriptures.info or purchased at scriptures.shop. Rumi, or Jalāl al-Dīn Muḥammad Rūmī, also known as Jalāl al-Dīn Muḥammad Balkhī, Mevlânâ/Mawlānā and Mevlevî/Mawlawī, was a 13th-century Persian poet, Hanafi faqih, Islamic scholar, Maturidi theologian and Sufi mystic originally from Greater Khorasan in Greater Iran. He was born September 30, 1207, and died December 17, 1273.

[3] OC Genesis 4:8.

[4] T&C 93:11.

captive by the Devil and led by his will down to destruction. Now this is what is meant by the chains of hell.[5]

In our fallen world, mankind is prone to wander and to stray. Joseph Smith taught that "so great the frailties and imperfections of men" that unless we come to understand and believe in the correct character, perfections, and attributes of God, "the faith necessary unto life and salvation could not exist. . . . For doubt would take the place of faith, and those who know their weakness and liability to sin would be in constant doubt of salvation."[6]

Those who do not harden their hearts have reason to hope, for the Lord has promised that to them is given the greater portion of the word, until it is given unto them to know the mysteries of God, until they know them in full.[7] The greatest mystery of Godliness that we can discover is who God is. Each of us can become a subject matter expert in coming to know the Lord for ourselves. As we do, the by-product is that our faith will increase by degrees until we no longer have faith, but an actual knowledge that He exists.

My family's journey toward the fullness of the Gospel has encompassed the study and research of a number of religious topics which we believe will help us come to know and better understand the Lord. This includes studying the lives and teachings of those who have been in God's presence and received words of Eternal Life from Him while in the flesh. We desire to know and give heed to whatever true messengers

---

[5] NC—BofM Alma 9:3.
[6] T&C 110 LoF 3:20 and 4:1.
[7] NC—BofM Alma 9:3.

teach and reveal about the mysteries of Godliness.

Two of those individuals are Joseph and Hyrum Smith.

In a prophecy delivered through Joseph of Egypt, the Lord mentioned Joseph Smith Jr. 22 times.[8] This should cause us to be much more circumspect about how we judge, criticize, and evaluate the life and teachings of a man whom the Lord trusted, loved, and called friend. My book *Joseph Smith Revealed: A Faithful Telling* came about because I had a yearning desire to know God, specifically, what They really think about Their daughters.[9] I also felt compelled to determine whether Joseph Smith was a true prophet or a fallen one. This led me into a deep dive on the issue of polygamy. I felt that in order to truly come to a full understanding of this topic, I needed to open myself up to source material from a multitude of perspectives.[10]

My most recent book, *Hyrum Smith: A Prophet Unsung*, was born out of a desire to know and learn from the man who followed Joseph's teachings and example until he, too, received a promise of Eternal life. As I researched Hyrum, I found that very little truth has been written, preserved, or even

---

[8] OC Genesis 12 and https://restorationarchives.net/audio/2021.06.26_4th-JSRC_Joseph-Joseph-Joseph.mp3.

[9] God's name in Hebrew is 'ĕlôhîym which is plural and can be understood as "male and female" or "father and mother."

[10] Some of the places I found sources for my books were: the Joseph Smith Papers Project, the LDS Church History Library, books published and sold through Restoration Bookstore, the Community of Christ Church History Library, the Harold B. Lee Library, Centerplace.org (maintained by the Restoration Branches of the former RLDS Church), and other blogs, websites, and libraries throughout the world. Many libraries have digital collections which I could peruse online. Others willingly sent pdf or digital copies of documents for a small fee. In some instances, in order to get to the original source material, I had to purchase published books.

understood, regarding the man whom the Lord loved because of the integrity of his heart, placed first in His Priesthood, and to whom the Lord made a promise that his name would be had in "honorable remembrance from generation to generation for ever and ever."[11]

As I have researched Joseph and Hyrum Smith, I have found that many LDS Church publications and writings use second and third hand accounts to justify their interpolations and unvirtuous narratives. In many cases, as I have dug further, I have discovered that original sources prove the exact opposite of the LDS Church's claims, and that, too often, mankind's philosophies, interpretations, agendas, and traditions color source material.[12]

It is human nature to see what we want to see, to believe what someone in authority tells us to accept as truth. The Lord has warned us that many leaders of religious institutions are "blind leaders of the blind, and if the blind lead the blind, both shall fall into the ditch."[13] The false traditions of our fathers, the cunning lies of the adversary, and the gospel of carnal security keeps many slumbering peacefully in the dark.[14]

Accepted academics, pedigreed theologians, and those placed in high positions of authority hold themselves up to be the only acceptable dispensers of light and truth to whom we should look. Yet, God has ordained truth to come to us without respect to persons. Whatever truths may exist, His true followers seek after these things and find they are freely

---

[11] T&C 141:32.
[12] See NC—NT Colossians 1:7.
[13] NC—NT Matthew 8:9.
[14] NC—BoM 2 Nephi 12:4.

given.[15]

God is no respecter of persons. As such, we are all authorized by the Lord to seek for light and truth. Joseph taught that all mankind has a mind susceptible of improvement and capable of instruction, as well as a faculty which may be enlarged in proportion to the heed and diligence given to the Light communicated from Heaven to the intellect.[16]

The Lord has promised that "those who have been blinded by falsehoods I can teach them to see, and for those claiming they see clearly, I will leave them in their blindness."[17] We do not need worldly acclaim, education, or credentials to seek after and discover Truth. We only need a desire and willingness to sacrifice what will be required. In fact, we might be in a better position to overcome the false traditions of our fathers than those who are "ever learning and never able to come to the knowledge of the truth."[18]

Coming to know the Lord begins with asking, seeking, and knocking.[19] God will speak to anyone, He will answer any earnest seeker. The First Vision came as a result of a specific vocal and private prayer in which [Joseph Smith Jr.] asked to know more.[20] Searching the mysteries of Godliness can be a scary prospect. This is partly because, while the truth will set you free, first it will tick you off. It is often painful to awaken

---

[15] T&C 159:33.

[16] Smith, Joseph F. (1976). *Teachings of the Prophet Joseph Smith*, p. 51. Salt Lake City, UT: Deseret Book Company.

[17] T&C Testimony of St. John 7:8 retrieved from https://scriptures.info/scriptures/tc/toj/7.

[18] NC NT—2 Timothy 1:8 retrieved from https://scriptures.info/scriptures/nt/2timothy/1.

[19] See T&C A Glossary of Gospel Terms, "Ask, Seek, Knock."

[20] See T&C A Glossary of Gospel Terms, "Ask."

and arise from a peaceful slumber into the full light of day. Sacrifice has no meaning if there is no consequence.

Yet, no matter the obstacles we are confronted with, each of us can overcome our blindness until we eventually stand in the full light of day. As we do so, we will inevitably uncover another great mystery—who we are: we will discover what is hidden in the deep recesses of our hearts, the beams in our eyes, the weaknesses of our flesh, and the sins and errors that keep us from piercing the veil and unlocking the record of Heaven that dwells within each of us.

> The nearer man approaches perfection, the clearer are his views, and the greater his enjoyments, till he has overcome the evils of his life and lost every desire for sin; and like the ancients, arrives at that point of faith where he is wrapped in the power and glory of his Maker and is caught up to dwell with Him.[21]

The Lord has promised that the day will come when His people shall no more teach every man his neighbor and every man his brother, saying, "Know the Lord"—for they shall all know Him.[22]

The path to discovering the great mysteries of godliness begins with listening, accepting, understanding, and living the first principles and ordinances of the Gospel.[23] Knowledge of the mysteries of godliness is obtained only through obedience to God. By obedience to what the Lord commands, we can qualify to receive greater Light and Truth. But, consider that

---

[21] Smith, Joseph Fielding, compiler, (1976) *Teachings of the Prophet Joseph Smith*, p. 51, Salt Lake City: Deseret Book.
[22] OC Jeremiah 12:9.
[23] T&C 110—LoF 3:4.

"this is a station to which no man ever arrived in a moment: he must have been instructed in the government and laws of that kingdom by proper degrees, until his mind is capable in some measure of comprehending the propriety, justice, equality, and consistency of the same."[24] When you climb a ladder, Joseph taught, you must begin at the bottom, and

> ascend step by step, until you arrive at the top; and so it is with the principles of the Gospel—you must begin with the first, and go on until you learn all the principles of exaltation. But it will be a great while after you have passed through the veil before you have learned them [all]. It is not all to be comprehended in this world; it will be a great work to learn our salvation and exaltation even beyond the grave.[25]

Since the days of Adam, the Lord has always sought to reestablish people of covenant among the living, and therefore has desired that man should love one another, not begrudgingly, but as brothers and sisters indeed, that He may establish His covenant and provide them with light and truth.[26] Jacob's great wrestle with God put his hip out of joint, nevertheless, he prevailed, and in the end received covenants, blessings, promises, and a new name from the Lord.

So, here we are, people who have woken up to a portion of light and truth. Some of us may be awake but still lying in bed. Others of us may have risen out of bed yet are still attempting to find the switch to fully turn on the Light. As we

---

[24] Smith, Joseph Fielding, compiler, (1976) *Teachings of the Prophet Joseph Smith*, p. 51, Salt Lake City: Deseret Book.
[25] Smith, Joseph Fielding, compiler, (1976) *Teachings of the Prophet Joseph Smith*, p. 348, Salt Lake City: Deseret Book.
[26] T&C 157:2.

stumble around, searching for truth, bumping into each other, remember that only God has all truth, so, let us be kind to each other and never give up on the wrestle to come to know the Lord.

Our lamps are different, but the Light is the same!

Essay 2

Joseph's Marvelous Experience: Lessons Learned from the First Vision[1]

Whitney N. Horning[2]

©June 20, 2020

"[W]hen man was created he stood in the presence of God . . . and had a most perfect knowledge of His existence."[3] Upon Adam and Eve's rebellion, but before they were cast out of the Garden of Eden, God taught them the law of sacrifice and obedience.[4] Once driven out of Eden to wander in a lone and dreary world, commonly referred to as the Fall of Adam, our first parents were separated from the presence of God by a veil. Though "separated . . . [Adam and Eve] still retained a knowledge of his existence, and that sufficiently to move them to call upon him."[5] Even though Adam and Eve had rebelled, they were not deprived of their previous knowledge of the existence of God and "no sooner was the plan of redemption revealed to man and he began to call upon God, than the holy

---

[1] Restoration Conference 2020: "Inviting all the branches of the Restoration to commemorate Joseph Smith's First Vision," Meridian, Idaho. This talk is a compilation of the various first-hand accounts of Joseph's First Vision. The scriptures referenced are from the KJV (King James Version of the Bible), LDS (The Church of Jesus Christ of Latter-Day Saints), and/or RE (Restoration Edition Scriptures found online at scriptures.info).

[2] I am a 7th generation Mormon, a member of The Church of Jesus Christ of Latter-Day Saints based in Salt Lake City, Utah.

[3] *Lectures on Faith* 2:62-66 (RE); see also Genesis 1:27-28 (KJV); Genesis 2:9 (RE).

[4] See Genesis 3 (KJV); Moses 4 (LDS *Pearl of Great Price*); Genesis 2:15-20 (RE).

[5] See *Lectures on Faith* 2:25 (RE).

spirit was given, bearing record of the Father and Son . . . notwithstanding they were separated from his immediate presence that they could not see his face, they continued to hear his voice."[6] After years of obedience, sacrifice, repentance, and calling upon the name of the Lord, Adam entered back into His presence and was redeemed from the Fall.[7]

We learn from the account of Adam and Eve:

Adam . . . being made acquainted with God, communicated the knowledge which he had unto his posterity; and it was through this means that the thought was first suggested to their minds that there was a God, which laid the foundation for the exercise of their faith, through which they could obtain a knowledge of his character and also of his glory . . . [It was by this means] that God became an object of faith among men after the fall . . . [which thing did stir] up the faith of multitudes to feel after him, to search after a knowledge of his character, perfections, and attributes until they became extensively acquainted with him; and not only commune with him and behold his glory, but be partakers of his power and stand in his presence . . . the whole faith of the world, from that time down to the present, is in a certain degree dependent on the knowledge first communicated to them by their common progenitor, [Father Adam]; and it has been handed down to the day and generation in which we live [through the sacred

---

[6] *Lectures on Faith* 2:30 (RE); see also Moses 5:4 (LDS *PofGP*); and Genesis 3:2 (RE).
[7] See Moses 5:1-12; 6:1-9, 64-68 (LDS *Pearl of Great Price*); Genesis 3:1-4, 14; Genesis 4:10 (RE).

records we call scripture].[8]

Adam and Eve were taught the gospel of Jesus Christ in a pure and unadulterated form by God, Himself. This entailed seeking for the fullness of the Gospel,[9] or in other words, being redeemed from the Fall by entering back into the presence of the Lord.[10] This, they plainly taught to their children,[11] calling upon them to repent.[12] But, Satan came among them, tempting them, and they loved Satan more than God and began to corrupt the pure religion of their father.[13] The conditions of this world are such that we are constantly involved in either restoring truth or apostatizing from it. Thus, ever since the days of Adam, mankind has experienced numerous cycles of apostasy from the correct knowledge of God. Whenever sufficient faith is found upon the earth, a restoration back to the

---

[8] *Lectures on Faith* 2:30-36 (RE).

[9] See T&C A Glossary of Gospel Terms: Fullness of the Gospel (RE): This is used a number of ways in scripture. . . . Joseph Smith used the term in his writings and teachings at different times with different meanings. "Learning these 'mysteries [of God]' is the fullness of Christ's Gospel." The fullness of the Gospel consists of asking God, receiving answers, revelations, knowledge, and finally, in the Second Comforter.

[10] Ether 3:13-16 (LDS); or Ether 1:13 (RE) "When he had said these words, behold, the Lord shewed himself unto him and said, Because thou knowest these things, ye are redeemed from the Fall. Therefore, ye are brought back into my presence; therefore I shew myself unto you." See also A Glossary of Gospel Terms: Redemption (RE).

[11] Because all restorations of the gospel necessarily begin with a redemption experience, it can be assumed that if Moses plainly taught this to the children of Israel, then so Adam did likewise to his. See D&C 84:23-24 (LDS); or T&C 82:13 (RE).

[12] See Genesis 4:25-26, 5:1-2 (KJV); Moses 6:1-9 (LDS *PofGP*); and Genesis 3:14 (RE).

[13] See Moses 5:13-16 (LDS *PofGP*); Genesis 3:5 (RE). The exceptions to this were Adam and Eve's sons, Cain, Abel, and Seth who rose up and entered back into God's presence.

truth becomes possible.

We can learn through Joseph's various first-hand accounts of his First Vision important, eternal truths about the nature of God. Joseph's "marvelous experience and . . . all the mighty acts which he [did] in the name of Jesus Christ"[14] began a little over 200 years ago. When "at about the age of twelve years [his] mind became seriously impressed with regard to the all important concerns for the welfare of [his] immortal soul."[15]

During this time, there was in the area in which his family resided, "unusual excitement on the subject of religion . . . It commenced with the Methodists, but soon . . . the whole district of country seemed affected by it, and great multitudes united themselves to the different religious parties, which created no small stir and division among the people."[16] Joseph had been born of "goodly parents who spared no pains to instructing [him]in the Christian religion."[17] They taught him to honor God and value the scriptures. His parents gave him the freedom to search truth out for himself and make his own decisions; even at a tender age. While the family did not belong to any particular church when Joseph was young, they taught their children what a true Christian should be.

This great religious revival stirred up a profound concern regarding his personal salvation. Joseph's anxiety led

---

[14] "History, circa Summer 1832," p. 1-4, The Joseph Smith Papers, accessed June 10, 2020, https://www.josephsmithpapers.org/paper-summary/history-circa-summer-1832/1.

[15] Ibid.

[16] At this time, the Smith family was living in Manchester, Ontario, New York. See History of Joseph Smith, *Times and Seasons*, Vol. 3, No. 10 (March 15, 1842), p. 727; T&C 1:11 (RE).

[17] T&C 80:2 (RE).

him to search the scriptures believing that they would help him identify which church to join. Joseph "[b]eliev[ed]the Bible to say what it means and mean what it says."[18] The Lord sent the scriptures forth "to be [His] warning to the world, [His] comfort to the faithful, [His] counsel to the meek, [His] reproof to the proud, [His] rebuke to the contentious, and [His] condemnation of the wicked. They are [His] invitation to all mankind to flee from corruption, repent and be baptized in [His] name, and prepare for the coming judgment."[19]

Joseph "concider[ed] it of the first importance that [he] should be right, in matters that involved eternal consequences."[20] Thus, for about two years, his "mind was called up to serious reflection and great uneasiness" regarding the subject of religion. God patiently waited for Joseph to sort through conflicting information, prompting him here and there to help guide him. Never forcing. Always inviting. Ultimately allowing him the freedom to choose for himself. As Joseph pondered the truths contained within the Bible, consulted various religious leaders, and observed his fellowman, he became more confused. He compared what the scriptures taught with how the people, who claimed to be God's servants and disciples, behaved. Joseph noticed that,

> [W]hen the converts began to file off, some to one
> party and some to another, it was seen that the

---

[18] ""Latter Day Saints," 1844," p. 404, The Joseph Smith Papers, accessed June 13, 2020, https://www.josephsmithpapers.org/paper-summary/latter-day-saints-1844/6.

[19] T&C 177:3 (RE).

[20] "Journal, 1835–1836," p. 23-24, The Joseph Smith Papers, accessed June 10, 2020, https://www.josephsmithpapers.org/paper-summary/journal-1835-1836/23; spelling as in original.

seemingly good feelings of both the priests and the converts were more pretended than real. For a scene of great confusion and bad feeling ensued, priest contending against priest and convert against convert, so that all their good feelings one for another (if they ever had any) were entirely lost in a strife of words and a contest about opinions.[21]

Joseph felt that their actions were in direct contrast to how a person who was truly converted to Christ should behave, for Christ taught that we can know people by their fruits and His disciples "have love, one to another."[22] The Apostle Paul encouraged the "elect of God...[to put on] hearts of mercies, kindness, humility...meekness, long-suffering, bearing with one another and forgiving one another...and above all these things put on charity...let the peace of God rule in your hearts."[23] Joseph lamented that "[the church leaders] did not adorn their profession by a holy walk and Godly conversation agreeable to what [he] found contained in that sacred depository."[24]

As Joseph labored under the extreme difficulties caused by the competing churches, he eventually began to feel

---

[21] "History, circa June 1839–circa 1841 [Draft 2]," p. [1], The Joseph Smith Papers, accessed June 10, 2020, https://www.josephsmithpapers.org/paper-summary/history-circa-june-1839-circa-1841-draft-2/1 See also Joseph's First Vision account found under History of Joseph Smith, printed in the *Times and Seasons*, Volume 3, Numbers 10 and 11 (March 15 & April 1, 1842), pp. 727-728, and 748; T&C Joseph Smith History Part 1-2 (RE).

[22] See John 13:33-35 (KJV); Testimony of St. John 10:7; and John 9:5 (RE).

[23] Colossians 3:12-17 (KJV); or Colossians 1:13 (RE).

[24] "History, circa Summer 1832," p. 1-4, The Joseph Smith Papers, accessed June 10, 2020, https://www.josephsmithpapers.org/paper-summary/history-circa-summer-1832/1.

"somewhat partial to the Methodist sect, and...felt some desire to be united with them."[25] Yet, he remained confused and perplexed in mind, unable to come to "any certain conclusion who was right and who was wrong"[26] or, if all of them were wrong how would he be able to know? As he studied the Bible, he recognized that mankind continually apostatized from the true and living faith. He perceived that contentions, divisions, wickedness, abominations, and darkness pervaded the minds of mankind[27] and gross darkness covered the earth.[28] This caused him to mourn for not only his own sins, but for those of the world. Though his "feelings were deep and often pungent,[29] still [he] kept himself aloof from all [the different] parties."[30]

---

[25] "History, circa June 1839–circa 1841 [Draft 2]," p. [1], The Joseph Smith Papers, accessed June 10, 2020, https://www.josephsmithpapers.org/paper-summary/history-circa-june-1839-circa-1841-draft-2/1 See also Joseph's First Vision account found under History of Joseph Smith, printed in the *Times and Seasons*, Volume 3, Numbers 10 and 11 (March 15 & April 1, 1842), pp. 727-728, and 748; and T&C Joseph Smith History Part 2:2 (RE).

[26] Ibid.

[27] "History, circa Summer 1832," p. 1-4, The Joseph Smith Papers, accessed June 10, 2020, https://www.josephsmithpapers.org/paper-summary/history-circa-summer-1832/1

[28] "Orson Hyde, *Ein Ruf aus der Wüste* (A Cry out of the Wilderness), 1842, extract, English translation," The Joseph Smith Papers, accessed June 11, 2020, https://www.josephsmithpapers.org/paper-summary/orson-hyde-ein-ruf-aus-der-wste-a-cry-out-of-the-wilderness-1842-extract-english-translation/1

[29] Pungent=piercing or sharp, acrimonious, biting.

[30] It is commendable, and something worth consideration, that his parents gave Joseph the time, space, and freedom to make this choice for himself. "History, circa June 1839–circa 1841 [Draft 2]," p. [1], The Joseph Smith Papers, accessed June 10, 2020, https://www.josephsmithpapers.org/paper-summary/history-circa-june-1839-circa-1841-draft-2/1 See also Joseph's First Vision account found under History of Joseph Smith, printed in the *Times and Seasons*, Volume 3,

Joseph

[L]ooked upon the sun...and also the moon rolling in their magesty through the heavens and also the stars shining in their courses and the earth also upon which [he] stood...the beast of the field and the fowls of heaven and the fish of the waters and also man walking forth upon the face of the earth in magesty and in the strength of beauty whose power and intiligence...even in the likeness of him who created them and when [he] considered upon these things [his] heart exclaimed well hath the wise man said it is a fool that saith in his heart there is no God my heart exclaimed all all these bear testimony and bespeak an omnipotant and omnipreasant power a being who makith Laws and decreeeth and bindeth all things in their bounds who filleth Eternity who was and is and will be from all Eternity to Eternity.[31]

Joseph trusted "that God was the same yesterday to day and forever that he was no respecter to persons for he was God."[32] When he considered all these things, Joseph sought to worship such a being and to "worship him in spirit and in truth."[33]

God promises that if we ask, we shall receive.[34] The

Numbers 10 and 11 (March 15 & April 1, 1842), pp. 727-728, and 748; and T&C Joseph Smith History Part 2:2 (RE).

[31] "History, circa Summer 1832," p. 1-4, The Joseph Smith Papers, accessed June 10, 2020, https://www.josephsmithpapers.org/paper-summary/history-circa-summer-1832/2.

[32] See Isaiah 9:4 (RE); Hebrews 13:7-9 (KJV); and Hebrews 1:59 (RE).

[33] "History, circa Summer 1832," p. 1-4, The Joseph Smith Papers, accessed June 10, 2020, https://www.josephsmithpapers.org/paper-summary/history-circa-summer-1832/2. Spelling, grammar, and punctuation as in original.

[34] See Matthew 7:6-8 (KJV); or Matthew 3:42 (RE).

Lord is the master teacher and desires to teach us, yet He patiently waits for us to come to Him. He gives us room to try to figure it out on our own and never encroaches upon our agency. He allows us to "taste the bitter that [we] may know to prize the good."[35] He has given us the light of Christ and the ability to know good from evil. We have the freedom to choose to either accept or reject Him. As we study things out in our minds,[36] learning to discern between truth and error, our faith grows.[37]

Eventually, Joseph came to the conclusion that "the teachers of religion of the different sects understood the same passage so differently as to destroy all confidence in settling the question by an appeal to the Bible."[38] No matter who we are, the Spirit of the Lord can influence us in our minds and in our hearts.[39] Through the words of God's own servant, the spirit gave Joseph a nudge in the right direction as he read James 1:5—"If any of you lack wisdom, let him ask of God, that giveth unto all men liberally and upbraideth not and it shall be given him."[40] Joseph marveled that in all his years of searching never had

---

[35] See Moses 6:53-56 (LDS *PofGP*); or Genesis 4:8 (RE).

[36] See D&C 9:7-9 (LDS); or T&C Joseph Smith History 13:26 (RE).

[37] Ibid.

[38] "History, circa June 1839–circa 1841 [Draft 2]," p. [1], The Joseph Smith Papers, accessed June 10, 2020, https://www.josephsmithpapers.org/paper-summary/history-circa-june-1839-circa-1841-draft-2/1   See also Joseph's First Vision account found under History of Joseph Smith, printed in the *Times and Seasons*, Volume 3, Numbers 10 and 11 (March 15 & April 1, 1842), pp. 727-728, and 748; T&C Joseph Smith History Part 1-2 (RE).

[39] See D&C 8:1-5 (LDS); or T&C Joseph Smith History 13:21 (RE).

[40] James 1:5 (KJV); or The Epistle of Jacob 1:2 (RE).

[A]ny passage of scripture come with more power to the heart of man than this did at this time to mine. It seemed to enter with great force into every feeling of my heart. I reflected on it again and again, knowing that if any person needed wisdom from God, I did, for how to act I did not know and unless I could get more wisdom than I then had would never know...At length I came to the conclusion that I must either remain in darkness and confusion or else I must do as James directs, that is, Ask of God...concluding that if he gave wisdom to them that lacked wisdom, and would give liberally and not upbraid, I might venture.[41]

After years of searching the scriptures, pondering on the many choices before him, learning and growing in knowledge and discernment, Joseph had done all he could to figure out his dilemma. He now knew exactly what the desire of his heart was, he knew exactly what he wanted from God—salvation, and he hoped that if he joined the right church, he might receive it. Therefore, on a beautiful spring morning in 1820, Joseph chose to act on God's promise and the feelings working in his heart. He retired to a previously chosen secret spot in a grove of trees. Looking around and finding himself alone he kneeled down and began to offer up the desires of his heart, crying unto the Lord for mercy for he knew that there

---

[41] "History, circa June 1839–circa 1841 [Draft 2]," p. [1], The Joseph Smith Papers, accessed June 10, 2020, https://www.josephsmithpapers.org/paper-summary/history-circa-june-1839-circa-1841-draft-2/1 See also Joseph's First Vision account found under History of Joseph Smith, printed in the *Times and Seasons*, Volume 3, Numbers 10 and 11 (March 15 & April 1, 1842), pp. 727-728, and 748; T&C Joseph Smith History Part 1-2 (RE).

was none else to whom he could go to obtain mercy.[42] Almost immediately he was seized by some power which bound his tongue so that he could not speak.

The Shouting Methodists had a tradition that a person shouting praises to God in hopes of obtaining some kind of spiritual manifestation would be seized upon by some marvelous, unseen power, and bound up to the point that they were unable to move. Joseph, having never prayed vocally before, was having the exact experience the Shouting Methodists described. To Joseph, though, it did not seem like the type of heavenly manifestation that was from God. Rather, he felt thick darkness gather around him and felt as if he was doomed to destruction.

Joseph's marvelous experience parallels those found in scripture and demonstrates that a major component of this earthly existence is to learn to discern between truth and error. It is an eternal law that whenever light is poured out upon this earth God allows darkness in equal measure in order that mankind may always have the freedom to choose between good and evil.[43] The false spirits of this world are manifested in part as traditions which fool the faithful into thinking they are obedient to God when they are merely misled. False traditions

---

[42] "History, circa Summer 1832," p. 1-4, The Joseph Smith Papers, accessed June 10, 2020, https://www.josephsmithpapers.org/paper-summary/history-circa-summer-1832/1.

[43] Adam and Eve walked and talked with God in the cool of the Garden and then Satan came as a serpent, tempting them. Moses vision at the burning bush; after the Lord had left him, Satan appeared which thing gave Moses an opportunity to choose between truth and deception. When Christ's 40 day fast was completed, Satan came tempting him. See Moses 1:1-26; 3:15-25; 4:1-13 (LDS *PofGP*); Genesis 2:15-25; 3:1-7 (KJV); Genesis 1:1-5; 2:13-16 (RE); Matthew 3:13-17; 4:1-4; and Matthew 2:4-5 (RE).

are as destructive to our souls as outright disobedience, holding us captive and leading us into darkness rather than into Christ's light.[44] The false traditions of our fathers cause us to fear and doubt, blinding us to the truth, and keeping us from accepting the greater light that is yet to be revealed.[45]

The scriptures teach that as we seek for Truth the Lord can set us free from everything that blinds us and binds us down.[46] In Joseph's battle with Satan in that grove, Joseph did not give up on God. He did not give in to the false traditions which would have kept him blinded and bound down. He persevered and exerted all of his power to call upon God to deliver him from his unseen enemy. After all Joseph could do, at the very moment when he was ready to sink into despair, God rescued him from that awful pit.[47] This appears to be the way God works in each of our lives. You're barely hanging on, you're completely exhausted and just when you are about to give in to total despair, that is when the answer comes.[48] And God allows it. He allowed Satan to have his way with Joseph because how else could Joseph learn the difference between God's glory and Satan? How else could Joseph prove his intent?

At the very moment when Joseph was ready to abandon

---

[44] See D&C 93:39 (LDS); T&C 93:11 (RE).

[45] See Matthew 15:14; John 8:12; 9:5; 12:36, 46 (KJV); Luke 2:32 (KJV); 2 Corinthians 4:4 (KJV); or Matthew 8:9; John 6:11-12, 17; 8:3, 6; (RE); Testimony of St. John 7:1; 9:4, 7 (RE); Luke 2:5 (RE); and 2 Corinthians 1:12 (RE).

[46] See John 8:32; 14:6 (KJV); John 6:14; 9:7 (RE); and Testimony of St. John 6:18; 10:9 (RE).

[47] See T&C The Testimony of St. John 3:4; 4:9; 5:18; 9:4 (RE).

[48] My husband and I refer to this as "Star Trek timing."

himself to destruction,[49] "the Lord heard [his] cry in the wilderness"[50] and a pillar of light above the brightness of the sun at noon day came down from above and rested upon him, filling him with the spirit of God[51] and unspeakable joy.[52] As Joseph looked up into the fiery conduit, the Lord opened the heavens upon him[53] and he was "enrapt in a heavenly vision, and saw two glorious personages, who exactly resembled each other in features and likeness, surrounded with a brilliant light."[54] Joseph's faith had led him to receive a correct knowledge of God. As he looked upon Them, his soul rejoiced to know that God does indeed live! Years later, in the *Lectures on Faith*, Joseph expounded,

> There are two personages who constitute the great matchless, governing, and supreme power over all things — by whom all things were created and

---

[49] "History, circa June 1839–circa 1841 [Draft 2]," p. [1], The Joseph Smith Papers, accessed June 10, 2020, https://www.josephsmithpapers.org/paper-summary/history-circa-june-1839-circa-1841-draft-2/1 See also Joseph's First Vision account found under History of Joseph Smith, printed in the *Times and Seasons*, Volume 3, Numbers 10 and 11 (March 15 & April 1, 1842), pp. 727-728, and 748; T&C Joseph Smith History Part 1-2 (RE).

[50] "History, circa Summer 1832," p. 1-4, The Joseph Smith Papers, accessed June 10, 2020, https://www.josephsmithpapers.org/paper-summary/history-circa-summer-1832/1.

[51] Ibid.

[52] "Journal, 1835–1836," p. 23-24, The Joseph Smith Papers, accessed June 10, 2020, https://www.josephsmithpapers.org/paper-summary/journal-1835-1836/23.

[53] "History, circa Summer 1832," p. 1-4, The Joseph Smith Papers, accessed June 10, 2020, https://www.josephsmithpapers.org/paper-summary/history-circa-summer-1832/1.

[54] "Latter Day Saints," 1844," p. 404, The Joseph Smith Papers, accessed June 13, 2020, https://www.josephsmithpapers.org/paper-summary/latter-day-saints-1844/1.

made...they are the Father and the Son: the Father being a personage of spirit, glory, and power: possessing all perfection and fullness; the Son, who was in the bosom of the Father, a personage of tabernacle, made or fashioned like unto man...or rather, man was formed after his likeness and in his image — he is also the express image and likeness of the personage of the Father, possessing all the fullness of the Father, or the same fullness with the Father, being begotten of him, and was ordained from before the foundation of the world to be a propitiation for the sins of all those who should believe on his name, and is called the Son because of the flesh.[55]

Joseph's vision included a view into heaven where he "saw many angels."[56] Whenever God the Father is on display it always includes the Heavenly Host.[57] Men and women may see Christ in vision or in an appearance as a solitary personage, but no person has ever seen God the Father without also seeing a host of others.[58] Throughout scripture, the Father is described as a God of Hosts, this is because God has a family, including a spouse. The image of God is male and female: "And I God, created man in my own image, in the image of my Only Begotten created I him. Male and female created I them."[59]

---

[55] T&C *Lectures on Faith* 5:2 (RE).

[56] "Journal, 1835–1836," p. 23-24, The Joseph Smith Papers, accessed June 10, 2020, https://www.josephsmithpapers.org/paper-summary/journal-1835-1836/23.

[57] Snuffer, D. (2012) *The Temple*. p. 2. Retrieved from https://www.dropbox.com/s/36vz6l2m7k3dnag/2012.10.28%20The%20Temple_transcript.pdf?dl=0.

[58] See T&C "A Glossary of Gospel Terms: Heavenly Host." The scriptures also refer to them as numerous angels or concourses of angels. See Luke 2:2 (RE). The Lord is called the "Lord of Hosts" throughout scripture.

[59] Genesis 1:24-28 (KJV); Moses 2:24-28 (LDS *PofGP*); or Genesis 2:8 (RE).

"That is the image of God. That is what God...should look like. He appears with the heavenly host because our God...is **this** image, male and female. They two are together."[60]

God knows each of us intimately "even the very hairs on [our] head are...numbered" by Him.[61] God desires to have a relationship with each of us. When He comes to you, He will call you by the name which your closest family and friends use. Joseph recorded that, "One of [the personages] spake unto me calling me by name."[62] The familiar use of Joseph's name brought comfort and peace to the young boy as he was welcomed into Their presence.

One of the personages pointed to the other one, saying, "This is my beloved Son, Hear him.'[63] This seemingly simple act of directing Joseph's attention to the Savior, Jesus Christ, emphasized in startling clarity that "there is no other way nor means whereby man can be saved, only in and through Jesus

---

[60] Snuffer, Denver (July 26, 2014), "Marriage and Family," *40 Years in Mormonism*, p. 2.

[61] Luke 12:7 (KJV); or Luke 8:19 (RE).

[62] "History, circa June 1839–circa 1841 [Draft 2]," p. [1], The Joseph Smith Papers, accessed June 10, 2020, https://www.josephsmithpapers.org/paper-summary/history-circa-june-1839-circa-1841-draft-2/1 See also Joseph's First Vision account found under History of Joseph Smith, printed in the *Times and Seasons*, Volume 3, Numbers 10 and 11 (March 15 & April 1, 1842), pp. 727-728, and 748; T&C Joseph Smith History Part 1-2 (RE).

[63] "History, circa June 1839–circa 1841 [Draft 2]," p. [1], The Joseph Smith Papers, accessed June 10, 2020, https://www.josephsmithpapers.org/paper-summary/history-circa-june-1839-circa-1841-draft-2/1 See also Joseph's First Vision account found under History of Joseph Smith, printed in the *Times and Seasons*, Volume 3, Numbers 10 and 11 (March 15 & April 1, 1842), pp. 727-728, and 748; T&C Joseph Smith History Part 1-2 (RE).

Christ."[64] Living in a fallen state, we need to be rescued by a Savior. That Savior is Jesus Christ. He died for each of us. His "atoning sacrifice is the means ordained by God to . . . rescue us from sin and death. Our salvation depends on knowing, confessing and worshiping Christ. Anything that distracts us from that can become an impediment to salvation."[65]

During that first vision, Joseph received the "testimony of Jesus" from Jesus, "behold I am the Lord of glory I was crucifyed for the world that all those who believe on my name may have Eternal life."[66] Jesus Christ testifies of who He is and what He has done for each and every one of us. "He is the one Moses prophesied would come and all Israel must give him heed or be cut off. God the Father loves and acknowledges Jesus as His Son and has made Him the steward over all creation. We are required to acknowledge God's Son to be rescued by him, for only the Son can rescue us from the Fall of Adam."[67]

Because he believed that his salvation was dependent

---

[64] See Alma 38:8-9 (LDS); or Alma 18:3 (RE).

[65] Snuffer, D. (2018) *Our Divine Parents*, p. 27. Retrieved from http://denversnuffer.com/wp/wp-content/uploads/2018/04/Our-Divine-Parents-FINAL.pdf.

[66] "History, circa Summer 1832," p. 1-4, The Joseph Smith Papers, accessed June 10, 2020, https://www.josephsmithpapers.org/paper-summary/history-circa-summer-1832/1. In 1843 Joseph taught, "Now if any man has the testimony of Jesus, has he not the spirit of prophecy? And if he has the spirit of prophecy, I ask, is he not a prophet? And if a prophet will, he can receive revelation. And any man that does not receive revelation for himself must be damned, for the testimony of Jesus is the spirit of prophecy for Christ says ask and you shall receive." Ehat & Cook (1980) *The Words of Joseph Smith*, p. 230, (Salt Lake City, UT: Bookcraft); spelling corrected; Smith, J. F. (1976) *The Teachings of the Prophet Joseph Smith*, p. 312 (Salt Lake City, UT: Deseret Book Company); emphasis added.

[67] T&C The Testimony of St. John 3:4 (RE).

upon choosing the correct church, until that moment, Joseph's main objective "in going to enquire of the Lord was to know which of all the sects was right, that [he] might know which to join."[68] As the veil was drawn back and the Heavens were opened Joseph was brought back into the presence of the Lord and received the salvation and redemption which he had so desperately desired. Truly Joseph learned that there is "no other name given, nor any other way nor means, whereby salvation can come unto the children of men, only in and through the name of Christ the Lord."[69]

Then Jesus Christ "spake . . . saying Joseph my son thy sins are forgiven thee go thy way walk in my statutes and keep my commandments."[70] The first thing the Lord does when a person enters back into His presence is to **immediately** forgive them of their sins. This gave Joseph the confidence to stand before Him.[71] Most of us believe that our sins and errors are too

---

[68] "History, circa June 1839–circa 1841 [Draft 2]," p. [1], The Joseph Smith Papers, accessed June 10, 2020, https://www.josephsmithpapers.org/paper-summary/history-circa-june-1839-circa-1841-draft-2/1 See also Joseph's First Vision account found under History of Joseph Smith, printed in the *Times and Seasons*, Volume 3, Numbers 10 and 11 (March 15 & April 1, 1842), pp. 727-728, and 748; T&C Joseph Smith History Part 1-2 (RE).

[69] See Mosiah 3:14-19 (LDS); or Mosiah 1:16 (RE).

[70] "History, circa Summer 1832," p. 1-4, The Joseph Smith Papers, accessed June 10, 2020, https://www.josephsmithpapers.org/paper-summary/history-circa-summer-1832/1.

[71] "God wants us to be comfortable in His presence. So much so, that it is a matter of course, that God invariably forgives your sins." Snuffer, Denver (September 10, 2013),"Be of Good Cheer, Be of Good Courage," *40 Years in Mormonism*, p. 9. Another example of this is the prophet, Isaiah. When Isaiah saw the Lord, he lamented, "Woe is me, for I am undone because I am a man of unclean lips, and I dwell in the midst of a people of unclean lips..." A seraphim immediately brought a live coal from off the altar and

serious an impediment to find acceptance from God. One of the greatest truths we learn from scripture, as well as Joseph's First Vision:

> [The Lord] doesn't want to judge [us]; He wants to heal [us]. He wants to give [us] what [we] lack, teach [us] to be better, and to bless [us]. He doesn't want to belittle, demean, or punish [us]. When [we] ask Him to forgive, He forgives. Even very serious sins. He does not want [us] burdened with sin . . . His willingness to leave [our] errors in the past and remember them no more is greater than [we] can imagine. It is a guiding principle for the atonement. Asking for forgiveness is almost all that is required to be forgiven. What alienates [us] from Him is not [our] sins — He will forgive those. What [we] lack is the confidence to ask in faith, nothing doubting, for His help.[72]

Joseph's eyes were now opened. He now knew, nothing doubting, that there is a God who died to set us free, for "[i]f the Son sets you free from sin, you are free indeed."[73]

While Joseph at first approached the Lord with a simple enough question: which church should he join, the Lord knew that what was truly in Joseph's heart was a desire for salvation and redemption. God is willing to meet us where we are at. No doubt there were others in Joseph's community who had asked

---

touched it to Isaiah's lips, symbolically cleansing him. See Isaiah 6:5 (KJV); or Isaiah 2:2 (RE).

[72] T&C "A Glossary of Gospel Terms, Forgiveness" (RE). Our Savior is willing to come and redeem us from the Fall. It is His work, His glory, and His success which culminates in our redemption. See also Snuffer, Denver (June 28, 2014), "Christ, the Prototype of the Saved Man," *40 Years in Mormonism*. Retrieved from http://denversnuffer.com/wp/wp-content/uploads/2015/02/07-Ephraim-Transcript-Christ.pdf.

[73] T&C The Testimony of St. John 6:19 (RE).

the same question in prayer and received a simple answer of which church they should join. How much more the Lord gives us is entirely dependent upon us. People don't get answers like Joseph's because at the core they don't actually know what it is they really want, or they stop short just before the breakthrough would have come.

God knows every minute detail about each and every one of us, including the desires of our hearts. We think we know what we want, but we are not always willing to put in the time, effort, and sacrifice to receive what it is that would actually be good for us. If you really want what the Lord offers, if you really want what Joseph received, then you've got to ask yourself if you want it badly enough to reorient yourself, in every possible way, to make the necessary sacrifice to obtain it. Asking for it isn't a whim or today's wish; you have to be deadly serious about it.[74] And then you have to go and live your life in faith that you will receive it because it is an eternal truth that no one receives a witness until after the trial of their faith: "For it was by faith that Christ shewed himself unto our fathers after he had risen from the dead, and he shewed not himself unto them until after they had faith in him."[75]

The Lord told Joseph, "the world lieth in sin at this time and none doeth good no not one they have turned aside from

---

[74] Excerpts and ideas taken from Peterson, J. B. (2020, May 24) *Biblical Series: Walking with God Noah and the Flood*. Retrieved from https://podcasts.apple.com/au/podcast/biblical-series-walking-with-god-noah-and-the-flood/id1184022695?i=1000475561528.

[75] See Ether 12:6-12 (LDS); or Ether 5:2 (RE).

the gospel and keep not my commandments."[76] Mankind not only struggles with violating commandments through addictions, compulsions, errors, weaknesses, and foolishness, but we also sin by our lack of knowledge and our willingness to put men and churches between us and a personal relationship with the Lord. The Greek word hamartia[77] defines sin "as missing the mark; not hitting the target; a mistake."[78] LDS Scholar, Hugh Nibley defined sin as "doing one thing when you should be doing other and better things for which you have the capacity. Hence, there are no innocent idle thoughts. That is why even the righteous must repent, constantly and progressively, since all fall short of their capacity and calling."[79]

Modern revelation defines commandments as communications that are sent by God: "If you love me, stand ready, watching for every communication I will send to you . . . He that treasures my teaching, and stands ready, watching for every communication I send him, is he who shows love for me."[80] Light and truth come to us from above as we keep the commandments in our lives, especially communications from the Lord. By keeping the commandments, we obtain from God light and truth as a by-product of obedience to them. The commandments reveal to us, in a very personal way, what the mind of God is for our life. It is intensely personal because it is

---

[76] "History, circa Summer 1832," p. 1-4, The Joseph Smith Papers, accessed June 10, 2020, https://www.josephsmithpapers.org/paper-summary/history-circa-summer-1832/1.

[77] Greek spelling: ἁμαρτία.

[78] Strong, James, *Strong's Expanded Exhaustive Concordance of the Bible* (Nashville: Thomas Nelson, 2009), G266.

[79] Nibley, H. (1989) *Approaching Zion*, p. 66-67 (Salt Lake City, UT: Deseret Book).

[80] T&C The Testimony of St. John 10:11–12 (RE).

all internal.[81] These truths were personified in the life of Joseph Smith.

The Lord told Joseph that "none doeth good." The Lord defined "good" as "they that are ready to receive the fullness of my gospel."[82] The "fullness of the gospel," as used in scripture, is defined: "First . . . [as] a collection of prophetic testimonies about Jesus Christ as . . . Redeemer and guide to salvation . . . and . . . Christ's role as universal Savior and Redeemer of mankind. Second, it is a way to identify Christ revealing Himself to mankind, thereby redeeming mortals from the fall . . . The ascent to God is the fullness of the gospel of Jesus Christ."[83] Joseph, while working on the inspired translation of the Bible, corrected the 14th Psalm to read, "The fool has said in his heart, There is no man that has seen God because he shows himself not unto us, therefore there is no God. Behold, they are corrupt. They have done abominable works and none of them does good."[84]

The Lord further instructed Joseph that he "must join none of [the churches], for they [are]all wrong . . . all their creeds [are] an abomination in [My] sight."[85] A creed is: "A brief

---

[81] T&C "A Glossary of Gospel Terms: Commandment" (RE).

[82] D&C 35:12 (LDS); or T&C 18:4 (RE).

[83] See T&C "A Glossary of Gospel Terms: Fullness of the Gospel" (RE); D&C 42:30-32; 76:11-17; 39:7-11; 45:9-14; 66:1-2 (LDS); 1 Nephi 10:11-16 (LDS); or T&C 26:7; 69:3; 23:3; 31:3; 52:1 (RE); and 1 Nephi 3:4 (RE).

[84] Psalm 14:1 (RE).

[85] "History, circa June 1839–circa 1841 [Draft 2]," p. [1], The Joseph Smith Papers, accessed June 10, 2020, https://www.josephsmithpapers.org/paper-summary/history-circa-june-1839-circa-1841-draft-2/1 See also Joseph's First Vision account found under History of Joseph Smith, printed in the *Times and Seasons*, Volume 3, Numbers 10 and 11 (March 15 & April 1, 1842), pp. 727-728, and 748; T&C Joseph Smith History Part 1-2 (RE).

summary of the articles of Christian faith . . . which are believed or professed."[86] The creeds of Christianity have been drawn up at times of conflict about doctrine. Their purpose is to provide a doctrinal statement of orthodoxy that has been voted on and accepted by the leaders of the churches.[87] In modern LDS vernacular, we would call that a Correlation Department. An abomination is "[t]he use of religion to suppress truth or impose a false form of truth [and] involves the religious justification of wrongdoing . . . [s]omething becomes abominable when it is motivated out of a false form of religious observance or is justified because of religious error."[88]

When the Bible first "proceeded forth from the mouth of a Jew, it contained the fullness of the gospel of the Lamb" and went forth to the gentiles in purity. When the "great and abominable" church was formed,

> [T]hey [took] away from the gospel of the Lamb many parts which are plain and most precious; and also many covenants of the Lord. . . . And all this have they done that they might pervert the right ways of the Lord, that they might blind the eyes and harden the hearts of the children of men . . . [After these] plain and precious things were taken away, [the Bible was sent] forth unto all the nations of the gentiles . . . [and] because of these things which are taken away out of the gospel of the Lamb, an exceeding great many do stumble, yea, insomuch that Satan hath great power

---

[86] http://webstersdictionary1828.com/Dictionary/creed.

[87] The original Christian creed was adopted in 325 AD by a council of Christian bishops at Nicaea to solve conflicts about the divine nature of God the Son and His relationship with God the Father. In modern terms, the Council of Nicaea was the first Christian Correlation Department.

[88] See T&C "A Glossary of Gospel Terms: Abomination" (RE).

over them.[89]

The Lord continued to awaken Joseph to the awful state of mankind, "they draw near to me with their lips, but their hearts are far from me; they teach for doctrines the commandments of men, having a form of godliness, but they deny the power thereof."[90] The Lord again forbade Joseph to join with any of them.[91] None of them knew the Lord. They sermonized and pontificated yet they lacked the keys of knowledge sufficient to plainly teach Christ's doctrine. They took power unto themselves, adding to and taking away from the Lord's commandments. They replaced an audience with the living Lord with rites and ordinances which they claimed were all that was necessary for salvation. All were wrong. All were in error. All were corrupt. They were blind leaders of the blind. They were ignorant guides, devoted to false traditions, claiming that their earthly institutions had the power to save them.

The Lord did not leave Joseph without hope. Many more things were revealed to him which he was commanded not to write at that time.[92] After this heavenly vision, Joseph's "soul was filled with love and for many days [he] could rejoice

---

[89] 1 Nephi 13:20-33 (LDS); or 1 Nephi 3:21-22 (RE).

[90] T&C 1—Joseph Smith History 2:5 (RE).

[91] "History, circa June 1839–circa 1841 [Draft 2]," p. [1], The Joseph Smith Papers, accessed June 10, 2020, https://www.josephsmithpapers.org/paper-summary/history-circa-june-1839-circa-1841-draft-2/1 See also Joseph's First Vision account found under History of Joseph Smith, printed in the Times and Seasons, Volume 3, Numbers 10 and 11 (March 15 & April 1, 1842), pp. 727-728, and 748; T&C Joseph Smith History Part 1-2 (RE).

[92] Ibid.

with great Joy and the Lord was with [him]."[93] **God is Love.** But many of us ask "If He loves us, then why did He send us down here to a world that is full of chaos and confusion? Why does He allow bad things to happen, especially to the pure and the innocent?"

Clinical psychologist, Jordan Peterson had a vision that he went to Heaven and was put in a roman amphitheater with Satan. It was rather a shock because he thought, "that's a hell of a thing to happen in Heaven." Well, he had his battle and he won. At the end, he came up to God and said: "You know, what's with the whole Roman Amphitheater thing," because he thought it was a little over the top, he said, "why would you put me in a ring with something like that?" God said, "Because I knew you could win."[94] As he has pondered on this vision, this is what he thinks it means:

> [I]f you want to make something strong you test it and maybe if you want to make something ultimately strong you test it ultimately . . .[Because of the Fall of Adam and Eve] we know good and evil now which allows us to be tested ultimately . . . Do you protect the people you love, or do you try to make them strong? It seems . . . that God [put us down here to be tested and that He] gave us Satan in order to make us strong. There is something about . . . consciousness through

[93] "History, circa Summer 1832," p. 1-4, The Joseph Smith Papers, accessed June 10, 2020, https://www.josephsmithpapers.org/paper-summary/history-circa-summer-1832/1; "You pray each time you partake of the sacrament to always have my spirit to be with you. And what is my spirit? It is to love one another as I have loved you." T&C 157:51 (RE).

[94] Peterson, J. B. (2020, May 3) *Biblical Series: Adam and Eve/ Self-Consciousness, Evil, and Death.* Apple Podcasts. Retrieved from https://podcasts.apple.com/us/podcast/biblical-series-adam-eve-self-consciousness-evil-and-death/id1184022695?i=1000473415047.

tragedy, clarity through suffering . . . that perfection that lurks as a potential in the future is something that has to be earned rather than given, maybe it has no value without free choice. Maybe we have to distinguish between good and evil now that we have the capacity to actually apprehend them. Maybe that's what life is about. Maybe that's the separating of the wheat from the chaff.[95]

Well, here we are today, celebrating and honoring the bicentennial of the First Vision.[96] What lessons have we learned about God through Joseph's first of many visions? What have we learned about God through our own grappling with Satan? What have we learned through the joys and sorrows of our own lives? Are we coming to know the Lord? If there was a young boy, or even a man, today who had the faith of Joseph and received a similar heavenly vision, would the Lord say much the same about us as He did about the people in Joseph's day?

The gospel of Jesus Christ has always been meant to teach mankind the correct character, perfections, and attributes of God in order that they might have the faith necessary to part the veil for themselves and enter back into His presence. Restoring ascension theology was Joseph's greatest gift to mankind. In order to make the fiery ascent back into the presence of the Lord, we must seek further light and knowledge from those who are sent from the presence of God to teach us. "There was a Pharisee named Nicodemus who was in darkness and came to visit with Jesus. He sought wisdom

---

95 Ibid.
96 June 20, 2020.

from Jesus and said, Enlightened heavenly guide, some of us know you have descended from the High Council of Heaven because signs confirm you have authority from God. Jesus answered I tell you, if you want to ascend to the Heavenly Council, you must first acknowledge and give heed to the messengers sent by them."[97]

Joseph was such a messenger. He was sent forth to declare the truth to the whole world.[98] Joseph's work must be remembered and preserved. The Lord revealed much through Joseph and we will be held accountable for the light and truth taught by him. Jesus Christ has declared that "**every soul** who forsakes their sins, and comes unto me, and calls on my name, and obeys my voice, and keeps all my commandments, shall see my face and know that I am. . . . for everyone that asks, receives; and he that seeks, finds; and to him that knocks, it shall be opened."[99] 200 years ago, on a beautiful spring morning, the Lord proved to the world that He does indeed keep His promises.[100]

---

[97] T&C The Testimony of St. John 2:1-3 (RE).

[98] T&C The Testimony of St. John 3:4 (RE).

[99] See D&C 93:1 (LDS); or T&C 93:1 (RE); emphasis added, and Matthew 7:6-8 (KJV); or Matthew 3:42 (RE).

[100] The Lord is no respecter of persons. Consider that He appeared to Adam who had previously rebelled and been cast out of His presence. He appeared to Moses, who had been a prince of Egypt and had committed murder to defend an innocent man. He appeared to Lehi who was a rich merchant in Jerusalem. He appeared to Alma the Elder who had been a wicked and corrupt priest. He appeared to Alma the Younger who had fought against the Lord's work. Each of these men repented and sought to be reunited with the Lord and received salvation and redemption. None of us are too far gone to have a relationship with Christ.

Removing the Stain of Polygamy from the Restoration[1]

Whitney N. Horning

© 2022

On June 27, 1844 Joseph Smith Jr., an authentic religious genius, was murdered in cold blood before the work of the Restoration was completed.[2] Joseph's ministry began during his fifteenth year when in faith he rose up out of the darkness and chaos of this world and into the Light of Christ.[3] He willingly chose to serve his God, laboring and sacrificing much to restore the fullness of the gospel of Jesus Christ to a hard-hearted and stiff-necked generation.[4]

---

[1] This talk was given at the Rescuing the Restoration Conference held in Meridian, Idaho on February 26, 2022.

[2] "[Joseph] Smith was an authentic religious genius, unique in our national history....I do not find it possible to doubt that [he] was an authentic prophet. Where in all of American history can we find his match?....In proportion to his importance and his complexity, [Smith] remains the least-studied personage, of an undiminished vitality, in our entire national saga." Harold Bloom, literary critic, religious scholar, and Professor of Humanities at Yale University. Bloom, H. (1992). *The American Religion: The Emergence of the Post Christian Nation*, p. 95. Simon and Schuster: New York.

[3] See Teachings and Commandments (T&C) 1—Joseph Smith History (JSH), Part 2. All scriptural references are from the Restoration Edition of the scriptures. They can be found online for free at https://scriptures.info/ or to purchase at https://scriptures.shop/.

[4] T&C A Glossary of Gospel Terms, "Hardness of Heart:" Hardness of heart is usually accompanied by a hardness of head; that is, people tend to not be willing to live in accordance with principles, even though they want to know about them. They are often more curious than they are obedient, becoming voyeurs rather than visionaries. Oddly enough, one's curiosity gets satisfied

In fulfillment of prophecy, the world has long spoken both good and evil of Joseph Smith.[5] Many people and many churches claim that they know Joseph. Historians, theologians, authors, and scholars have produced an exhaustive number of volumes on the subject. The majority of these works are based upon the historical narrative put forth by the largest and most well-known branch of Joseph's Restoration: The Church of Jesus Christ of Latter-day Saints. They assert that Joseph was commanded by God to enter into plural marriage using a priesthood ordinance called sealing, secretly teaching the doctrine to a select group of men and women in Nauvoo.[6] The LDS Church bases their claims upon the lies of John C. Bennett, the polygamy of Brigham Young and his followers, and the "revelation on marriage" known as LDS Doctrine and Covenants section 132.[7]

On April 6, 1860, Joseph Smith III, the oldest living son

---

as he obeys — but man is usually unwilling to make that exchange (New Covenants [NC] Book of Mormon [BofM]—Alma 9:3,10; 1 Nephi 3:26). Man determines whether he has a hard heart or an open heart. Anciently, the "heart" was considered the seat of understanding rather than emotion; therefore, an "open heart" belonged to the seeker, the asker, the knocker on the door (New Covenants [NC] New Testament [NT]—Matthew 3:42,44). And "Stiffneckedness:" When a person is 1 — in error and 2 — decidedly committed to remaining so. He won't budge, won't humble himself, and won't ask the Lord to remove his scales of darkness. He remains a devoted disciple of unbelief, leading to wickedness that is borne upon the shoulders of his ignorance.

[5] See T&C 1—JSH, 3:3 and T&C 139:7.

[6] The Church of Jesus Christ of Latter-day Saints also calls the marriage covenant "Celestial marriage," or the new and everlasting covenant of marriage.

[7] See *Saints*, Vol. 1, Ch. 40, "United in an Everlasting Covenant." Retrieved from https://www.churchofjesuschrist.org/study/history/saints-v1/40-united-in-an-everlasting-covenant?lang=eng.

of Joseph and Emma Smith, established the second largest branch founded upon the Restoration: The Reorganized Church of Jesus Christ of Latter Day Saints. Joseph III spent his life exonerating his father from the accusation of plural marriage and was instrumental in persuading the United States Congress to pass laws making the practice of polygamy illegal.[8] For over 100 years the RLDS Church believed and taught that Joseph Smith was a faithful and honorable monogamist.

In 1918, RLDS Patriarch Elbert A. Smith, grandson of Joseph and Emma, made the observation that the LDS Church in Utah included two remarkable statements made by Joseph Smith in their official History.[9] The first on May of 1844, stated,

---

[8] See Launius, Roger D. (1987) Methods and Motives: Joseph Smith III's Opposition to Polygamy, 1860-90. *Dialogue: A Journal of Mormon Thought*, Vol. 20, No. 4 (Winter 1987), pp. 105-120. Retrieved from https://www.jstor.org/stable/45228113?seq=1#metadata_info_tab_conte nts.

[9] The Church of Jesus Christ of Latter-day Saints contends that *A Comprehensive History of The Church of Jesus Christ of Latter-day Saints* in six volumes was written by Joseph Smith and compiled by B. H. Roberts. This is not a true statement. Joseph Smith had only written his and the Restoration's history up to June 1830 before he was killed. After his death, Brigham Young, Heber C. Kimball, and other men undertook to "correct" the history of the Church. Many alterations, additions, deletions, and corrections were made before the LDS Church published the six-volume series. One of the largest alterations regarded plural marriage. Joseph was decidedly against it and was laboring to eradicate it from the Church when he was killed. The LDS Church's history was edited to show that Joseph and Hyrum approved of, taught, and practiced plural marriage. Many examples of these changes can be seen at https://www.josephsmithpapers.org/. One example is the changes Brigham had made to Joseph journal entry for October 5, 1843. The original journal entry denouncing polygamy can be seen here (as of February 21, 2022): https://www.josephsmithpapers.org/paper-summary/journal-december-1842-june-1844-book-3-15-july-1843-29-february-1844/123#xbbbe971c-8c89-4ea1-b1af-c88a5eb316fb. The doctored version of Joseph's journal

"What a thing it is for a man to be accused of committing adultery, and having seven wives, when I can find only one." The second was stated ten days before he died, "I have taught all the strong doctrines publicly, and always taught stronger doctrines in public than in private." Patriarch Smith concluded that these two statements,

> [E]ffectually disposes of the Utah claim that [Joseph] taught the strong (and rank) doctrine of polygamy in private, not daring to teach it in public. Salt Lake can hardly repudiate its own version of these sermons. . . . There is no halfway ground. Either Joseph Smith was true and clean, open and above board . . . or else he was a hypocrite and a fraud through and through . . . The Utah Mormons cannot long continue seriously to contend that he was a real prophet of God, and a good man, yet blowing hot in private and cold in public, a monogamist in the pulpit and press and a polygamist in his home, a pure milk of the word man by daylight and a strong meat man after dark.[10]

In 2001, the RLDS Church officially changed their name to the Community of Christ. Because the historical preponderance of the LDS Church regarding Joseph and polygamy is widely accepted as fact today, the Community of Christ Church has now begun to sway toward believing the LDS Church's portrayal of Joseph Smith.[11]

---

entry promoting polygamy can be seen here (as of February 21, 2022): https://www.josephsmithpapers.org/paper-summary/history-draft-1-march-31-december-1843/143#source-note.

[10] See *Saints' Herald* 65 [February 27, 1918]: 204. See also Price, P. and R. (2000). *Joseph Smith Fought Polygamy, Vol. 1*, Ch. 10. Independence, MO: Price Publishing Co.

[11] Per private conversation with Community of Christ apostle, Lachlan E. Mackay, summer of 2019 at the Sunstone Symposium in Salt Lake City, Utah.

Several years ago, as an active, faithful, seventh generation Latter-day Saint, I concluded that my church's position on Joseph and polygamy showed him to be the worst kind of hypocrite, yet I could not deny that his words filled me with light and a hunger to know the Lord. I became determined to reconcile this paradox and find the truth. I researched, studied, pondered, and prayed for a process of time. One day a quiet thought entered my mind, "what if Joseph meant what he said?"

As I opened my mind to this new and startling idea, I began to come to know the real Joseph. He was a brilliant theologian. He was never one to back down or hesitate to proclaim all of the doctrines of the gospel, regardless of the persecution and opposition he encountered. He was a religious revolutionary who shared deep and often poignant thoughts and feelings on a number of difficult to understand topics without apology. On the subject of plural marriage, whenever he spoke about it, he emphatically denounced it and condemned it.

In the eastern United States, there were other new religious groups that arose around the same time that Joseph began the Restoration. Some of these new religions espoused divergent sexual and marital practices such that polygamy began to be associated with religious reform.[12] Whenever God

---

[12] The plurality of wives became associated with religious reform in the 1500's. Radical reformers in Munster, Germany in the 1530's practiced polygamy. Plural marriage became the subject of theological and social debates and was a significant aspect of Enlightenment thinking throughout Europe in the 1700's. Martin Madan published a pro-polygamy treatise in

begins a work to renew and restore truth there is always opposition in order to preserve mankind's right to choose.[13] Opposition presents itself in a myriad of ways. One of those is through the false spirit of adultery. Because adulterous hearts require signs to believe, the introduction of sexual promiscuity into a Restoration is one of the easiest ways for Satan to derail it.[14]

The adversary seemed aware that Joseph was destined to prove a disturber and an annoyer of his kingdom, and thus oppression and persecution arose against Joseph almost from his infancy.[15] He was often accused of adultery and polygamy and it quickly became commonplace for Mormon missionaries to be asked if they believed in having more wives than one.[16]

England in 1780. See Pearsall, Sarah. (2013). "Polygamy and Bigamy." Retrieved from http://www.oxfordbibliographies.com/view/document/obo-9780199730414/obo-9780199730414-0119.xml. Some of the groups who practiced divergent marriages in the United States were the Cochranites, John Humphrey Noyes' communities, and others. Their sexual practices reignited the idea that polygamy is part of religious reform.

[13] See NC BofM—2 Nephi 1:8.

[14] See NC NT—Matthew 6:15.

[15] See T&C 1—JSH 2:7-8.

[16] Joseph Smith, as editor of the *Elders' Journal*, listed frequently asked questions in the November 1837:28 edition. He listed the questions again along with the answers in the July 1838:43 edition, "In obedience to our promise, we give the following answers to questions, which were asked in the last number of the Journal." Question number seven was, "***Do the Mormons believe in having more wives than one. Answer. No, not at the same time. But they believe, that if their companion dies, they have a right to marry again.*** But we do disapprove of the custom which has gained in the world, and has been practiced among us, to our great mortification, of marrying in five or six weeks, or even in two or three months after the death of their companion. We believe that due respect ought to be had, to the memory of the dead, and the feelings of both friends and children." Emphasis added.

In 1834, Joseph was a member of a committee organized to publish a work "arranged from the items of the doctrine of Christ" and titled the Doctrine and Covenants.[17] Published in 1835 and unanimously accepted by the saints, it contained a section which became known as the Statement or Law of the Church on Marriage. It stated in part,

> [A]s this church of Christ has been reproached with the crime of fornication, and polygamy: we declare that we believe, that one man should have one wife; and one woman, but one husband, except in case of death, when either is at liberty to marry again.[18]

By 1842, Doctor John C. Bennett's sexual escapades in Nauvoo added fuel to the ongoing adultery rumors adding a new twist that Joseph was secretly preaching and practicing polygamy and giving Bennett and other select men permission to do likewise. When Joseph discovered Bennett's sexual indiscretions and duplicity he confronted him,

> Doctor! why are you using my name to carry on your hellish wickedness? Have I ever taught you that fornication and adultery was right, or polygamy or any

---

[17] The Kirtland high council appointed the following men to the committee: Joseph Smith, Oliver Cowdery, Sidney Rigdon, and Frederick G. Williams. The book was titled Doctrine and Covenants because the first part was comprised of the seven *Lectures on Faith* and the second part contained the revelations of the Lord revealed through Joseph. Oliver Cowdery was tasked with writing the section on marriage. Joseph had the Law of the Church on Marriage reprinted several times in the *Times and Seasons* between 1841-1844 and chose to include it in his 1844 edition of the Doctrine and Covenants. *Times and Seasons* can be found online at centerplace.org.

[18] 1835 edition Doctrine and Covenants section 101; see also "Doctrine and Covenants, 1835," p. 251, The Joseph Smith Papers, accessed February 10, 2022, https://www.josephsmithpapers.org/paper-summary/doctrine-and-covenants-1835/259.

such practices? . . . Did I ever teach you any thing that was not virtuous—that was iniquitous, either in public or private?[19]

Bennett responded, "You never did." He swore out an affidavit affirming that Joseph had only taught the strictest principles of the gospel and of virtue both in public and in private.[20]

Bennett was excommunicated for his misconduct, yet this did not stop the cancer of secret abominations from spreading throughout Nauvoo and the Church. As Joseph and Emma began to understand just how deeply the putridity of Bennett's behavior and teachings had seeped into the minds of the saints, they determined that since adultery takes two willing participants that the women of the Church would benefit from their own instruction. A society for the females, where they could meet regularly to learn truth straight from Joseph and Emma's mouths, was organized on March 17, 1842.[21] The primary purpose of the Female Relief Society was to strengthen and promote virtue and chastity among the

---

[19] *Times and Seasons*, Vol. 3, No. 19, (August 1, 1842), p. 871. Bennett stated in his affidavit that he "never was taught any thing in the least contrary to the strictest principles of the Gospel, or of virtue, or of the laws of God, or man, under any occasion either directly or indirectly, in word or deed, by Joseph Smith; and that he never knew the said Smith to countenance any improper conduct whatever, either in public or private; and that he never did teach . . . in private that an illegal illicit intercourse with females was, under any circumstances, justifiable, and that I never knew him so to teach others."

[20] Ibid.

[21] The official name voted on by the women present when the Society was first organized on March 17, 1842, was the Female Relief Society of Nauvoo. Joseph and Emma desired the people to be virtuous, morally good, chaste, to abstain from vice, and to conform to the moral, divine law of chastity. See *Nauvoo Relief Society Minute Book* found online at the Joseph Smith Papers Project website.

women.[22]

Joseph and Emma soon realized that the women of the Church had become so dependent upon the prophet and other leading men that they were susceptible to evil persuasion by any who claimed, "Joseph said it is right." Joseph encouraged the women to learn the scriptures and to think for themselves, stating that "If the people departed from the Lord, they must fall—that they were depending on the prophet hence they were darkened in their minds from neglect of themselves."[23] Joseph did not want the women to "trust in the arm of flesh," specifically men's adulterous advances. He and Emma hoped that a closer connection to Emma would empower women to "just say no" when approached by men making false claims. Joseph asked Emma to:

> [T]ell the sisters of the society that if any man, no matter who he was, undertook to talk such stuff [as the doctrine of polygamy] to them in their houses, to just order him out at once, and if he did not go immediately, to take the tongs or the broom and drive him out, for the whole idea was absolutely false and the doctrine an evil and unlawful thing.[24]

---

[22] Joseph often instructed the women to be pure of heart, exhorting them to live up to their privileges so that the angels could not be restrained from being their associates. He instructed them, "for what is more pleasing to God than innocence; you [women of the Relief Society] must be innocent, or you cannot come up before God; if we would come before God, we must keep ourselves pure, as He is pure." See Smith, Joseph F. (1976). *Teachings of the Prophet Joseph Smith*, p.226. Salt Lake City, UT: Deseret Book Company (hereafter denoted as TPJS).

[23] See the entry for the May 26, 1842, meeting in the *Nauvoo Relief Society Minute Book* found online at the Joseph Smith Papers Project website.

[24] Vienna Jaques' reminiscence as found in *The Memoirs of President Joseph Smith III*, p. 170; and *The Saint's Herald*, October 15, 1935, p. 1329.

Despite their crusade to eradicate polygamy and excommunicate those who were practicing and promoting it, the crime and sin of polygamy was taking a strong hold upon the saints and rapidly infiltrating the Restoration. Rumors that Joseph was secretly involved continued to increase. Joseph, Emma, and Hyrum intensified their efforts to eradicate the plural wife doctrine from the Church. On October 5, 1843, Joseph "gave instruction to try those who were preaching, teaching" or practicing this law, stating, "[I] forbid it and the practice thereof. No man shall have but one wife."[25] He and Hyrum excommunicated men and women, published names of guilty persons in the paper, and answered countless letters from saints who asked if "men having a certain priesthood, may have as many wives as he pleases."[26] Joseph and Hyrum's answer was firm: "that man teaches false doctrine, for there is no such doctrine taught here."[27]

When polygamy rumors spread to include Hyrum,

---

[25] "Journal, December 1842–June 1844; Book 3, 15 July 1843–29 February 1844," p. [117], The Joseph Smith Papers, accessed February 7, 2022, https://www.josephsmithpapers.org/paper-summary/journal-december-1842-june-1844-book-3-15-july-1843-29-february-1844/123.

[26] See *Times and Seasons*, Vol. 5, No. 3, (February 1, 1844), pp. 416-431 for the notice of the excommunication of Hiram Brown. The notice stated: "As we have lately been credibly informed, that an Elder of the Church of Jesus Christ, of Latter-day Saints, by the name of Hyram Brown, has been preaching polygamy, and other false and corrupt doctrines, in the county of Lapeer, state of Michigan. This is to notify him and the Church in general, that he has been cut off from the church, for his iniquity; and he is further notified to appear at the Special Conference, on the 6th of April next, to make answer to these charges. JOSEPH SMITH. HYRUM SMITH."

[27] See T&C 152 and *Times and Seasons*, Vol. 5, No. 6, (March 15, 1844), pp. 464-479. This letter was written by President Hyrum Smith on March 15, 1844, to the saints living on China Creek, in Hancock County, Illinois.

Joseph and Emma directed the publication of the pamphlet *A Voice of Innocence*. Their aim was to defend and exonerate Hyrum while publicly denouncing the plural wife practice.[28] The document was presented to several thousand saints who voted unanimously:

> [To] raise our voices and hands against John C. Bennett's 'spiritual wife system,' as a grand scheme of profligates to seduce women . . . let polygamy, bigamy, fornication, adultery, and prostitution, be frowned out of the hearts of honest men to drop into the gulf of fallen nature. . . . And let all the saints say, Amen![29]

LDS Church History and D&C section 132 teach that there are times when God may command a man to enter into polygamy, yet Joseph Smith consistently denied that he practiced plural marriage and spoke out against it, both publicly and privately. On April 8, 1844, co-president, co-prophet, and Patriarch of the Church Hyrum Smith spoke at length against the "spiritual wife system" during a special meeting for the Elders. He was decidedly against the idea in every form, calling it the "damned foolish doctrine of polygamy." Hyrum declared that God had never commanded any man to enter into plural marriage and promised that any

---

[28] Orsamus F. Bostwick leveled accusations of polygamy, adultery, and prostitution at Hyrum Smith. See *Times and Seasons*, vol. 3, p. 940, [October 1, 1842]. See also the document *A Voice of Innocence from Nauvoo*.

[29] On March 7, 1844, the pamphlet was presented to a "vast assembly of saints" who unanimously accepted it. The document was then presented to the Female Relief Society. The meetings were so well attended that it was necessary to hold four sessions to accommodate all who wished to participate. Two meetings were held on March 9, 1844, and two were held on March 16, 1844. The document was unanimously accepted by all of those in attendance and published in the *Nauvoo Neighbor* on March 20, 1844.

elder discovered teaching, preaching, or living it would be called home, their preaching license removed, and their name published in the paper.[30]

A few weeks before his death, Joseph asked William Marks, president of the Nauvoo Stake and high council, to help bring leading men and women "in high places" to stand trial and be expelled for secretly practicing polygamy. Joseph stated that polygamy would ruin the church and lamented that he had been deceived by these men.[31] Joseph was killed before he

---

[30] Up to Joseph's death some of the men whose names were published in the paper include John C. Bennett and Hiram Brown. The Joseph Smith Papers (2015). *Journals, Vol. 3, May 1843-June 1844*, p. 224. Salt Lake City, UT: The Church Historian's Press and Hyrum Smith, April 8, 1844, Conference address, "Minutes and Discourses, 6–9 April 1844, as Reported by Thomas Bullock," p. 30-32, The Joseph Smith Papers, accessed February 12, 2022; https://www.josephsmithpapers.org/paper-summary/minutes-and-discourses-6-9-april-1844-as-reported-by-thomas-bullock/33. *After giving this talk and publishing my book on Hyrm Smith, *Hyrum Smith A Prophet Unsung*, the Joseph Smith Papers removed this document. The only place an original can be seen as of today is the LDS Church History Library, Historian's Office general Church minutes, 1839-1877; 1839-1845; Nauvoo, Illinois, 1844 April 6-9; Church History Library, https://catalog.churchofjesuschrist.org/assets/daa151c4-7bae-49d0-8cef-d281a70f1d32/0/0?lang=eng (accessed: January 2, 2024).

[31] Emma told Joseph that some of the sisters in the Relief Society claimed that Brigham Young and some of his fellow apostles were involved in the secret polygamy ring in Nauvoo. Brigham, who was on his way back East, was called on by Joseph to delay his departure and come speak with him (see letter from William Smith to his nephew, Joseph Smith III, printed in *The Saints' Herald* 26 [April 15, 1879]: 117. The letter revealed that John Taylor, Willard Richards, and Brigham Young were the ones responsible for privately teaching and practicing polygamy and that Joseph had been deceived by them). See *RLDS History of the Church* 2:733 and William Marks, "Epistle," *Zions Harbinger and Baneemy's Organ* 3 (July 1853), pp. 52-54. Published in St. Louis by C. B. Thompson.

could follow through on bringing the guilty parties to trial.[32] It is worth the effort to reconcile these contradictions. We live in a great day and age where truth long since hidden is coming forth into the light of day.[33] "The things of God are of deep import," taught Joseph,

> and time, and experience, and careful and ponderous and solemn thoughts can only find them out. Thy mind, O man! If thou wilt lead a soul unto salvation, must stretch as high as the utmost heavens, and search into and contemplate the darkest abyss, and the broad expanse of eternity--thou must commune with God.[34]

There is a growing movement within Mormonism to believe that Joseph meant it when he said a few weeks before he died,

> I had not been married scarcely five minutes, and made one proclamation of the Gospel, before it was reported that I had seven wives... I can only find one. I am the same man, and as innocent as I was fourteen years ago; and I can prove them all perjurers.[35]

---

[32] At the time of Joseph's death eight members of the quorum of the Twelve were secretly involved in polygamy, and according to William Marks, without Joseph's prior knowledge or approval. Those men were: Brigham Young, Heber C. Kimball, Parley P. Pratt, Willard Richards, John Taylor, George A. Smith, Orson Hyde, and Orson Pratt. Shortly after Joseph's murder two more entered into the practice with the other eight taking on even more wives. Those two were Lorenzo Snow and Wilford Woodruff.

[33] The evidence which proves that Joseph fought polygamy has always existed in newspapers, documents, journals, etc. We are indebted to those who have made this information available through digitization, the internet, books, articles, blogs, etc.

[34] TPJS, p. 137.

[35] Ehat, Andrew F. & Cook, Lyndon W. (1980). *The Words of Joseph Smith*, pp. 375-77. Provo, UT: Religious Studies Center Brigham Young University (hereafter denoted as WJS).

Critics cry out that in the effort to exonerate Joseph and prove that he was a faithful monogamist two main pieces of evidence are overlooked: LDS Doctrine and Covenants 132, known as the "polygamy revelation," and the many testimonies of women who claimed to have been "married or sealed" to Joseph.[36]

In June 1844 the first and only edition of the *Nauvoo Expositor* was published as an expose on Joseph and polygamy. It contained language similar in nature to LDS D&C 132. Seriously concerned that the *Expositor* would stir up angry mobs, the Nauvoo City Council consulted together for two days to determine what action they should take, if any, against the paper. Testimony was given by both Joseph and Hyrum concerning the purported polygamy revelation which had been written down one year earlier on July 12, 1843, most likely in preparation for a sermon Joseph gave on July 16th during which

---

[36] Critics who state that the women should be believed are generally referring to affidavits from dozens of women who claimed that they were "married or sealed" to Joseph Smith. The wording in these affidavits is such that if the woman had been sealed as a daughter to Joseph and Emma rather than as a wife to Joseph, her affidavit was still technically accurate. Also, consider that Brigham Young and Heber C. Kimball "married or sealed" dozens of women to Joseph and a few women to Hyrum as wives in January 1846, one and a half years *after* their deaths. Many of the affidavits collected by Joseph F. Smith in 1869 do not include a date of woman's marriage or sealing to Joseph Smith, thus the women were not technically lying when they stated that they had been "married or sealed" to Joseph as they could have been referring to the post-martyrdom sealings performed by Brigham Young and Heber C. Kimball. The few affidavits referring to Hyrum Smith are very suspect, not being affirmed until after all of the purported witnesses to the event were deceased. Additionally, Hyrum's sister-in-law Mercy Fielding Thompson stated that she was the only plural wife of Hyrum and that he had no others. Mercy was never sealed to Hyrum while he was living, rather, he stood as proxy for her deceased husband, Robert Blashel Thompson, so that she could be sealed to Robert.

he publicly taught the concepts of the revelation.[37]

Joseph testified before the City Council on June 8 and 10, 1844 that the *Expositor* transformed the truth of God into a lie, that he never preached the revelation in private as he had in public and had not taught [polygamy] to the anointed in the Church, either in public or in private. Many men confirmed this statement. Joseph explained that he had been pondering on the passage in the Bible "[I]n the resurrection they neither marry nor are given in marriage, but are as the angels of God in Heaven" and received for an answer that a man and his wife must be married in view of eternity in this life or he will have no claim on her in the next, and that was the full amount of the content of the revelation.[38] Hyrum testified that he read the marriage revelation to the high council in August 1843, and "that it was in answer to a question concerning things which transpired in former days and had no reference to the present

---

[37] The revelation Joseph received in answer to his question regarding the scripture "neither are they married nor given in marriage in the resurrection" was written down July 12, 1843, most likely in preparation for a talk he gave on the subject on July 16, 1843 (see WJS, pp. 232-233).

[38] See NC NT—Matthew 10:22 and Mark 5:43, Dinger, John S., editor. (2011). *The Nauvoo City and High Council Minutes*, p. 255-256. Salt Lake City, UT: Signature Books and WJS, pp. 232-233. Joseph taught the concepts of the eternal marriage revelation publicly to the saints in a sermon on July 16, 1843, "[A] man must enter into an everlasting covenant with his wife in this world or he will have no claim on her in the next." He told the saints that he "could not reveal the fullness of these things until the [Nauvoo] Temple is completed." According to Joseph's journal, on May 28, 1843, the very first Eternal marriage covenant of the Restoration took place between Joseph and Emma. The next day, Hyrum entered into an Eternal marriage covenant with his deceased wife, Jerusha, who had died several years earlier. Hyrum's second wife, Mary Fielding Smith declined the opportunity to be eternally married to Hyrum and had chosen instead to stand as proxy for Jerusha.

time."[39]

The original revelation is no longer in existence. Brigham Young and his followers claimed that Joseph Kingsbury, a store clerk, made a copy of the original revelation before Emma burned it. That copy was kept locked in Brigham's desk drawer until it was read for the first time in public during a special conference in Salt Lake in 1852, eight years after Joseph's death. Many people who had seen or listened to the original revelation testified that the one Brigham brought forth was nothing like the one Joseph had received.[40] In 1876 Brigham had The Law of the Church on Marriage which stated that "one man should have but one wife" removed from the Doctrine and Covenants and replaced it with what is now known as section 132.[41] D&C 132 is an altered copy of a copy with a dubious history.

The second criticism regards believing the testimony of women.[42] Misled by church leaders' and husbands' incorrect

---

[39] Dinger, John S., editor. (2011). *The Nauvoo City and High Council Minutes*, p. 241. Salt Lake City, UT: Signature Books.

[40] See *Abstract of Evidence Temple Lot Case U.S.C.C.*; The Temple Lot Case [trial and appeal transcripts] (Lamoni, Iowa: Herald Publishing House, 1893); https://archive.org/details/TempleLotCase; and various statements of Emma Smith.

[41] In 1876 under Brigham Young's direction, 26 sections were added; one of those was section 132, the "polygamy" revelation, while the former Law of the Church on Marriage was removed. In 1921 *Lectures on Faith* was removed.

[42] The strongest anti-polygamy sermon ever given by a prophet of the Lord recorded in scripture revealed that the Lord heard the mourning of the daughters of His people in Jerusalem and in all the lands of His people because of the wickedness and abominations of their husbands who had broken the hearts of their tender wives and lost the confidence of their children and whose sobbings ascended up to God against their husbands and fathers. See NC BofM—Jacob 2:8-9.

interpretations of scripture, false beliefs, and a wrong understanding of what Joseph was really doing, many early Mormon women who agreed to plural marriage suffered terribly.

Helen Mar Kimball, daughter of Heber and Vilate, had lived thirty years in polygamy when she bemoaned: "Nothing would induce me to lose . . . that crown which awaits all that have laid their willing, but bleeding hearts upon the altar!"[43]

Sarah Pratt, first wife of Orson Pratt, left Mormonism when Orson, at age fifty-seven, took his tenth wife, a young girl of sixteen. Sarah called his venture into polygamy "sheer fanaticism."

A daughter of Jedediah M. Grant said, "Polygamy is alright when it is properly carried out—on a shovel!"[44]

Phebe Woodruff, first wife of Wilford Woodruff shared with a close friend why she publicly supported polygamy,

> I loathe the unclean thing with all the strength of my nature, but Sister, I have suffered all that a woman can endure. I am old and helpless, and would rather stand up anywhere, and say anything commanded of me, than to be turned out of my home in my old age which I should be most assuredly if I refused to obey counsel.[45]

Emmeline B. Wells, Daniel H. Wells' seventh wife, prominent writer and editor defended plural marriage in

---

[43] *The Saints' Advocate* 6 (June 1884): pp. 449-451.

[44] Van Wagoner, R. S. (1986). *Mormon Polygamy: A History,* p. 94. Salt Lake City, UT: Signature Books.

[45] Pearson, C. L. (2016) *The Ghost of Eternal Polygamy,* p. 113. Pivot Point Books. See also, Van Wagoner, R. S. (1986). *Mormon Polygamy: A History,* p. 101. Salt Lake City, UT: Signature Books.

public, but inwardly was full of sorrow. She recorded in her journal:

> O, if only my husband could only love me even a little and not seem to be perfectly indifferent to any sensation of that kind. He cannot know the cravings of my nature; he is surrounded with love on every side, and I am cast out. . . . How much sorrow I have known in place of the joy I looked forward to.[46]

Brigham Young said the following about the struggles women had in polygamous unions:

> A few years ago one of my wives, when talking about wives leaving their husbands said, "I wish my husband's wives would leave him, every soul of them except myself." That is the way they all feel, more or less, at times, both old and young.[47]

Of all the testimonies women have given regarding Joseph and polygamy, there is one whose holds the greatest value. She was the only woman whose life intertwined intimately with his. In all of scripture, there are only two women given the title Elect Lady by the Lord. Emma Smith was one of them.[48] Despite the suspicion, turmoil, and poverty that accompanied Joseph from the beginning of the Restoration, Emma chose to unite her life to his. She was his greatest support and truest friend. Driven from state to state by

---

[46] Van Wagoner, R. S. (1986). *Mormon Polygamy: A History,* p. 94. Salt Lake City, UT: Signature Books.

[47] *Journal of Discourse*, vol. 9, p. 195.

[48] Emma is the only woman of the Restoration to be given the title elect lady by the Lord. In all of scripture there are only two women referred to as "elect lady:" Mary, the wife of Christ (NC NT—2 John 1:1, T&C 171—The Testimony of St. John 8:1, 13; 11:16; and 12:1, 4) and Emma Smith (T&C 5:1).

persecution, the struggles to provide the necessities of life, the deaths of six children, caring for their family while Joseph was imprisoned or forced into hiding, what Emma experienced in her young married life would have emotionally and spiritually crippled most ordinary women.[49]

Joseph's mother, Lucy, said of Emma,

> I have never seen a woman in my life, who would endure every species of fatigue and hardship, from month to month, and from year to year, with that unflinching courage, zeal, and patience, which she has ever done; for I know that which she has had to endure ... would have borne down almost any other woman.[50]

Emma suffered great sorrows and afflictions, yet she remained faithful and true to Joseph, to the Lord, and to the work of the Restoration.

Those who advocated plural marriage in Nauvoo and later altered the LDS Church's history described Emma as a thorn in Joseph's side, opposing his plural marriage policies, burning the polygamy revelation, and leading him an ill life. According to Joseph, Emma, their children, and others who knew her, these accusations were absolutely not true.[51] Joseph and Emma had a respectful, loving, and affectionate

---

[49] During their marriage, Emma gave birth to nine children, five of whom were stillborn or died as infants, and adopted twins, one of whom died as an infant, for a total of six out of eleven who died.

[50] Smith, Lucy Mack (1853). *History of Joseph Smith*, pp. 190-191. Liverpool, England.

[51] Anderson, M. S. (1832-1914) *The Memoirs of President Joseph Smith III*, p.35.

marriage.[52] Asked if she and Joseph had ever quarreled or if she had opposed him where polygamy was concerned, Emma replied,

> I never had any reason to oppose him, for we were always on the best of terms ourselves. . . . There was no necessity for any quarreling. He knew that I wished for nothing but what was right; and, as he wished for nothing else, we did not disagree . . . It was quite a grievous thing to many that I had any influence with him.[53]

Regarding D&C 132, Emma declared,

> [T]he statement that I burned the original of the copy Brigham Young claimed to have, is false, and made out of whole cloth, and not true in any particular. . . .I never saw anything purporting to be a revelation authorizing polygamy until I saw it in the *Seer*, published by Orson Pratt.[54]

Emma was considered "of the purest and noblest intentions herself, she never submitted to be made a party to anything low, wrong, or evil, was absolutely fearless where the right was concerned."[55] She was a woman of great compassion, honor, integrity, and truthfulness. If anyone knew what Joseph

---

[52] Joseph adored Emma, publicly remarking on several occasions that she was a wonderful wife. He said of her, "Oh, what a commingling of thought filled my mind for the moment, again she is here, even in the seventh trouble—undaunted, firm, and unwavering—unchangeable, affectionate Emma." See Newell and Avery. (1994) *Mormon Enigma Emma Hale Smith*. Champaign, IL: University of Illinois Press.

[53] Briggs, E. C., *Early History of the Reorganization*, pp. 88, 93-95 and *The Saints' Herald*, Vol. 26, pp. 289, 290.

[54] Briggs, E. C., *Early History of the Reorganization*, pp. 88, 93-95.

[55] Newell and Avery. (1994) *Mormon Enigma Emma Hale Smith*. Champaign, IL: University of Illinois Press.

was about, it was Emma, who stood by his side as his partner, companion, and helpmeet.[56]

Emma stood shoulder to shoulder with Joseph to fight iniquity, both in public and in private, and consistently championed him as a man of honor and virtue.[57] Toward the end of her life, she said of Joseph, "He did not have improper relations with any woman that ever came to my knowledge."[58]

Emma

[S]poke so endearingly of Joseph, in confidence, tears filling her eyes that [you] could see she reverenced his

---

[56] Emma's support of Joseph began early in their courtship. She accompanied Joseph the night he retrieved the Gold Plates at the Hill Cumorah. She rode to warn Joseph about a group of men that were searching the woods to find the plates which he had hidden. Emma served as Joseph's scribe for a time while he translated the plates into the Book of Mormon. Once Oliver Cowdery became the scribe, Emma would relieve Oliver when he grew tired. Emma never broke the Lord's confidence: she lived with the Gold Plates in her home for almost two years under a command from God that she was not to look at them, even while the plates were kept in a little trunk on her dresser or covered by a linen tablecloth, she kept her word.

[57] A few of the ways Emma joined with Joseph in the fight against polygamy: she and Joseph filed a slander lawsuit against Chauncey Higbee, he supported her in forming the Relief Society to help teach the woman the commandments of God so they would have the knowledge to turn away men seeking to engage them in polygamy, and she edited the pamphlet, *A Voice of Innocence*, and during the succession crisis which took place after Joseph's death, Emma supported William Marks, and not Brigham Young. When Brigham's followers headed West, Emma remained in Nauvoo where she continued to denounce polygamy and defend Joseph's innocence. Emma stated, "I was threatened by Brigham Young because I opposed and denounced his measures and would not go west with them. At that time, they did not know where they were going themselves, but he told me that he would yet bring me prostrate to his feet" (Briggs, E. C., *Early History of the Reorganization*, pp. 88, 93-95).

[58] Newell and Avery. (1994) *Mormon Enigma Emma Hale Smith*, p. 301. Champaign, IL: University of Illinois Press.

very memory, and had full faith in Joseph's inspiration as a prophet of God, and she always denied. . . in the most emphatic language that he taught or practiced polygamy.[59]

Joseph had assured Emma that if she heard rumors about spiritual marriages, or anything of the kind, that "they were without foundation; that there was no such doctrine, and never should be with his knowledge, or consent." [60] She recalled that Joseph told her polygamy was "contrary to the will of Heaven" and always led to violence.[61] Emma, who knew Joseph best, was firm: "he had no other wife or wives other than myself, in any sense, either spiritual or otherwise."[62]

After Joseph's death the Restoration shattered into dozens of off-shoots and began to fall into ruin and decay.[63] Polygamy entered Brigham Young's branch unchecked and proceeded to destroy lives and shatter faith. Since God's definition of adultery includes sexual relations outside the bounds of a monogamous marriage, if we are going to rescue, preserve, and live the Restoration begun by Joseph, we ought

---

[59] Briggs, E. C., *Early History of the Reorganization*, pp. 88, 93-95.

[60] *The Saints' Herald*, Vol. 26, pp. 289, 290.

[61] See interview with Emma Smith as reported in *The Saints' Herald*, vol. 26, pp. 289-290. Too often, violence is a product of adultery/polygamy as wicked and ambitious men wrestle for control over wives, children, and followers. "Linking murder and adultery together in the list that Alma provides [NC BofM—Alma 11:8] is not just happenstance. Preaching against adultery and guarding yourself against that may keep you also distant from the kind of anger and violence that results in the shedding of blood and the misery of many souls, just like the Answer to the Prayer for Covenant mentions" (Snuffer, Denver [2021] *Equality*, p. 8).

[62] *The Saints' Herald*, Vol. 26, pp. 289, 290.

[63] See dream given to Joseph Smith, Jr. June 26, 1844, as contained in T&C 153.

to know what that entails, including the truth behind polygamy.[64]

Joseph was one of this world's greatest Christian thinkers. He laid a foundation that would revolutionize the whole world.[65] His audacious and unorthodox religion was a

---

[64] See T&C—A Glossary of Gospel Terms, "Adultery:" To look on a woman to lust after her...or...commit adultery in their hearts (T&C 50:4; see also NC NT—Matt 3:21; NC BofM— 3 Nephi 5:27; T&C 26:8) means the actual scheming or mental planning to engage or seduce. It is not just a passing biological attraction that is subdued by one's will to obey God, nor is it a whispered temptation from a mischievous spirit. Subduing and rejecting that temptation is part of living righteously. Divorce also leads to adultery. When forced away by the man she loves, a woman is then adulterated by the act of the man. He is accountable for the treachery involved in dissolving the marriage that the woman wanted and forcing her into the relation with either no one or with another man. In either case, it is adulterating the marriage which she had with him. He is accountable for that uncharitable, unkind, and unjustified treatment of the woman. On the other hand, when she has lost affection for him and the union has become hollow and without love, then the marriage is dead, and continuation of the relation is a farce. It is not a marriage. In fact, it is a pretense and an abomination unworthy of preservation. It will not endure. "We reject adultery by any name or description. It is morally wrong, even if you call it plural wives, polygamy, 'celestial marriage,' or any other misnomer. Adultery is prohibited in the Ten Commandments and remains an important prohibition for any moral society." There is a reason why such a serious sin as adultery ought to be altogether avoided; even if it is only as a foolish temptation contemplating the possibility of a plural wife. All need greater light and knowledge. The only way it can be acquired is by heed and diligence to the commandments of God. Any other path is a diversion, intended to waylay a person and prevent him or her from developing as God intends. Those who think they can follow God and yet commit adultery are deceived and giving heed to a false spirit. It is impossible to be both on the path to greater light and also engaged in such a serious sin. In addition to referring to a physical act involving sexual union with another, the term adultery is often used with the connotation of unfaithfulness, as in Israel becoming unfaithful and playing the part of an adulteress, worshiping other gods (see OC—Jeremiah 2:1).

[65] See WJS, p. 367. The Lord promised Joseph that his people would never be turned against him by the testimony of traitors (T&C 139:7).

gift from God intended for all mankind.[66] Yet, God's voice through Joseph has largely been silenced by the stain of polygamy. Honest seekers for truth disregard and discount Joseph's marvelous message in part because they believe he was a liar, hypocrite, sexual deviant, and pedophile.

Opposing information preserves our right to choose. On one side are the testimonies of known liars, traitors, and enemies of Joseph, the men and women who embraced the "damned foolish doctrine of polygamy" placing the blame of their own sins upon the shoulders of Joseph, and the LDS Church's long-standing historical traditions. On the other side are the testimonies of Joseph, a prophet of God, who declared a few weeks before his death,

> It is our purpose to build up and establish the principles of righteousness, and not to break down and destroy. The Great Jehovah has ever been with me, and the wisdom of God will direct me in the seventh hour. I feel in closer communion and better standing with God than ever I felt before in my life.[67]

And Emma, the Elect Lady, who lamented,

> [T]he Utah Mormons had by their acts, since the death of her husband, made true all the slanders and vile things charged against the Church.[68]

---

[66] One of Joseph Smith's greatest teachings was the audacious idea that God desired to have a personal relationship with each and every person. Joseph taught that "every soul" who forsakes their sins, and comes unto the Lord, and calls on His name, and obeys His voice, and keeps all His commandments, could ascend up to the throne of God, to see His face and know that He is! See T&C 93:1.

[67] WJS, pp. 375-77.

[68] *The Saints' Herald*, Vol. 26, pp. 289, 290.

Either Joseph and Emma were telling the truth or they were not.[69]

John C. Bennett's lies, and Brigham Young's doctrine of polygamy have stained the Restoration long enough. The Lord promised Joseph,

> [Y]our people shall never be turned against you by the testimony of traitors . . . you shall be had in honor. And but for a small moment, and your voice shall be more terrible in the midst of your enemies than the fierce lion, because of your righteousness, and your God shall stand by you for ever and ever.[70]

I invite you to come to know the correct character, perfections, and attributes of the Lord through the revelations, teachings, and writings of Joseph Smith.[71] Together, we can rescue the Restoration and help move it toward its glorious, prophesied conclusion.[72]

---

[69] There is enough information published and recorded in Joseph's day that is readily available to us today that can inform us concerning Joseph's repeated denials and condemnation of polygamy. The public and private words of Joseph reveal that he taught nothing but what was right and reveal that he was decidedly opposed to the plural wife system.

[70] T&C 139:7, emphasis added.

[71] See Old Covenants (OC) "Foreword," retrieved from https://scriptures.info/scriptures/oc/ocforeword, and T&C A Glossary of Gospel Terms, "Know the Lord."

[72] On January 19, 1841, the Lord promised the saints that if they built a temple wherein He could dwell, that he would "come and restore again that which was lost unto you, or which he has taken away, even the fullness of the Priesthood." The Nauvoo Temple was never completed, and the promised fullness was not restored. All Restoration attempts are meant to culminate with the establishment of Zion. This has not yet happened. See T&C A Glossary of Gospel Terms, "Zion."

Essay 4

Joseph vs. Polygamy:
The Raging Storm in Nauvoo[1]

Whitney N. Horning

© March 21, 2022

Storms rage around us and a diverse legion of voices surround us.[2] There is a great war of words and contest of opinions on almost every matter. This can make discerning truth from error difficult. "Truth is knowledge of things as they are, and as they were, and as they are to come; and whatever is more or less than these is the spirit of that wicked one who was a liar from the beginning."[3] False spirits, false ideas, false prophets, and imitative religions all vie for our attention.

False spirits take the form of ignorant, incomplete, or incorrect ideas that are easily conveyed from one person to another. They are spirits that mislead and confuse. And they infect every religious tradition on earth.[4] Many early saints of the Restoration could not discern between false spirits and true ones, disregarding and discarding the voice of the Lord in favor of more enticing ones. The heeding of false spirits in Nauvoo created a raging storm that culminated in Joseph Smith's

---

[1] I would like to thank the organizers of this conference for inviting me to speak here today. This talk is a companion to one I gave last month at the Rescuing the Restoration conference held in Boise, Idaho on February 26, 2022. *This talk was given at the Hear and Trust the Lord in the Storm conference held on March 25-27, 2022, in Lexington, Kentucky.

[2] Teachings and Commandments, Joseph Smith History (T&C JSH) 1:11.

[3] T&C 93:8.

[4] T&C—A Glossary of Gospel Terms, "False Spirit."

death.

If we fail to learn from history, we are doomed to repeat it.[5]

In the beginning, Adam and Eve were created in God's image, male and female.[6] Marriage was established at the beginning as a covenant by the word and authority of God, between the woman and God, the man and the woman, and the man and God, and was ordained by His word to endure for ever. God intended it to remain so for the sons of Adam and the daughters of Eve that they might multiply and replenish the earth.[7] God commanded that there should not any man have save it be one wife, and concubines he should have none, for the Lord "delights in the chastity of women, and in the respect men have for their wives."[8]

Upon Eve's creation, Adam prophesied,

This I know now is bone of my bones and flesh of my flesh. She shall be called woman because she was taken out of man; therefore shall a man leave his father and his mother and shall cleave unto his wife, and they shall be one flesh.[9]

---

[5] Winston Churchill said, "Those that fail to learn from history are doomed to repeat it."

[6] Joseph Smith taught that the Hebrew word for God, Elohim, ought to be plural throughout the entire Bible. Male and female, husband and wife, an eternal couple. See Ehat, Andrew F. & Cook, Lyndon W. (1980). *The Words of Joseph Smith*, p. 379. Provo, UT: Religious Studies Center Brigham Young University (hereafter denoted as WJS).

[7] See T&C 157:34-35.

[8] New Covenants Book of Mormon (NC BofM)—Jacob 2:7, T&C 157:34.

[9] See Old Covenants (OC) Genesis 2:14. Besides the unity between a man and his wife which makes them "one," consider that when a child is conceived the father's DNA and the mother's DNA combines to create one flesh.

It was God's will that all marriages would follow this pattern, and therefore all other marriages would be ordained as at the first.

Adam and Eve understood that they reflected God's image because they stood in God's presence and had a most perfect knowledge of God's existence.[10] Upon their transgression, Adam and Eve were driven out of Eden and separated from God. For several generations, mankind remained faithful to God's image as Adam and Eve's descendants divided two and two in the land.[11] Not many generations passed, however, before Lamech, one of Adam and Eve's descendants through Cain, apostatized from God's image and commandments when he took two wives.[12] Lamech's works were abominations and began to spread among all the sons of men.[13]

Fallen men refused God's marriage covenant, did not hearken to His word, nor receive His promise, and marriage fell outside His rule, disorganized and without Him, therefore unable to endure beyond the promises made between the mortal man and the mortal woman, to end when they are dead.[14] Mankind deliberately, intentionally, and willfully rejected the pure gospel of Jesus Christ and in doing so, lost correct knowledge and understanding.[15]

Nothing remains stagnant in this world of change,

---

[10] OC Genesis 2:8-9 and T&C 110—Lectures on Faith (LoF) 2:3 and 634.

[11] OC Genesis 3:1.

[12] Lamech became Master Mahon. See OC Genesis 3:11.

[13] OC Genesis 3:12.

[14] See New Covenants New Testament (NC NT)—Matthew 10:22, Mark 5:43, Luke 12:10; and T&C 157:36.

[15] This world has experienced numerous cycles of apostasy and restoration.

either growth or decay are at work at all times, everywhere. Since the days of Adam, whether as a group or as an individual, mankind has either been restoring light and truth or apostatizing from it.[16] Whenever there is a man, or even a boy, with the faith necessary to ascend above this world and into His light, it becomes possible for God to restore truth. In 1820 God's image was uncovered when Joseph Smith Jr. parted the

---

[16] Whenever mankind departs from the word of God and apostatizes from truth, one of the many sins that is embraced is sexual immorality, including, but not limited to, the taking of multiple wives and concubines. During Jesus Christ's mortal ministry, He attempted to elevate the mind, heart, and spirit of mankind. "To look on a woman to lust after her," he said, is akin to committing adultery in the heart. This means the actual scheming or mental planning to engage or seduce and not just a passing biological attraction that is subdued by one's will to obey God, nor is it a whispered temptation from a mischievous spirit. Subduing and rejecting that temptation is part of living righteously. See NC NT—Matthew 3:21; NC BofM—3 Nephi 5:27; T&C 26:8, 50:4; and T&C A Glossary of Gospel Terms, "Adultery." Therefore, whenever God undertakes to restore His will and pleasure, it necessarily includes revealing His correct character, attributes, and perfections, including His image. Such was the case with Moses as well as with Joseph Smith. When Moses saw God, he saw a "burning bush." This is symbolic of the mother, or the female deity. See OC Genesis 1:3 and Exodus 2:2. See also T&C A Glossary of Gospel Terms, "Apostasy:" When mankind limits what they will permit God to reveal, setting boundaries to His teachings, they rebel. But that rebellion only limits themselves. Mankind, whether as a group or a single person, is either gaining (restoring) light and truth or losing (apostatizing) from light and truth. This world is a world of change. Nothing remains the same. Either growth or decay are at work everywhere. They are also at work within every person. One either searches out new truth — finds it, lives it, and thereby becomes restored to truth — or one backs away from it. If one is backing away, losing it, neglecting it, and discarding it, one is in the process of apostasy. With respect to God's people, apostasy is always marked by a change of ordinances and breaking of the covenant. "In ancient times, apostasy never came by renouncing the gospel, but always by corrupting it.... The great apostasy in the time of the apostles was not a renouncing of faith but its corruption and manipulation."

veil and entered Their presence.[17]

Through a process of time and experience, Joseph became a servant of God, clothed with power and authority. He was a man who sought to be morally sound, pure of heart, incorrupt, upright, genuine, unadulterated, and honest. He strove to obey the Lord's commands with exactness.[18] When Joseph said he believed something, he demonstrated his belief by example. When he said he would do something, he did it.[19] He was a man of integrity who respected, honored, and loved his wife Emma and was faithful to her in every way.

As a servant of God, Joseph labored to elevate and uplift the minds, hearts, and souls of the people. As a brilliant and

---

[17] Joseph taught a correct understanding of that image to his people and expected them to honor God by keeping all the commandments, including God's law of marriage and chastity. See T&C A Glossary of Gospel Terms, "Heavenly Host:" "Men and women may see Christ in vision or in an appearance as a solitary personage, but no person has ever seen God the Father without also seeing a host of others. They are referred to in scriptures as a Heavenly host or numerous angels or concourses of angels. 'There is a reason that a company is always shown at the appearance of the Father. You should look into the matter. Within the answer lies a great truth about God the Father.' Throughout scripture, the Father is described as the God of Hosts. Seeing Him includes an accompanying host or concourses of angels or train or a similar reference to others with Him. He appears with the Heavenly Host because God has a family, including a spouse." See also NC NT—Epistle of Jacob 1:2.

[18] See Webster's 1828 Dictionary: Integrity.

[19] See RLDS Patriarch Elbert A. Smith. *Saints' Herald* 65 [February 27, 1918]: 204. In addition, see Price, P. and R. (2000). *Joseph Smith Fought Polygamy, Vol. 1*, Ch. 10. Independence, MO: Price Publishing Co. In a sermon on May 26, 1844, Joseph declared, "I had not been married scarcely five minutes, and made one proclamation of the Gospel, before it was reported that I had seven wives. . . . what a thing it is for a man to be accused of committing adultery, and having seven wives, when I can only find one. . . . I am the same man, and as innocent [of all these charges] as I was fourteen years ago." WJS pp. 375-377.

inspired revelator, he was prolific in dictating God's voice to mankind. Each of the works touched by his hand, the Holy Inspired Translation of the Bible, the Book of Mormon, the Book of Commandments, the 1835 and 1844 editions of the Doctrine and Covenants, and the Book of Abraham reveal and emphasize God's law of marriage:

> You shall love your wife with all your heart and shall cleave unto her and none else, and he that looks upon a woman to lust after her shall deny the faith, and shall not have the spirit, and if he repent not he shall be cast out.[20]

Beginning with our first parents, the Lord plainly taught that sexual relations outside the bounds of a monogamous marriage is adultery. Sexual sins are some of Satan's easiest and most effective tools employed to corrupt the very image of God. These sins damage souls, shatter faith, and devour the faithful. Adultery divides the unity which God requires of the man and his wife and is one sure way to bring about the destruction of ideals. Because Zion requires a pure and holy people who are of one heart, one mind, and dwell in righteousness, sexual sin thwarts its establishment.[21]

Joseph exhorted both men and women to be honorable and virtuous and to remove immorality from their hearts and from the Church. "For what is more pleasing to God than innocence," he taught, "you must be innocent, or you cannot come up before God; if we would come before God, we must

---

[20] See T&C 26:6; NC BofM—Jacob 2:7.
[21] See OC Genesis 4:14.

keep ourselves pure, as He is pure."[22]

Joseph taught the saints to live the strictest of moral codes including honor, fidelity, and faithfulness, and was adamant that the sin of polygamy had no place in God's Kingdom. He commanded the saints to reject it in all its forms, warning them that it was not to be accepted, tolerated, or embraced.[23]

Plural marriage contradicts everything the Lord exemplifies and is in opposition to God's image.[24] Because the

---

[22] Smith, Joseph F. (1976). *Teachings of the Prophet Joseph Smith*, p. 226. Salt Lake City, UT: Deseret Book Company. (Hereafter denoted as TPJS).

[23] Joseph Smith fought the practice of polygamy from the very beginning of the Restoration. The Utah-based LDS Church claims that Joseph practiced plural marriage, secretly teaching it to a handful of "inner circle" saints. They base their history on the lies of John C. Bennett, Brigham Young, Heber C. Kimball, and other members of the Twelve who blamed Joseph for their own sins. The book *Joseph Smith Revealed: A Faithful Telling, Exploring an Alternate Polygamy Narrative* lays out Joseph's personal fight against the crime of polygamy and his battle to prove his innocence. Additional research, especially into the journals and letters of Heber C. Kimball and other documents contemporary with Joseph and Hyrum's day, further exonerate Joseph and Hyrum. Joseph, Emma, and Hyrum told the truth when they adamantly denied any involvement in what Hyrum called the "damned foolish doctrine of polygamy."

[24] God has never commanded any man to enter into plural marriage. Members of the Church of Jesus Christ of Latter-day Saints believe that Joseph Smith revealed D&C 132, the "polygamy revelation." He testified weeks before his death that his eternal marriage revelation had nothing to do with polygamy. D&C 132 as it stands today is an altered document that did not surface until 1852. See Hyrum Smith, April 8, 1844, Conference address, "Minutes and Discourses, 6–9 April 1844, as Reported by Thomas Bullock," p. 30-32, The Joseph Smith Papers, accessed February 12, 2002; https://www.josephsmithpapers.org/paper-summary/minutes-and-discourses-6-9-april-1844-as-reported-by-thomas-bullock/33. *After giving this talk and publishing my book on Hyrm Smith, *Hyrum Smith A Prophet Unsung*, the Joseph Smith Papers removed this document. The only place an original can be seen as of today is the LDS Church History Library, Historian's

adulterous and predatory victimize and destroy and will rarely reform, the Lord commanded the saints to cast out those who commit adultery and refuse to repent.[25] Joseph's feelings were strong on the matter, "If a man commit adultery he cannot receive the celestial kingdom of God. Even if he is saved in any kingdom, it cannot be the celestial kingdom."[26]

Whenever God begins to establish His kingdom upon the earth "the devil always sets up his kingdom at the very same time in opposition to God."[27] While this preserves our right to choose between the bitter and the sweet, we must be cognizant that there are both seen and unseen forces that want to stop our progression with any means possible.[28] Satan's opposition presents itself in a myriad of ways which can derail the honest seeker from God's word and His work.

As an individual opens their heart and mind to new truths, zealousness, impatience, and arrogance leaves them vulnerable to deception. Hugh Nibley observed that nothing can excite mankind to action like the contemplation of the eternities.[29] A little bit of knowledge can be heady stuff, but it "easily leads to an excess of zeal! — to illusions of grandeur and

---

Office general Church minutes, 1839-1877; 1839-1845; Nauvoo, Illinois, 1844 April 6-9; Church History Library, https://catalog.churchofjesuschrist.org/assets/daa151c4-7bae-49d0-8cef-d281a70f1d32/0/0?lang=eng (accessed: January 2, 2024).

[25] T&C 26:6 and A Glossary of Gospel Terms, "Cast Out."

[26] Documentary History of the Church (DHC) Vol. 6, p. 81.

[27] WJS, p. 367.

[28] See OC Isaiah 1:17; NC NT—Ep. Of Jacob 1:13; NC BofM2 Nephi 1:7-8, 8:15; and T&C 9:11.

[29] Nibley, Hugh W. (1989). *Approaching Zion*, p. 69. Salt Lake City, UT: Deseret Book Company.

a desire to impress others and achieve eminence."[30] Men and women get a little knowledge, as they suppose, and set themselves up as authorities. Paul taught that such people

> [H]ave a zeal of God, but not according to knowledge; for they, being ignorant of God's righteousness, and going about to establish their own righteousness, have not submitted themselves unto the righteousness of God.[31]

False spirits mislead those seeking to know the Lord into foolish errors. "One great evil," Joseph taught, "is that men are ignorant of the nature of spirits: their power, laws, government, intelligence, etc., and imagine that when there is anything like power, revelation, or vision manifested, that it must be of God."[32]

Pretenders and deceivers imitate truth as closely as possible. Hard-hearted and stiff-necked people too often require signs in order to believe. False prophets attract attention and followers by the "signs" they produce. Joseph Smith warned that an adulterous heart has an inability to accept truth without a sign, requiring something coarse to convince them because they lack faith.[33]

---

[30] Nibley, Hugh W. (1989). *Approaching Zion*, p. 70. Salt Lake City, UT: Deseret Book Company.

[31] See NC NT—Romans 1:46.

[32] See T&C 147:4, "Try the Spirits." People are too accepting and not patient enough to try the spirits or test the teacher's fruits, leaving them open to a host of false teachings and false spirits.

[33] While he was preaching in Philadelphia on February 9, 1843, a Quaker called out for a sign. Joseph told him to be still. After the sermon, the Quaker again asked for a sign. Joseph told the congregation that "the man was an adulterer; that a wicked and adulterous generation seeketh after a sign; and

When signs attract followers, the resulting congregation is vulnerable to the sin of adultery.[34] Among the converts to the Restoration were those who sought signs and those who were susceptible to the influence of false spirits which presented themselves among the saints in "jarrings, and contentions, and envyings, and strifes, and lustful and covetous desires."[35]

With the outpouring of greater light at the dedication of the Kirtland Temple, and the appearance of the Lord a few days later, an equal measure of darkness was manifested among the saints.[36] The saints' impatience and inability to discern between the Lord's voice and false ones created a storm in Kirtland which cost those who were true to the Restoration their homes and their temple as they fled to safety in Missouri.[37]

Rather than learning from their mistakes, humbling

---

that the Lord had said to [him] in a revelation, that any man who wanted a sign was an adulterous person. 'It is true,' cried one, 'for I caught him in the very act,' which the man afterwards confessed when he was baptized. See TPJS, p. 278 and DHC Vol. 5, p. 268.

[34] See NC NT-Matthew 8:15.

[35] T&C 101:2. This may be because the Restoration began with Joseph's marvelous First Vision experience and the translation of the Book of Mormon. Many converts were attracted to the "signs" rather than the truth of the Lord's message.

[36] The Kirtland, Ohio Temple was dedicated on March 27, 1836. The Lord accepted that temple when He personally appeared to Joseph Smith and Oliver Cowdery on April 3, 1836. See T&C 157:26-32. Greater light versus greater darkness was exemplified when Moses saw the Lord, after which Satan "came tempting him, saying, Moses, son of man, worship me." Moses was able to discern between the Lord and Satan by the difference in their messages. See OC Genesis 1:1-5.

[37] One of the greatest storms revolved around the Kirtland Safety Society, an anti-banking financial institution.

themselves, and repenting, the saints continued the same pattern in Missouri. In their pride and arrogance, they contended with each other and with their neighbors, igniting an already simmering storm into a full out Mormon War.[38] In yet another attempt to humble them, the Lord allowed the saints to be driven again and their prophet cast into prison.[39]

The saints were welcomed and offered refuge by the state of Illinois. They hoped to enjoy a time of peace and succeed in establishing Zion: a prophesied last-days community where Christ would dwell.[40] But, the hoped-for peace did not come. The storms that had developed in Kirtland and Missouri were small in comparison to the storms that would form in Nauvoo.

As Joseph labored to restore truth, he was beset by opposition: aspiring and conspiring men, liars, traitors, and hypocrites circled around him, claiming close association and friendship and using his name to promote their own agendas, indulging in all manner of iniquity.[41] A survey of crime showed that Joseph and his brother Hyrum were dealing with major problems, including, but not limited to: thievery, counterfeiting, post office fraud, theft of monetary Temple donations and lumber, murder, adultery, and polygamy.[42]

While Joseph worked to discover and cast out guilty

---

[38] See https://en.wikipedia.org/wiki/1838_Mormon_War.

[39] Joseph was imprisoned on false charged in the Liberty Jail. Those who witnessed against him were once fellow friends and saints.

[40] See T&C A Glossary of Gospel Terms, "Zion."

[41] See T&C A Glossary of Gospel Terms, "Iniquity."

[42] Godfrey, K. W. (1991). Crime and Punishment in Mormon Nauvoo, 1839-1846. *Brigham Young University Studies*, 32(1/2), pp. 195–227. Retrieved from http://www.jstor.org/stable/43044971.

parties, he simultaneously focused on teaching correct principles and denouncing sin. He often addressed marriage over the pulpit and in print, reminding members, and teaching non-members, that:

> All legal contracts of marriage made before a person is baptized into this church, should be held sacred and fulfilled. Inasmuch as this church of Christ has been reproached with the crime of fornication, and polygamy: we declare that we believe, that one man should have one wife; and one woman, but one husband, except in case of death, when either is at liberty to marry again.[43]

---

[43] When asked, "Do the Mormons believe in having more wives than one." Joseph's answer was firm, "No, not at the same time. But they believe, that if their companion dies, they have a right to marry again." See *Elders' Journal*, July 1838," p. 43, The Joseph Smith Papers, retrieved from https://www.josephsmithpapers.org/paper-summary/elders-journal-july-1838/11. In April 1838, Oliver Cowdery was excommunicated from the Church for several charges including his accusation that Joseph was an adulterer. Oliver believed that Joseph had an affair with a young girl named Fanny Alger who did housework for Joseph and Emma. At Oliver's Church court, Joseph explained what had happened between he and Fanny. The council was satisfied that Joseph did nothing improper or immoral. Latter-day Saint historians today claim that Fanny Alger was Joseph's first plural wife. They base their sources on the testimonies of William McLellin, a known adulterer, and Mosiah Hancock, a Utah polygamist, who claimed in the 1890's that his father, Levi, had performed a sealing between Joseph and Fanny. Neither Joseph, Emma, nor Fanny left any record of what actually happened. There are contemporary sources that claim that a teenage Fanny, who had a crush on Joseph, made an improper attempt to get his attention. Joseph rebuffed her and she was taken straightway to her parents who immediately left Kirtland. This scenario makes much more sense in conjunction with the Far West High Council decision as well as Joseph and Emma's consistent denials regarding plural marriage. It also fits with Fanny's response when asked by her brother about what happened between her and Joseph. Fanny responded, "That is all a matter of my own. And I have

Joseph and Emma Smith stood side by side in their unwavering fight to root out sexual perversion and immorality from the Church. They desired to correct the morals and strengthen the virtues of the community, instructing the women that "it was high time for Mothers to watch over their Daughters & exhort them to keep the path of virtue."[44] They charged the women to learn God's commandments, and promised that if they lived up to all their privileges the angels could not be restrained from being their associates.[45]

Despite Joseph's example of unflinching courage in speaking truth and in doing God's will, some men began to wrest the scriptures to their own destruction.[46] The false spirit of polygamy entered on at least two different fronts: John C. Bennett's group and Brigham Young and Heber C. Kimball's inner circle, which included other members of the Twelve.[47] These groups became the two most influential and significant

---

nothing to communicate." Very few, if any, women would admit to a brother that they had made improper advances to a married man.

1835 Doctrine and Covenants 101:4, emphasis added. It is printed in the appendix of this work. Brigham Young's Latter-day Saint Church removed it from their scriptures in 1876 replacing it with their section on plural marriage which they claim came from Joseph Smith. In-depth research into this claim reveals that their D&C 132 was more than likely altered from its original state by Brigham Young's followers to promote their pro-polygamy agenda and is not the original revelation Joseph Smith received which promoted monogamy.

[44] *Nauvoo Relief Society Minute Book* which can be found online at the Joseph Smith Papers Project website.

[45] TPJS, p. 226.

[46] See NC BofM—Alma 10:2; and T&C A Glossary of Gospel Terms, "Wrest."

[47] It was expected and common for non-Mormons to spread lies and rumors about Joseph, but it was incomprehensible to Joseph and Emma that lies and rumors regarding his involvement with polygamy were being spread by the very men who claimed to be his closest friends and confidants.

parties to use Joseph's name in order to gratify their own lustful ambitions. Their positions within the Church and the city lent credibility to their lies.

Brigham Young, Heber C. Kimball, and other members of the Twelve arrived in Liverpool, England on April 6, 1840, poor and penniless.[48] While in England, Brigham, who was "trying to become like [Abraham], a Father of many Nations" was deceived by a false spirit when he accepted as truth a personal revelation concerning the principle of plural marriage.[49] He began teaching select others "It is lawful and right for a man to have two wives; for, as it was in the days of Abraham, so it shall be in these last days."[50] He taught select women that if they did not love their husbands, polygamy could give them one they would love.[51]

---

[48] When Brigham and Heber arrived in England they were poorly dressed and penniless. When they left for home one year later, on April 19, 1841, they were well-dressed and had gold in their pockets. Members of the Twelve often received gifts of money, silk fabric and handkerchiefs, and other items from their converts. Lorenzo Snow testified that while in England in the 1840's he gained a "perfect knowledge of the principle of plural marriage, its holiness and divinity." See Deseret Semi-weekly News, June 6, 1899.

[49] See Brigham Young's *Mission Notebook #2 of 1840* and Brigham Young's reflections of his mind regarding his personal revelation on plural marriage in *The Deseret News*, July 1, 1874, p. 4. It is possible that Brigham Young was influenced by the Cochranites in his beliefs and teachings on plural marriage and the united order. Brigham met Augusta Adams Cobb, who had been baptized in 1832 by Samuel Harrison Smith and Orson Hyde, during his journeys into the Boston area beginning in 1835.

[50] Martha Brotherton letter to John C. Bennett, July 13, 1842.

[51] One of Brigham's first plural wives, Augusta Adams Cobb, an already married woman from Boston, told a friend that "the [plural wife] doctrine taught by Brigham Young was a glorious doctrine, for if she did not love her husband [Henry], it gave her a man she did love." *Boston Post* in the *Quincy Whig*, December 22, 1847, p. 2. Testimony given by George J. Adams during the Henry Cobb vs. Augusta Adams Cobb divorce proceedings.

Before leaving the United States, Heber C. Kimball converted twenty-something Ellen Belfour Redman in New York. She followed Heber to England where she became a fixture in his journal and in his bed.[52] Heber wrote his wife Vilate that he was taught many marvelous mysteries by Dr. and Mrs. Copeland concerning a true system of salvation which required men to have many wives and children.[53] Heber called this idea "the principle . . . the Law that leads to the Celestial world," and claimed that he had received it "as from the Lord."[54] Heber fully embraced this false idea, coming to believe that he had been called of God to be a "Father of Lives,"

---

[52] Beginning in December 1840, Heber C. Kimball's personal journals and letters reveal that he spent a significant amount of time alone with a variety of different women while on his second mission in England. Some of these women performed a type of ordinance which involved the combing and cutting of his hair as well as the washing of his feet. Ellen Balfour Redman was a convert from New York who followed Heber C. Kimball to England to serve as a missionary alongside him and Wilford Woodruff (see Ellen Balfour Redman letter to Vilate Kimball, January 14, 1841). Ellen is mentioned twelve times in Heber's journal in a two-month period. On January 21, 1841, Ellen came to Heber's apartment and stayed with him through the evening. Heber recorded that "Sister Ellen combed my head we washed our feet and went to bed." The 1987 compilation of Heber's Journals, *On the Potter's Wheel: The Diaries of Heber C. Kimball,* published by Spencer B. Kimball left out the words "we washed our feet and went to bed." Someone tried to erase these words in the original journal, however, they are still readable. In a letter to Vilate on February 17, 1841, two months into his affair with Ellen Redman, Heber began to reveal his beliefs regarding polygamy, wanting to know if Vilate would accept "the principle . . . when I come home, a hint is sufficient." Heber C. Kimball letter to Vilate Kimball, February 17, 1841, and *Journal 20 December 1840-17 November 1845.*

[53] Beginning in 1841 and on many of the letters between Heber and Vilate Kimball reveal their beliefs, acceptance of, and practice of plural wives. See Heber C. Kimball letter to Vilate Kimball, February 17, 1841.

[54] Heber C. Kimball letter to Vilate Kimball, February 17, 1841.

that he must "give life" to any woman who was willing to receive it from him, and that God had put power into his hands for the purpose of getting women for himself.[55]

When John C. Bennett was baptized in September 1840, he was already living an immoral, duplicitous life.[56] He had left his wife and children behind when he came to Nauvoo where he pretended to be a single man. Bennett put himself in a position to gain the confidence and friendship of both Joseph

---

[55] February 12, 1849, Heber C Kimball apology letter to Vilate, "no one can supersede you . . . what I have done is according to the mind and will of god for his glory and mine so it will be for thine. Let me say unto you V. K Evry son and daughter that is brought forth by the wives that are given to me will add to your glory as much as it will to them. They are given to me for this purpus, and for no other. I am a Father of lives to give lives to those that wish to receive. Woman is to receive from the Man. What I have done has been by stolen moments for the purpus to save your feelins and that alone on the a count of the love I have for you. I beg of you to consider my case. As you cannot do the work that God has required of me no one can do my work but my self. No Vilate look look and see that god has pute power in to my hands for the purpus to get women to my self and those that he has given to me."

[56] Soon after it was known that Bennett had become a member of the Church, a communication was received from a person of respectable character who resided in the vicinity where Bennett had lived. The letter cautioned Joseph and Hyrum against Bennett, setting forth that he was a very mean man, and had a wife, and two or three children in McConnelsville, Ohio. Regarding this letter, Joseph said, "but knowing that it is no uncommon thing for good men to be evil spoken against, the above letter was kept quiet, but held in reserve." Joseph did keep an eye on Bennett and when he discovered that Bennett was courting a woman who was ignorant that he was a married man, threatened to expose him. Bennett broke off his publicly wicked actions only to continue to sink deeper into depravity in private. See *Times and Seasons*, Vol. 3, No. 17, (July 1, 1842), pp. 839-840. One year later, Hyrum met a man in Philadelphia who knew Bennett and gave him more information regarding him. Hyrum sent a letter to Joseph who confronted Bennett. Bennett admitted it was true and attempted suicide to "escape the censures of an indignant community" but was revived. See *Times and Seasons*, Vol. 3, No. 17, (July 1, 1842), p. 840.

and Hyrum. He rose quickly in the ranks of both Church and civic government and used his trusted status as a leader and a doctor to seduce women. His group of intimate acquaintances participated in adultery, "spiritual wifery," "buggery," and abortions.[57]

Brigham and Heber arrived back in Nauvoo around July 1, 1841, well-dressed, with gold in their pockets, bringing with them their new-found polygamous beliefs along with thirty-year-old Sarah Peak Noon. Sarah was a pregnant, married woman when she left her husband to follow Heber to Nauvoo where she secretly lived as his first polygamous wife.

Over the next few years, Joseph and Hyrum had scarcely dealt with one man or woman guilty of adultery when another would come to their attention. John C. Bennett was not

---

[57] Some of Bennett's known associates were Francis and Chauncey Higbee and Brigham Young. Francis was also a friend to Heber C. Kimball. When Heber was in Boston in the summer of 1843 he recorded on June 22, "Frances Higbey come to us on the 22 and on the twenty third he left us." Bennett and associates would calm women's concerns about being "found out" in their adulterous affairs by offering to perform abortions, if necessary, in order to hide their sins. On May 21, 1842, the Nauvoo High Council met and, "[A] charge [was] [preferred] against Chauncey L. Higbee by George Miller for unchaste and un-virtuous conduct with the widow [Sarah] Miller, and others." At the trial, "Three witness[es] testified that he had seduced [several women] and at different times [had] been guilty of unchaste and unvirtuous conduct with them and taught the doctrine that it was right to have free intercourse with women if it was kept secret &c and also taught that Joseph Smith authorised him to practice these things &c." Dinger, John S. (2011) *The Nauvoo City and High Council Minutes*, pp. 414-415. Salt Lake City, UT: Signature Books. Another tactic Bennett used to convince women that it was safe to engage in unmarried relations was to offer to perform abortions if their actions resulted in a pregnancy, thus making sure no one knew of their indiscretion. Violence and murder are often the by-product of sexual sin. See Hyrum Smith, Affidavit, *Time and Seasons*, Vol. 3, No. 19, (August 1, 1842), pp. 870-871.

as discrete as Brigham and Heber were in his sexual excesses and debauchery. When several saints finally reported Bennett's actions, he was brought to trial and excommunicated.[58] He did not go away quietly.

Imbued with a spirit of malevolence, Bennett published exposés smearing Joseph's character and stirring up enemies. Joseph took to the stand where he "spoke his mind in great plainness concerning the iniquity & wickedness" of Bennett and "exposed him before the public."[59] Concerned that Bennett's lies would incite mobs, Joseph published a pamphlet which contained dozens of affidavits and statements testifying

---

[58] Hyrum swore out an affidavit that he was a witness to the following conversation between Joseph and John C. Bennett: "Dr. Bennett . . . reached out his hand to Br. Joseph and said will you forgive me . . . I am guilty, I acknowledge it, and I beg of you not to expose me, for it will ruin me; Joseph replied, Doctor! why are you using my name to carry on your hellish wickedness? Have I ever taught you that fornication and adultery was right, or polygamy or any such practices? He said you never did. Did I ever teach you any thing that was not virtuous-that was iniquitous, either in public or private? He said you never did. Did you ever know anything unvirtuous or unrighteous in my conduct or actions at any time, either in public or in private? he said, I did not; are you willing to make oath to this before an Alderman of the city? he said I am willing to do so. Joseph said Dr. go into my office, and write what you can in conscience subscribe your name to, and I will be satisfied-I will, he said, and went into the office, and I went with him." See *Times and Seasons*, Vol. 3, No. 19, (August 1, 1842), pp. 870-871. The June 15, 1842, edition of the *Times and Seasons* ran a notice that the hand of fellowship had been "withdrawn from General John C. Bennett, as a christian, he having been labored with from time to time, to persuade him to amend his conduct, apparently to no good effect." See *Times and Seasons*, Vol. 3, No. 16, (June 15, 1842), p. 830.

[59] See Wilford Woodruff *Journal*, 18 June 1842. The *Times and Seasons* dedicated several pages to more fully exposing Bennett's lies in the August 1, 1842, edition. It included the affidavits of several leading citizens of Nauvoo who declared that Joseph was a "good, moral, virtuous, peaceable and patriotic man, and a firm supporter of law, justice and equal rights." See *Times and Seasons*, Vol. 3, No. 19, (August 1, 1842), p. 869.

to Bennett's guilt and Joseph's innocence.[60] It was "thought wisdom in God that every Elder who can, should ... go forth to every part of the United States, and take proper documents with them setting forth the truth as it is."[61] About 380 elders volunteered for this special anti-polygamy mission.

Bennett's deceptions paled in comparison to Brigham and Heber's. The sin and crime of polygamy was taking root in the Restoration and spreading. Joseph and Hyrum had hoped that excommunicating Bennett would send a strong message and put an end to the plural wife practice.[62] But those involved in Brigham and Heber's polygamy ring did not repent and end their mischief. Instead, the strong and decisive measures taken with Bennett only served to drive the unrepentant practitioners and proponents of plural marriage further underground.

With storms brewing on every side, there was yet another problem growing among the saints: converts were leaving husbands, wives, and even children behind when they gathered to Nauvoo because their companions were unbelievers or they were too poor to travel together.[63] In a few weeks or months after arriving in Nauvoo they were finding themselves new husbands or wives. The result of this practice,

---

[60] See a photo image of the original pamphlet "Affidavits and Certificates, Disproving the Statements and Affidavits contained in John C. Bennett's Letters," retrieved from https://archive.org/details/AffidavitsCertificates/mode/2up.

[61] The Joseph Smith Papers (2011). *Journals, Vol. 2, December 1841-April 1843*, pp. 121-122.

[62] The Nauvoo high council minutes from the Nauvoo years are filled with cases of adultery and polygamy which often ended in excommunication for adultery.

[63] See T&C 149 and *The Latter-day Saints' Millenial Star*, Vol. 3, No. 7, (November 7, 1842), pp. 115-116.

according to Joseph and Hyrum, was producing evil fruits of polygamy and adultery and they were obliged to cut the perpetrators off from the church.[64]

Joseph and Hyrum warned the saints that "this is a wicked generation, full of lyings, and deceit, and craftiness."[65] They believed that if taught correct principles, the saints would amend themselves. To this end, Hyrum wrote:

> [Do] not suffer families to be broken up on no account whatever, if it be possible to avoid it. Suffer no man to leave his wife because she is an unbeliever, nor no woman to leave her husband because he is an unbeliever. . . . You know not but the unbeliever may be converted and the Lord heal him. But let the believers exercise faith in God, and the unbelieving husband shall be sanctified by the believing wife, and the unbelieving wife by the believing husband, and families are preserved and saved from a great evil. . . . [If he or she is a bad man or woman] and if the law will divorce them, then they are at liberty. Otherwise, they are bound as long as they two shall live, and it is not our prerogative to go beyond this. . . .These are the things in plainness which we desire should be publicly known.[66]

Even though sin and iniquity persisted within the Church, God did not abandon those who deserved to be called saints. The Restoration continued to unfold.[67] During the spring of 1843, Joseph was pondering on the Bible passage "in the resurrection they neither marry, nor are given in marriage,

---

[64] Ibid.
[65] Ibid.
[66] Ibid.
[67] See T&C 31:4, 157:19, and 177:5.

but are as the angels of God in Heaven." He received for an answer:

> No man can obtain an eternal Blessing unless the contract or covenant be made in view of Eternity. All contracts in view of this Life only terminate with this Life. . . . Those who keep no eternal Law in this life or make no eternal contract are single & alone in the eternal world and are only made Angels to minister to those who shall be heirs of Salvation never becoming Sons of God having never kept the Law of God.[68]

---

[68] The new and everlasting covenant was "new" only as a consequence of it having been restored to Joseph's attention. Joseph was restoring lost truths which had been established in the beginning by the Lord with Adam. The new and everlasting covenant of marriage was also called the Eternal marriage covenant or Celestial marriage, referring to the idea that a man could not inherit the Celestial Kingdom unless he had entered into an Eternal marriage covenant with his wife. Eternal marriage was established in the beginning by God with Adam and Eve. It began between one man and one wife and was intended to remain so for all mankind. Brigham Young, who was already practicing polygamy at this time based on his belief that Abraham had more than one wife, took this new revelation and conflated it to add authority to his doctrine of plural marriage. The original revelation regarding the Eternal marriage covenant no longer exits, in a form that we are aware of today. The LDS Church claims that Emma burned the original but not before it was copied by William Clayton, whose copy was then copied by Joseph Kingsbury. When Brigham published his copy in 1852, he told the saints that he had kept it locked away for safe keeping. Several men and women who had lived in Nauvoo in 1843 and had seen the original stated that the revelation Brigham published did not resemble the original which they had seen. On July 14, 2017, the Lord revealed that the original revelation had been altered. See T&C 157:33; Ehat, Andrew F. & Cook, Lyndon W. (1980). *The Words of Joseph Smith*, pp. 232-233. Provo, UT: Religious Studies Center Brigham Young University; and Dinger, John S., editor. (2011). *The Nauvoo City and High Council Minutes*, p. 255-256. Salt Lake City, UT: Signature Books. According to Joseph's journal, the very first Eternal marriage covenant of the Restoration took place between he and his Elect Lady, Emma on May 28, 1843. The next day, Hyrum entered into an Eternal marriage covenant with his deceased wife, Jerusha. Because Jerusha

This restoration of light and truth revealed a necessary step for a man and his wife to be reconnected to the family of God and was preparatory for the fullness that was promised to be restored if the Nauvoo Temple was completed.[69]

The ideas presented in the marriage revelation were new, startling, and contrary to the long-standing Christian tradition "till death do us part." For those saints who desired their marital relationship to endure past death, the revelation brought joy and excitement. For others, it caused them to "fly to pieces like glass" and turn against Joseph and the Restoration.[70] For those who had been married more than once due to the death of a spouse, the new revelation created stress and anxiety as they were confronted with the decision of which spouse they should choose.[71] Other saints added to the revelation, transforming the truth of God into a lie by making it "a criminality for a man to have a wife on the earth while he

---

was deceased, a living proxy needed to stand in her place. Hyrum's second wife, Mary Fielding, chose to be proxy for Jerusha. See The Joseph Smith Papers (2015). *Journals, Vol. 3, May 1843-June 1844*, pp. 24-25. Salt Lake City, UT: The Church Historian's Press.

[69] T&C 141:10, 13, and see T&C A Glossary of Gospel Terms, "Sons and Daughters of God."

[70] Ehat, Andrew F. & Cook, Lyndon W. (1980). *The Words of Joseph Smith*, p. 319. Provo, UT: Religious Studies Center Brigham Young University. Hyrum and Joseph were aware that, just like Kirtland and Far West, their greatest threat came from within the Church. Joseph preached all day on July 16, 1843 "concerning a man's foes being they of his own house, such as having secret enemies in the city, intermingling with the saints." See The Joseph Smith Papers (2015). *Journals, Vol. 3, May 1843-June 1844*, p. 61. Salt Lake City, UT: The Church Historian's Press.

[71] This was the case with Hyrum Smith. Hyrum gave his second wife, Mary Fielding Smith, the choice. Mary chose to stand as proxy for Jerusha so that Hyrum could be eternally married to his first wife, who was dead.

has one in heaven." And still others whispered rumors that the new revelation sanctioned polygamy.[72]

That spring, Hyrum formulated a plot to entrap the so-called "brethren of the secret priesthood" who were teaching and practicing polygamy.[73] Hyrum naively and unknowingly trusted the very men who were involved. William Clayton, a clerk for Joseph, was one of Heber C. Kimball's converts from England and was involved in Brigham and Heber's plural wife scheme. Clayton alerted Kimball to Hyrum's plan, thus

---

[72] Brigham Young explained his new ideas on Joseph's revelation to a non-Member using the example of one man having seven wives: the man marrying the next wife after the previous one died and so on until he had married seven times (See *Manuscript History of Brigham Young* 1801-1844: July 9, 1843). Ironically, the example in the scripture which inspired Joseph's revelation on the Eternal marriage covenant (NC NT—Matthew 10:22) refers to one woman married to seven different men. Brigham Young's misinterpretation is somewhat understandable as he was one of those saints who was placed in the position of having to choose between spouses. His first wife, Miriam Works, had died in 1832 and at the time the Eternal marriage covenant was revealed to Joseph, Brigham had remarried a woman named Mary Ann Angell. It is possible that Brigham felt that he should be able to have all of his spouses as wives in Heaven. It is purported that on August 12, 1843, at a meeting of the Nauvoo High Council, Lewis Wilson "made enquiry in relation to the subject of a plurality of wives as there were rumors afloat respecting it." To clear up the confusion, Hyrum supposedly went home and retrieved a copy of the revelation which he read aloud and explained to the high council, testifying to its truth. The original minutes of this meeting do not mention anything about Hyrum reading this revelation. However, one year later, during a Nauvoo City Council meeting, Hyrum testified that he had read the revelation the previous year to the high council. See Dinger, John S., editor. (2011). *The Nauvoo City and High Council Minutes*, pp. 254-255, 467-468 fn 61. Salt Lake City, UT: Signature Books. Brigham Young and his associates transformed the eternal marriage revelation into a polygamy revelation which is now in the LDS Doctrine and Covenants as section 132.

[73] T&C 152: 1. William Clayton recorded in his journal on May 23, 1843, "conversed with H.C.K. [Heber C. Kimball] concerning plot that is being laid to entrap the brethren of the secret priesthood by bro. H[yrum] and others."

enabling his group to continue to escape detection.[74]

Joseph and Hyrum, who believed that "no person that is acquainted with our principles" would ever embrace the "damned foolish doctrine of polygamy," accepted as truth the pretended ignorance and innocence of the very men and women who were involved as they signed their names to epistles and legally binding affidavits supporting monogamy and denouncing plural marriage.[75]

---

[74] While he received letters that alerted Hyrum that the sexual depravities had not ended with Bennett, they did not help him to discover who was at the core of these false teachings. William Clayton, who worked as a clerk for Joseph was able to alert Brigham and Heber to Hyrum's plan, which enabled them to continue to escape detection. While on a mission in England, Clayton had recorded in his journal on several occasions that a woman named Sarah Crooks would "wash his feet" after which they would go to bed. Clayton secretly took his first plural wife, his sister-in-law Margaret Moon, in 1843, thereby inducting him into the "spiritual wifery" ring. William worked as a clerk for Joseph from 1842-1844 which gave him access to information regarding Joseph and Hyrum's plans. Clayton recorded in his journal on May 23, 1843, "conversed with H.C.K. [Heber C. Kimball] concerning plot that is being laid to entrap the brethren of the secret priesthood by bro. H[yrum] and others."

[75] Brigham Young and Heber C. Kimball signed their names or testified for monogamy and against polygamy several times, a few of which were: March 31, 1842 epistle to the Relief Society denouncing immorality, the crime of polygamy, and giving the sisters permission to expose anyone who taught such evils; April 1842 affidavit (also signed by Vilate Kimball) that seventeen-year-old Martha Brotherton had lied when she claimed that Brigham and Heber had tried to persuade her to believe in plural marriage and in their right to have two wives; April 6, 1842 in Joseph's home, testified before others "to the principles of virtue which they had invariably heard taught by Joseph;" June 15, 1842 notice of Bennett's excommunication; August 1, 1842 City Council affidavit testifying of "Joseph Smith's innocence, virtue, and pure teaching;" May 1844 testified on behalf of Joseph's purity and innocence in a law-suit between Francis Higbee and Joseph. *Times and Seasons*, Vol. 3, No. 12 (April 15, 1842), pp. 751-766. At this time, Joseph did not know that Brigham Young, Heber C. Kimball, and other members of the

Brigham Young and Heber and Vilate Kimball were key players in the underground polygamy ring.[76] As Brigham and Heber traveled for their church duties, they sent teenage girls and women who were converted to their "principle" of plural marriage to live with Vilate.[77] She was responsible for matching them with the men who came to the Kimball home to "get a girl."[78]

In June of 1843, Parley P. Pratt was taught "the

Quorum of the Twelve were secretly practicing polygamy. About three weeks before his death, Joseph lamented to William Marks that he had been deceived by men "in high places" whom he had trusted. Hyrum Smith April 8, 1844, conference address. "Minutes and Discourses, 6–9 April 1844, as Reported by Thomas Bullock," pp. 30-32, The Joseph Smith Papers, https://www.josephsmithpapers.org/paper-summary/minutes-and-discourses-6-9-april-1844-as-reported-by-thomas-bullock/33. *After giving this talk and publishing my book on Hyrm Smith, *Hyrum Smith A Prophet Unsung*, the Joseph Smith Papers removed this document. The only place an original can be seen as of today is the LDS Church History Library, Historian's Office general Church minutes, 1839-1877; 1839-1845; Nauvoo, Illinois, 1844 April 6-9; Church History Library, https://catalog.churchofjesuschrist.org/assets/daa151c4-7bae-49d0-8cef-d281a70f1d32/0/0?lang=eng (accessed: January 2, 2024).

[76] In the vernacular of our day, we would define what Brigham Young, Heber C. Kimball, and Vilate Kimball were doing as being facilitators in the sex-slave trade.

[77] See Vilate Kimball letters to Heber C. Kimball, June 9 and 30, 1844.

[78] Letters home reveal that Brigham Young and Heber C. Kimball were spending time with their current plural wives as well as future ones. Brigham spent time with his plural wife, Augusta Cobbs, who was back in Boston where her husband was suing her for divorce. Heber visited and stayed with female converts. Vilate wrote letters alerting both Heber and Brigham that all was not safe in Nauvoo. She told them about the *Nauvoo Expositor* and the arrests and murders of Joseph and Hyrum. When Heber found out about Joseph and Hyrum's deaths, his first concern was for his own safety. Vilate had sent him another letter stating, "I have no doubt but your life will be sought." She based her belief on statements of William Law, that he was determined to have members of the Twelve killed. See Vilate Kimball letters to Heber C. Kimball, June 9 and 30, 1844.

principle" by a polygamy insider. He inquired of Vilate if it was true that it was "his privilege" to take as many wives as he chose.[79] Vilate was hesitant to teach Parley more or to convince his wife Mary Ann to accept it, concerned that Parley would "run too fast." She warned him that "these were sacred things and he better not make a move until he got more instruction."[80] But, Parley did not heed Vilate's warning, quickly marrying his first plural wife, Elizabeth Brotherton.[81]

As the year 1844 dawned, Joseph and Emma called on the citizens of Nauvoo to take a stand against the corruption and wickedness that had entered the "only city in the world that **pretends** to work righteousness in union." [82] As the April 1844 general conference approached, Joseph and Hyrum were concerned that if they could not eradicate polygamy it would prove to be the downfall of the entire Restoration movement.[83]

---

[79] Vilate wrote Heber that Parley Pratt was taught "the principle" by "J. K." This most likely stood for Joseph Kingsbury, a close friend of Brigham Young and Heber C. Kimball and the key player in the coming forth of the "polygamy revelation" in 1852 known as D&C 132. See Vilate Kimball letter to Heber C. Kimball, June 24, 1843.

[80] See Vilate Kimball letter to Heber C. Kimball, June 24, 1843.

[81] Apparently, whichever woman had been "appointed" to be Parley's plural wife was a woman who Heber had been considering taking as one of his wives. See Vilate Kimball letter to Heber C. Kimball June 24, 1843. The thought of entering into polygamy was very distressing for Parley's wife, Mary Ann Frost, and she eventually left him.

[82] *Nauvoo Neighbor*, Vol. 1, No. 47 (March 20, 1844). Retrieved from http://boap.org/LDS/Nauvoo-Neighbor/1844/3-20-1844.pdf. Emphasis added.

[83] A week or so before Joseph and Hyrum's deaths, Joseph confided in William Marks, Nauvoo Stake President, that he had been deceived by many leading men of the Church. Joseph had recently discovered that these men were secretly practicing the "spiritual wife" system (plurality of wives). Joseph stated that it would prove the Church's destruction and overthrow.

In another effort to end the speculation and practice among the saints, and to strengthen the men spiritually so that only those elders "who knew how to preach nothing but the truth" would be sent out on missions, Joseph and Hyrum called every elder to Nauvoo.[84] During that conference Joseph called upon all men to repent and obey the gospel, warning them that if they did not, they would be damned.[85] He told the people, "you never knew me, you do not know my heart. . . . when I am called at the trump and weighed in the balance you will know

---

To stop this from happening, Joseph was going to prefer charges against those practicing it and bring them up for trial before the Nauvoo High Council. He asked Marks to "try them by the laws of the Church, and cut them off, if they will not repent and cease the practice." Joseph said that he would "**go into the stand and preach against it, with all my might, and in this way we may rid the Church of this damnable heresy**." Emphasis added. See *RLDS History of the Church* 2:733 and William Marks, "Epistle," *Zions Harbinger and Baneemy's Organ* 3 (July 1853), pp. 52-54. Published in St. Louis by C. B. Thompson.

[84] The following notice was printed in the *Times and Seasons* on March 1, 1844: "A special conference of the Church of Jesus Christ of Latter Day Saints will be held at Nauvoo, near the Temple, commencing on Saturday, the 6th of April next. All the elders abroad who can by any means make it convenient to attend, are requested to be present on the occasion, as there is business of importance to attend to." *Times and Seasons*, Vol 5, No. 5, (March 1, 1844), pp. 455-456. See also Hyrum Smith, April 7, 1844, Conference address. See "Minutes and Discourses, 6–9 April 1844, as Reported by Thomas Bullock," pp. 12-14. The Joseph Smith Papers, https://www.josephsmithpapers.org/paper-summary/minutes-and-discourses-6-9-april-1844-as-reported-by-thomas-bullock/33. *After giving this talk and publishing my book on Hyrm Smith, *Hyrum Smith A Prophet Unsung*, the Joseph Smith Papers removed this document. The only place an original can be seen as of today is the LDS Church History Library, Historian's Office general Church minutes, 1839-1877; 1839-1845; Nauvoo, Illinois, 1844 April 6-9; Church History Library, https://catalog.churchofjesuschrist.org/assets/daa151c4-7bae-49d0-8cef-d281a70f1d32/0/0?lang=eng (accessed: January 2, 2024).

[85] WJS, p. 343.

me then."[86] Hyrum delivered a bold and strong stand against polygamy, leaving no room for doubt: repent and end the practice now or you will be cut off from the Church and publicly exposed.

One month later, Joseph emphatically declared to a congregation of thousands that Emma was his only wife and that he was innocent of the charges of adultery and polygamy.[87]

Despite Joseph and Hyrum's efforts to teach truth, the secret polygamy group refused to accept that they had been listening to and embracing false spirits. In June of 1844, regardless of the upheaval and difficulties rumors of polygamy were causing the Smith's and the entire city of Nauvoo, Brigham and Heber continued to direct both member and non-member men to the Kimball home to obtain wives and mistresses.[88] Brigham, Heber, and their associates chose to follow the voices they believed were from God over the voice that was God as delivered through Joseph, Hyrum, and the scriptures.

A few weeks before his death, Joseph learned that

---

[86] WJS, p. 355.

[87] In Joseph's sermon on May 26, 1844, he emphatically testified "This spiritual wifeism! Why, a man dares not speak or wink, for fear of being accused of this. . . . I am innocent of all these charges, and you can bear witness of my innocence, for you know me yourselves. . . . What a thing it is for a man to be accused of committing adultery, and having seven wives, when I can only find one. I am the same man, and as innocent as I was fourteen years ago; and I can prove them all perjurers." Ehat, Andrew F. & Cook, Lyndon W. (1980). *The Words of Joseph Smith*, pp. 375-377. Provo, UT: Religious Studies Center Brigham Young University. It had been a practice since the founding of the *Times and Seasons* newspaper to report on the conference by giving a synopsis of the talks. These talks by Joseph and Hyrum condemning plural marriage were never reprinted, or even mentioned in any way, in the newspaper.

[88] See Vilate Kimball letters to Heber C. Kimball, June 9 and 30, 1844.

among those who called him friend were some who had been deceiving him regarding polygamy. He made a plan to go into the stand and preach against the plural marriage doctrine with all his might while also preferring charges against all who practiced it. If the men and women would not repent and cease the practice they would be cut off. He believed that in this way he could rid the church of the damnable heresy.[89]

As time marched closer to June 27, 1844, Joseph and Hyrum's efforts to campaign for political office while cleansing the Church and the city of the raging storms of thievery, counterfeiting, polygamy and all other unholy and impure practices served to create a host of enemies and fan the flames of dissent in those who became determined to end the Smith families' lives.[90] The cold-blooded and willful murders of Joseph and Hyrum Smith were caused by the direct actions of those who they had once called friends.[91]

---

[89] William Smith claimed that Joseph learned from Emma that John Taylor, Willard Richards, and Brigham Young had been teaching some doctrines among the saints that were contrary to the laws and rules governing the church. *The Saints' Herald, Official publication of the Reorganized Church of Jesus Christ of Latter Day Saints*, Vol. 26, No. 8, Plano, Ill., April 15, 1879. See also RLDS History of the Church 2:733 and William Marks, "Epistle," Zions Harbinger and Baneemy's Organ 3 (July 1853), pp. 52-54. Published in St. Louis by C. B. Thompson.

[90] Some of the former friends and Church members who were plotting to kill Joseph, Hyrum, and their families were Joseph H. Jackson, William Law, Wilson Law, Robert Foster, and Charles Foster. In addition, the judgment against Bostwick combined with *The Voice of Innocence*, which personally called him out, further inflamed his furor toward Hyrum and led to his plotting to seek revenge by murdering Hyrum.

[91] Joseph was surrounded by traitors throughout his ministry. See T&C 139:7 and The Joseph Smith Papers (2017). *Documents, Vol. 6: February 1838-August 1839*, pp. 300-301, 306. Salt Lake City, UT: The Church Historian's Press.

To be clear, polygamy in any form is in opposition to the image of God and is a false spirit.[92] Plural marriage is not substantiated as a Godly form of marriage anywhere in scripture. Nor has God ever commanded any man or woman to enter into it.[93]

The saints in Joseph's day could not discern between the voice of the Lord and false ones. Are we any wiser today? Do we suffer from vain imaginings, believing that when there is anything like power, revelation, or vision manifested, that it must be of God? Are we as ignorant of the nature of spirits in our day as the saints were in Joseph's? Do we take time to study out a matter, to try the spirits, and to test a teacher's fruits?[94] False spirits are actively involved whenever God begins a work. There are many false spirits at work in the world today.[95]

Satan was "an angel of God who was in authority in the presence of God before he was cast down. Such a being does not look vile. Visually, he may appear to have light and glory. Because he is a liar, he uses his appearance as a pretense to be an angel of light."[96] Satan is the father of all lies and desires to take us into a dark and dreary waste.[97]

We all need greater light which requires that we open

---

[92] When a person is working at cross-purposes to God they are working iniquity. Because polygamy is in opposition to the purpose of God it is iniquity. See T&C A Glossary of Gospel Terms, "Iniquity."

[93] Hyrum Smith pointed this out in his conference address to the elders on April 8, 1844.

[94] See NC NT—Matthew 3:46 and T&C 147, "Try the Spirits."

[95] Joseph Smith taught that when a person has an association with heavenly angels, they are not apt to be misled by fallen, false spirits.

[96] T&C A Glossary of Gospel Terms, "Angel of Light."

[97] T&C A Glossary of Gospel Terms, "Angel of Light." See also Lehi's vision in NC BofM—1 Nephi 2:7-11.

our heart and mind to new truths. Similar to being in a deep and peaceful slumber when someone turns on the light, awakening to our awful situation can be a painful experience.[98] Yet, it is imperative that we do so if we are to arise and connect with the source of all light and truth.[99] Do not be afraid of the light, but be wise as you search for it.

To avoid deception:

1.   Keep yourself unspotted from the world; meaning that we avoid those things we know to be wrong. If we understand it is wrong, we refuse to do or participate. This does not mean we always know enough to avoid all wrongdoing, but we avoid deliberate wrongdoing.

2.   Read/study the scriptures. They provide us with a background of information that allows us to compare what we are told with what God has told others and revealed or commanded. If the answer conflicts with scripture, it ought to be seriously questioned or rejected.

3.   Test it to see if it produces pride or instead produces humility. If it is self-aggrandizing, it should be questioned or rejected. If it produces humility, it should be considered carefully or accepted.

4.   Realize that answers are from the question, not from an absolute position. If we ask about the apple in our hand, we won't get an answer about the orchard it came from. We limit the scope and we get a limited scope answer. So, an answer does not mean we have yet been given the whole there is to know about a matter.

---

[98] See NC BofM—2 Nephi 1:3, 2 Nephi 3:8, and T&C A Glossary of Gospel Terms, "Awake and Arise."
[99] See T&C 93:1.

5. Does it lead to faith in Christ and recognition of Him as our Savior, or does it raise doubts about Him and His commandments/mission/status. If it affirms Christ and produces faith in Him and confidence in His commandments, it ought to be accepted or carefully considered. If it does not, it should be rejected.

The most important thing we can do is to obey what we know to be good, true, and right.[100]

To avoid deception, we must have light which comes by keeping God's commandments. Any other path is a diversion, intended to waylay a person and prevent him or her from developing as God intends. If we are immoral and know it to be wrong, then we are compromising our ability to avoid deception.[101] As we come to know better, we ought to repent and do better.

Anyone who claims to follow Christ will:

[R]eject adultery by any name or description. It is morally wrong, even if you call it plural wives, polygamy, "celestial marriage," or any other misnomer. Adultery is prohibited in the Ten Commandments and remains an important prohibition for any moral society. There is a reason why such a serious sin as adultery ought to be altogether avoided; even if it is only as a foolish temptation contemplating the possibility of a plural wife. . . . Those who think they can follow God and yet commit adultery are deceived and giving heed to a

---

[100] Taken from a personal email from Denver C. Snuffer, Jr. to Vernon and Whitney Horning on July 6, 2018.
[101] Personal email from Denver C. Snuffer, Jr. to Vernon and Whitney Horning on July 6, 2018.

false spirit. It is impossible to be both on the path to greater light and also engaged in such a serious sin.[102]

The scriptures condemn polygamy and, when it is done in the name of religion, refer to it as an abomination.[103] All men and women are subject to temptations of the flesh. All are weak when they are unwise. Sin and temptation are more difficult to withstand when justification for such sin is first considered, then accepted, then practiced, and finally rendered into a religious sacrament.[104] The chains of adultery can only be avoided by removing adulterous thoughts from the heart. Anything claiming to be more or less than the Lord's Law of Marriage is designed to encircle and bind you down with the chains of hell. Joseph taught that from all such sin and temptation turn away. "The Church must be cleansed," he declared, "and I proclaim against all iniquity."[105]

The truth cannot long be hidden.

It matters whether or not it was Joseph Smith, a servant of God with a direct connection to Heaven, or others, misled by false spirits, who were responsible for introducing and incorporating polygamy into the fabric of the Restoration.

---

[102] T&C A Glossary of Gospel Terms, "Adultery."

[103] See Lamech, the first polygamist; Noah, the son of Zeniff who "did not keep the commandments of God, but did walk after the desires of his own heart. And he had many wives and concubines. And he did cause his people to commit sin and do that which was abominable in the sight of the Lord" (NC BofM—Mosiah 7:1; and Riplakish, who did "afflict the people with his whoredoms and abominations" (NC BofM—Ether 4:10-11).

[104] A religious sacrament is a rite or observance which is believed to have been ordained by Christ. Anyone who teaches that polygamy is necessary for exaltation, or that it is commanded of God, has turned polygamy into a religious sacrament.

[105] TPJS, p. 217.

Faithful men and women, misled by false traditions, are actively entering into polygamy today. Joseph and Emma testified that he had no other wife or wives other than her, in any sense, spiritual or otherwise.[106] The Church of Jesus Christ of Latter-day Saints still teaches and believes that polygamy is practiced in heaven. Hyrum Smith disavowed this false notion in 1844 when he explained that although he had remarried after the death of his first wife, he was sealed in an eternal marriage covenant to only one.[107] False spirits are manifested in false traditions which can fool the faithful into thinking they are obedient to God when they are merely misled. False traditions are as destructive to our souls as outright disobedience. Joseph warned us:

A man is saved no faster than he gets knowledge, for if

---

[106] *The Saints' Herald*, Vol. 26, pp. 289, 290.

[107] During his sermon, Hyrum explained that his first wife had died before Joseph was given authority from God to seal a man to his wife for eternity. When Joseph received the marriage revelation and explained it to Hyrum, he was remarried and wondered what he should do. Essentially, Hyrum had to choose between his two wives, the living one or the deceased one. He decided to let his current, living wife, Mary Fielding, have the opportunity to choose. She chose not to be sealed to Hyrum but to stand as a proxy, so that Hyrum could be eternally married, or sealed, to his first wife, Jerusha, who was dead. See Hyrum Smith, April 8, 1844, Conference address, "Minutes and Discourses, 6–9 April 1844, as Reported by Thomas Bullock," p. 30-32, The Joseph Smith Papers, accessed February 12, 2002; https://www.josephsmithpapers.org/paper-summary/minutes-and-discourses-6-9-april-1844-as-reported-by-thomas-bullock/33. *After giving this talk and publishing my book on Hyrm Smith, *Hyrum Smith A Prophet Unsung*, the Joseph Smith Papers removed this document. The only place an original can be seen as of today is the LDS Church History Library, Historian's Office general Church minutes, 1839-1877; 1839-1845; Nauvoo, Illinois, 1844 April 6-9; Church History Library, https://catalog.churchofjesuschrist.org/assets/daa151c4-7bae-49d0-8cef-d281a70f1d32/0/0?lang=eng (accessed: January 2, 2024).

he does not get knowledge, he will be brought into captivity by some evil power in the other world, as evil spirits will have more knowledge, and consequently more power than many men who are on the earth. Hence it needs revelation to assist us, and give us knowledge of the things of God.[108]

It matters what we believe and say about Joseph Smith. The Lord promised Joseph,

> Cursed are all those that shall lift up the heel against my anointed . . . and cry, They have sinned! — when they have not sinned . . . and those who swear false against my servants . . . woe unto them. . . . They shall be severed from the ordinances of my house . . . [and] they shall not have right to the Priesthood, nor their posterity after them, from generation to generation.[109]

It matters because we must know the Lord's commandments in order to be able to repent and be obedient to them. The Lord promised Noah that when men should keep all His commandments, when his "posterity shall embrace the

---

[108] See Hyrum Smith, April 8, 1844, Conference address, "Minutes and Discourses, 6–9 April 1844, as Reported by Thomas Bullock," p. 30-32, The Joseph Smith Papers, accessed February 12, 2002; https://www.josephsmithpapers.org/paper-summary/minutes-and-discourses-6-9-april-1844-as-reported-by-thomas-bullock/33. *After giving this talk and publishing my book on Hyrm Smith, *Hyrum Smith A Prophet Unsung*, the Joseph Smith Papers removed this document. The only place an original can be seen as of today is the LDS Church History Library, Historian's Office general Church minutes, 1839-1877; 1839-1845; Nauvoo, Illinois, 1844 April 6-9; Church History Library, https://catalog.churchofjesuschrist.org/assets/daa151c4-7bae-49d0-8cef-d281a70f1d32/0/0?lang=eng (accessed: January 2, 2024).

[109] T&C 138:13. The Lord further promised Joseph that all those who say that Joseph has sinned, [and the Lord considers polygamy a sin], when he has not will be cut off from the ordinances and denied priesthood.

truth and look upward, then shall Zion look downward, and all the heavens shall shake with gladness and the earth shall tremble with joy."[110]

Ultimately, it is what we can learn from Joseph's testimony of the risen Lord that matters. A last day's Zion will come, but it can only be inhabited by those who know the Lord.[111] "If men do not comprehend the character of God," taught Joseph, "they do not comprehend themselves . . . if man does not know God, [he] has not Eternal life" for Eternal life is to know the only true and living God.[112] Joseph and Emma Smith emulated God's image and in so doing taught by example what we must all become in order to be called good.[113]

Though storms rage around us and a diverse legion of voices surround us, the Lord wants us to remember to "Be comforted, be of good cheer, rejoice, and look up, for I am with you who remember me, and all those who watch for me, always, even unto the end."[114]

---

[110] OC Genesis 5:22.
[111] See NC NT—Hebrews 1:23.
[112] See WJS, p. 340; and NC NT—1 John 1:15.
[113] See OC Genesis 2:13, "And I, the Lord God, said unto my Only Begotten that it was not good that the man should be alone; wherefore, I will make a help meet for him." To be "good" a man must have a wife and the two should work to emulate a godly relationship.
[114] T&C 157:66. See also NC NT—Matthew 4:7, 8:6, Mark 4:6, John 9:18, Acts 12:22, NC BofM 3 Nephi 1:3, T&C 48:9, 55:2, 70:5, 124:1, 175:52.

Essay 5

A Servant's Heart[1]

Whitney N. Horning

©August 2022

I adored and idolized my father. I was the proverbial "Daddy's little girl." Despite his father's lack of religious commitment, my dad gained his own testimony of the Savior and the restored Gospel at the age of 14, he attended church faithfully, and prepared himself to serve a mission. At 19 he was interviewed by an LDS general authority who refused him a mission call, advising him to marry his high school sweetheart, my mother, instead. My father misunderstood this to mean he was not worthy to serve as a missionary. This was a deep and painful wound for my father who never quite felt he was considered a truly worthy priesthood holder after that experience. My dad sacrificed and served much to provide for our family and to help build the Kingdom of God on the earth. He led our family in early morning scripture study and family home evening, pronounced father's blessings upon us, and demonstrated by faithful service his love for the Gospel.

My parents' marriage was somewhat difficult and tumultuous. While my father was faithful to my mother and completely committed to their union and our family, he was not necessarily an easy spouse to be married to. In his younger years he was arrogant and prideful in ways that damaged my

---

[1] This talk was given at the You Never Knew My Heart conference on August 20, 2022, in Hildale, Utah. It was a very special day to me. It fell on the same day as our daughter and her husband's wedding anniversary and my dad's birthday.

mother's own self-worth.

My parents' lives were filled with intense humbling opportunities. My dad was an accomplished artist and provided for our family as a graphic designer.[2] These careers take steady hands. He was diagnosed with early on-set Parkinson's at the age of 50. The doctors calculated that it had begun ravaging his mind and his body in his mid-thirties. By age 50 the effects were noticeable and could no longer be ignored. Parkinson's seriously affected his quality of work and is a very noticeable disease. His hands shook and jerked, his body swayed, his gait was staggered and stumbling. He commented once to me that those who did not know him thought he was an alcoholic drunk. It was an embarrassing and humiliating disorder for him. My once handsome, strong, proud, commanding father was brought low by this disease.

When I was a young teen, my mother became enveloped in debilitating mental illness and difficult struggles with medication. In her early 50's she was diagnosed with stage 4, rapid growth breast cancer. Her chances of survival were slim. Fasting, prayer, blessings, radical surgery, chemotherapy, and radiation successfully combated the cancer, but the stress, trauma, and treatment added to her mental distress and illness.

My parents' lives were punctuated by many years of uncertainty and fear.

My father accepted the Lord's humbling and allowed it to work within him to become more like the Savior. He became

---

[2] Many of my father's paintings were purchased by the LDS Church, and some were featured in the *Ensign* and other LDS publications.

kinder and more thoughtful, more loving and gentler. He strove to heal the damage his pride and arrogance had done to my mother and their marriage. He grew to truly love her more than himself. He desired her happiness above all else and labored to earn her love, respect, and admiration in return. My dad had always exhibited qualities of faith, loyalty, and commitment. Through the lessons learned in his suffering, and that of my mother's, my father began to become a man with a Christ-like, servant's heart. Qualities of meekness, grace, compassion, and mercy developed and deepened within him.

My father served and cared for my mother through her many illnesses for many decades with tender patience and great love. When she died suddenly, I came to understand that the notion it is possible to die of a broken heart is real. It took one year and one week for Parkinson's and the devastation of losing my mother to break down my father's body and his will to the point that it became possible for him to join her in death.

My parents taught me to love and honor the Lord, the Prophet-presidents of the Church of Jesus Christ of Latter-day Saints, and the Book of Mormon. I developed a love for the scriptures and LDS Church history and sought to become a greater follower of righteousness.

Several years ago, I recorded in my journal Doctrine and Covenants 93:1 which states that every soul who forsakes their sins, and comes unto the Lord, and calls on His name, and obeys His voice, and keeps all His commandments, **shall see His face and know that He is.**[3]

---

[3] This is the testimony of Jesus, the spirit of prophecy, spoken about by John in the Book of Revelation.

I recognized that since this promise had not yet come to pass in my life there must be commandments that I was unknowingly and unintentionally not obeying. I set out on a quest to figure out what those were. As I expressed my sincere desire to obtain this mercy, the Lord went to work to prove the desires of my heart. He began to open the eyes of my understanding, showing me that even though I was active in the LDS Church, nevertheless, I was in a state of iniquity, unbelief, and apostasy.

Living and acting in a state of iniquity can be the consequence of following traditions that are culturally, socially, or religiously acceptable ways mankind worships God, but are working against what God is trying to do in our day. The traditions of our fathers can cause us to become blind to true doctrine and religion. Religious leaders who teach the traditions and philosophies of men as truth, who do not have an actual connection with Heaven, are described in the scriptures as the blind leaders of the blind, "and if the blind lead the blind, both shall fall into the ditch."[4]

One who does not understand and has not accepted true doctrine is in a state of unbelief.[5] Unbelief also means:

[T]o accept false doctrine or to have an incomplete and inaccurate understanding of correct doctrine. Unbelief is often used in conjunction with losing truth, forsaking doctrine, and 'dwindling.' The phrase dwindling in unbelief is the Book of Mormon's way to describe moving from a state of belief, with true and

---

[4] See NC NT—Matthew 8:9.
[5] Snuffer, Denver C. (July 6, 2010). "1 Nephi 14:5, blog post comment. Retrieved from https://denversnuffer.com/2010/07/1-nephi-14-5/.

complete doctrine, to a state of unbelief, where the truth has been discarded.[6]

The limits set upon this earth at the Fall of Adam and Eve when death entered the world sent it into a state of entropy and decay. Since the beginning, mankind has been involved in either gaining or restoring light and truth or losing and apostatizing from it. Almost every single person living in this world today is in varying degrees of apostasy and most do not even realize it. It may be most difficult for those born into families, cultures, or religions who claim they are the Lord's chosen people, or are the "only true church," to recognize the state they are in. When speaking of religious institutions, apostasy is always marked by a change of ordinances and breaking of the covenant. Apostasy rarely comes by renouncing the Gospel, but by the corruption of it.

In addition to changing ordinances, the vocabulary of godly things is corrupted, causing a "confusion of tongues" which leads people further away from Light and Truth.

I was like Father Lehi in the Book of Mormon who was in a dark and dreary wilderness, following a man dressed in a white robe through a dark and dreary waste. Like Lehi, after the space of many hours in darkness I began to awaken to my awful state and prayed to the Lord for mercy.[7]

The Lord heard my cries and went to work in a variety of ways and means to help me course correct and repent.[8] Part of that correction led me to a greater understanding of the

---

[6] See T&C—A Glossary of Gospel Terms, "Unbelief."

[7] NC BofM—1 Nephi 2:7.

[8] Much of my awakening was brought about through my husband as he opened the scriptures. I consider myself his most important convert.

foundational revelations and teachings of Joseph Smith Jr. I came to the conclusion that not one of the churches that claims to be founded upon the Restoration has stayed true to the original. What is taught in almost, if not all, churches today regarding Joseph Smith is a mere caricature of the man.

My journey to greater Light and Truth has not been easy. I have always had a deep respect, love, and trust in the scriptures which contain the words, revelations, teachings, and stories of men and their families who came into contact with the divine. Having my eyes opened included discovering that well-meaning, but disillusioned leaders have been perpetuating lies regarding Joseph Smith, and even more disturbingly to me, about the very character, perfections, and attributes of God. This realization shook me to my core, and I went through a period of time where I trusted no one but God. I did not want to be deceived or fooled ever again. I repeated Nephi's warning often to myself, "I will not put my trust in the arm of flesh . . . Yea, cursed is he that putteth his trust in man or maketh flesh his arm."[9]

When Vern began to convert me to the Lord's work now underway, I wrestled for some time with what seemed to me a conundrum: receive words, teachings, commandments, and covenants directly from the Lord for myself versus giving heed to and accepting the messengers He sends. I eventually discovered that Nephi also appeared to have wrestled with this same paradox. Much later in 2 Nephi, he amended his earlier warning with this caveat: "Cursed is he that putteth his trust in man . . . **save their precepts shall be given by the power of the**

---

[9] NC BofM 2 Nephi 3:8.

holy ghost.”[10]

I have come to understand that it is an eternal principle that if we want to ascend to the Heavenly Council, we must first acknowledge and give heed to the messengers sent by them.[11] This includes both dead prophets as well as living ones.

Men who have safely navigated the pitfalls, dangers, and beasts of this world to ascend to the top of the mountain and back into the Lord's presence can offer guidance to help us in our own personal journeys along the strait and narrow path. Men who have done so and been given a ministry to go forth as the Lord's servant, must necessarily have a wife, in part because in essence the Lord's Priesthood, or Holy Order, is intended to create of flesh and blood a living, mortal surrogate for the Father and Mother. It is the Mother's right to choose the birthright heir, as seen when Eve chose Cain, Able and then Seth. As well as when Rebecca chose Jacob over Esau. The Mother watches how her sons treat her daughters and how they treat their children.

In this world there are a host of pretenders. Seeking for messengers who have been sent from the presence of the Father to teach us puts the onus squarely upon our own shoulders. We are here to learn to choose between the bitter and the sweet, to discern between truth and error. In our search for greater light and truth, we must test the fruits of those claiming an association with Heaven, whether they be a man, a woman, or an angel.[12] The things of God are of **"deep import; and time, and experience, and careful and ponderous and**

---

[10] NC BofM 2 Nephi 12:6.

[11] T&C 171—Testimony of St. John 2:3.

[12] See Joseph Smith's editorial, "Try the Spirits," reprinted in T&C 147.

solemn thoughts can only find them out."[13]

For most of my life I had been reading the scriptures and LDS Church history through an apologetic lens, forcing them to fit my religion. Several years ago, the Lord led Vern and I into close friendship with an elderly neighbor named Don who had been excommunicated from the LDS Church 40 years earlier. The death of his wife led Don into rebaptism in the LDS Church. On the morning of his rebaptism, Don heard the voice of the Lord speak to him, "Don, many churches and many men may excommunicate you, but only you can excommunicate yourself from me."

Don's rebaptism awakened a hunger and thirst to come to know the Lord for himself. He read the Book of Mormon for the first time in his life. Unencumbered by decades of LDS Church leaders' interpretations and teachings, Don read the scriptures with the eyes of a child, pure and believing. Vern and I would visit in Don's home almost weekly. He would ask us every single time why the LDS Church taught such and such when the scriptures taught it a different way. Don's questions and desire to know the Lord challenged us to open our eyes and ears, to reconsider long-held beliefs and traditions. Don had a profound impact upon us, helping us to believe that the scriptures actually mean what they say, even when they go against widely accepted Church traditions and beliefs.

For me, one of those traditions dealt with plural marriage. The LDS Church teaches that Joseph Smith was commanded by God to marry a plurality of wives as part of the restoration of all things. They assert that whenever he

---

[13] *Teachings of the Prophet Joseph Smith*, p. 137.

condemned plural marriage and denounced it, he was "lying for the Lord," using "carefully worded denials," and "pretzeled language." They have brought forth a multitude of records they assert proves Joseph's involvement in the practice.

After years spent studying, praying, and searching the Lord led me to a conclusion regarding His nature, Joseph Smith, and plural marriage that was as welcome as it was surprising.[14]

The scriptures teach in plainness that the Lord's law of marriage is monogamy. He taught it to Adam and Eve, reiterated it with Jacob's sermon in the Book of Mormon, restated it in Joseph's day, and has clarified it for us again in our day:

> Marriage was, in the beginning, between one man and one woman, and was intended to remain so for the sons of Adam and the daughters of Eve, that they may multiply and replenish the earth. I commanded that there shall not any man have save it be one wife, and concubines he shall have none. **I, the Lord your God, delight in the chastity of women, and in the respect of men for their wives.**[15]

A close examination of the scriptures reveals that only two Patriarchal Fathers might be considered polygamists: Father Abraham and Father Jacob. In Abraham's case, after years of longing for a child, Sarah invoked the rights and laws acceptable in their culture to use one of her handmaids as a surrogate mother. It was the pleadings of a wife desperate to be

---

[14] I have written my conclusions in the book *Joseph Smith Revealed: A Faithful Telling; Exploring an Alternate Polygamy Narrative.*
[15] T&C 157:34.

a mother that persuaded Abraham to father a child through Hagar. Ishmael, born of Hagar, should have been Sarah's child under this law.

In Jacob's case, he loved Rachel and had made vows and commitments with her. Tricked by a dishonorable father-in-law, Jacob was married to Leah instead of Rachel. Out of respect for Leah's reputation and what it would mean in their culture and society for her to be put away, he maintained his marriage with her. Because of his great love for Rachel, and the commitments already made between them, Jacob also married her.

Neither Abraham nor Jacob was commanded by God to take a plural wife. A few weeks before he died, Hyrum Smith spoke to a conference of elders, stating "I wish the Elders of Israel to understand it is lawful for a man to marry a wife but it is unlawful to have more, and God has not commanded anyone to have more."[16]

There is, in fact, only one document in all of scripture which promotes the idea of plural marriage. It is found only in the scriptures of the churches born out of the Utah Mormon

---

[16] Hyrum Smith, April 8, 1844, conference address. See "Minutes and Discourses, 6–9 April 1844, as Reported by Thomas Bullock," pp. 30-32, The Joseph Smith Papers, accessed on July 20, 2022, https://www.josephsmithpapers.org/paper-summary/minutes-and-discourses-6-9-april-1844-as-reported-by-thomas-bullock/33. Grammar, punctuation, and spelling corrected and modernized. *After giving this talk and publishing my book on Hyrm Smith, *Hyrum Smith A Prophet Unsung*, the Joseph Smith Papers removed this document. The only place an original can be seen as of today is the LDS Church History Library, Historian's Office general Church minutes, 1839-1877; 1839-1845; Nauvoo, Illinois, 1844 April 6-9; Church History Library, https://catalog.churchofjesuschrist.org/assets/daa151c4-7bae-49d0-8cef-d281a70f1d32/0/0?lang=eng (accessed: January 2, 2024).

Church: Doctrine and Covenants 132. These churches attribute the authorship of this document to Joseph Smith. Joseph testified before the Nauvoo City Council that the revelation he had received had nothing to do with polygamy. Rather, it taught that in order for a man to lay claim upon his wife in the next life he must be married to her in view of eternity, for no man sits on a throne in eternity unless he has a wife that is willing to make covenants with him to put him there.[17] D&C 132 does not support any other scripture or teachings from the Lord.[18]

---

[17] According to Joseph's journal, the very first Eternal marriage covenant of the Restoration took place between him and his Elect Lady, Emma on May 28, 1843. The next day, Hyrum entered into an Eternal marriage covenant with his deceased wife, Jerusha. Because Jerusha was dead, a living proxy needed to stand in her place. Hyrum's second wife, Mary Fielding, chose to be proxy for Jerusha. See The Joseph Smith Papers (2015). *Journals, Vol. 3, May 1843-June 1844*, pp. 24-25. Salt Lake City, UT: The Church Historian's Press. See T&C 157:42.

[18] Investigation into its provenance suggests that it is an altered document. The original revelation regarding the Eternal marriage covenant no longer exists in a form that we are aware of today. The LDS Church claims that Emma burned the original but not before it was copied by William Clayton, whose copy was then copied by Joseph Kingsbury. When Brigham published his copy in 1852, he told the saints that he had kept it locked away for safe keeping. Several men and women who had lived in Nauvoo in 1843 and had seen the original stated that the revelation Brigham published did not resemble the original which they had seen. On July 14, 2017, the Lord revealed that the original revelation had been altered. See T&C 157:33; Ehat, Andrew F. & Cook, Lyndon W. (1980). *The Words of Joseph Smith*, pp. 232-233. Provo, UT: Religious Studies Center Brigham Young University; and Dinger, John S., editor. (2011). *The Nauvoo City and High Council Minutes*, p. 255-256. Salt Lake City, UT: Signature Books. See also T&C 157: 33. The Lord has revealed in our day that conspiracies have corrupted the scriptures beginning with the Bible and again following the time of Joseph and Hyrum. See T&C 157:15. A little over five years ago, an independent group of people came together to restore the scriptures as accurately as humanly possible. These people had a desire to get back to the original teachings of the Lord

When Hyrum learned about the principle of eternal marriage, sometime in the spring of 1843, he was concerned what it would mean for him as he had been married to two different women. His first wife, Jerusha, had died after the birth of their sixth child. After her death, he had married Mary Fielding and had two children with her. Hyrum asked Joseph what could be done. Joseph replied that Hyrum had to choose between the two. Out of respect for Mary, Hyrum left the choice up to her. For reasons unknown, Mary chose not to be sealed to Hyrum but to stand as a proxy so that he could be sealed to his first wife, Jerusha.[19] Both Joseph and Hyrum understood the nature of eternal, monogamous marriage.

as revealed to Joseph Smith. This included printing, for the first time ever, the Inspired Translation of the Bible, the Book of Mormon, and the revelations and doctrines as Joseph had intended. This entailed much research, sacrifice, time and money. We owe an enormous debt of gratitude to the many people involved. Part of restoring truth includes restoring correct definitions and meanings of the Gospel. The Restoration Edition of the scriptures includes a Glossary of Gospel Terms which is as interesting as it is enlightening. I used to love reading the encyclopedia and as a teen would read Bruce R. McConkie's' Mormon Doctrine and the Encyclopedia of Mormonism. I have learned more about God and His ways from studying the Glossary of Gospel Terms than almost any other book. The Restoration Edition of the scriptures is available for free online at scriptures.info. You can purchase print copies, sold at the cost, at scriptures.shop.

[19] See Hyrum Smith, April 8, 1844, Conference address, "Minutes and Discourses, 6–9 April 1844, as Reported by Thomas Bullock," p. 30-32, The Joseph Smith Papers, accessed February 12, 2002; https://www.josephsmithpapers.org/paper-summary/minutes-and-discourses-6-9-april-1844-as-reported-by-thomas-bullock/33. *After giving this talk and publishing my book on Hyrm Smith, *Hyrum Smith A Prophet Unsung*, the Joseph Smith Papers removed this document. The only place an original can be seen as of today is the LDS Church History Library, Historian's Office general Church minutes, 1839-1877; 1839-1845; Nauvoo, Illinois, 1844 April 6-9; Church History Library, https://catalog.churchofjesuschrist.org/assets/daa151c4-7bae-49d0-8cef-d281a70f1d32/0/0?lang=eng (accessed: January 2, 2024).

Rather than sanctioning and justifying plural marriage, the stories of Abraham and Jacob demonstrate God's great mercy. The Lord willingly extends grace and forgiveness, even to those of us who have been living and participating in societies, cultures, and religions burdened with false traditions, iniquity, and unbelief.

The common thread that weaves through the pages of scripture beginning with Genesis down to our day are the stories of men who in faith rose up out of the lies and darkness of this world and into the Light of Christ. While the world groaned under the weight of generations of apostasy, Joseph Smith became such a man. He then spent the rest of his life ministering to teach and persuade others to do as he had done.

I have found that Joseph Smith was a man of honor, integrity, and virtue who loved the Lord and his family. I believe had no other wives or concubines than his one wife, Emma. It saddens me to know that because of the many lies which have been and continue to be spread about him, Joseph could say to the saints in our day, "You don't know me; you never knew my heart."[20]

Joseph's great work of the Restoration was intended to restore the family of God, to elevate mankind from our fallen state back into full fellowship with the Lord.[21] Of all of Joseph's

---

[20] *Teachings of the Prophet Joseph Smith*, p. 361.

[21] Before the return of Christ, everything — including the original Priesthood with all its components — must be restored. It will necessarily include men and women, as husband and wife, because in essence, the Holy Order Priesthood is to create of flesh and blood a living, mortal surrogate for the Father and Mother. It is the nature of this Holy Order that it is conferred upon the man and woman jointly (see 1 Corinthians 1:44). The Holy Order is familial. It does not involve establishing a church but, instead, connecting

disciples there is record of only one other man who accepted and acted upon Joseph's teachings with a heart of integrity until he, too, had obtained the faith necessary to rise up and was crowned by the Lord with the same blessings Joseph had received.

Our desires are what initiates the call of God to those who are willing to labor in His vineyard. The Lord is interested in discovering what it is we truly desire, what it is that is hidden in the recesses of our hearts, to help us root out and burn away anything that keeps us from being exactly and precisely what He is. The Lord "will judge all men according to their works, according to the desires of their hearts."[22] This life is a perfect laboratory whereby our hearts are tested and proven. Each day is an opportunity to reflect to the Lord, as well as to others, the condition of our hearts.

Hyrum Smith was born with a servant's heart. He and Joseph were extremely close. Theirs was a love and a bond forged out of the fiery furnaces of affliction. When Joseph was a small child brought low by Typhus and the accompanying surgery which removed part of his leg, 11-year-old Hyrum sat next to his bed for hours each day, holding his little brother's hand, trying to soothe his great agony of pain. Hyrum was not absent from [Joseph] at any one time, not even the space of six months since his birth.[23]

---

together the Family of God. See T&C—A Glossary of Gospel Terms, "Holy Order."

[22] T&C 122:5.

[23] The hearing began on January 2, 1843, and ended with Judge Pope's decision on January 5, 1843. Pope presided over the federal courtroom in Springfield, Illinois, located on the second floor of what is now the Lincoln-

As Hyrum sacrificed and supported Joseph in the work of the Restoration, he waited patiently upon the Lord, serving in meekness, laboring by the sweat of his brow, grateful for all the Lord had revealed, seeking to obtain God's word, and honoring God by exact obedience to every word that proceeded forth from His mouth. Hyrum had an earnest desire to serve the Lord at any cost, declaring that all he had was the Lord's and he was ready to do his will continually.[24] The Lord declared, "I came unto my own and my own received me not, but unto as many as received me gave I power to do many miracles and to become the sons of God, and even unto them that believed on my name gave I power to obtain eternal life."[25]

In the history of the Restoration, Hyrum is pivotal. Joseph's ascension, redemption and call to minister followed the pattern of men who rise up out of obscurity and outside religious hierarchy to connect with God after generations of

---

Herndon Law Office building. Among the throng of spectators were a large number of women, Mary Lincoln among them, who for lack of space were seated on the judge's platform. Abraham Lincoln was one of the Illinois state representatives who voted in favor of the Nauvoo City Charter. He and Mary were newlyweds when Joseph's case was heard in Springfield. Hyrum and Joseph Jr.'s father, Joseph Sr., had passed away two years earlier, therefore, the Prophet Joseph was legally referred to as Joseph Smith Sr. after his father's passing. See *Times and Seasons*, Vol. 4, No. 16, (July 1, 1843), pp. 242-256 and Holst, Erika (2016, October 13). When Joseph Smith stood trial in Springfield, *Illinois Times*; retrieved from https://www.illinoistimes.com/springfield/when-joseph-smith-stood-trial-in-springfield/Content?oid=11443543.

[24] Cannon, Donald Q. and Cook, Lyndon W. (Eds.) (1983). *Far West Record: Minutes of The Church of Jesus Christ of Latter-day Saints, 1830-1844*, November 7, 1837, p. 21. Salt Lake City, UT: Deseret Book Company.

[25] See T&C 31:2. A true Prophet is one who has been in the presence of the Lord and who goes forth crying repentance and teaching the rest of us how we can obtain the same blessings for ourselves.

apostasy. Hyrum accepted Joseph as the Lord's servant and rose up inside a religious institution to lay hold of God's promises. God invites each of us to rise up and become one of His "many sons and daughters."

Joseph loved and admired his older brother, seeking his counsel and guidance throughout their lives, stating that he never knew Hyrum to say he ever had a revelation and it failed.

In September 1840, as Joseph Smith Sr., Patriarch of the Smith family and the Church, lay on his death bed, he gave each of his children a final father's blessing. He laid his hands upon Hyrum's head and sealed his patriarchal blessing upon him.[26] Joseph Sr. then said,

> You shall have a season of peace, so that you shall have sufficient rest to accomplish the work which God has given you to do. You shall be as firm as the pillars of heaven unto the end of your days. I now seal upon your head the patriarchal power, and you shall bless the people. This is my dying blessing upon your head in the name of Jesus. Amen.[27]

On January 19, 1841, the Lord ratified Hyrum's ordination, declaring that His servant Hyrum should take:

> [T]he office of Priesthood and Patriarch, which was appointed unto him by his father by blessing, and also by right, that from henceforth he shall hold the keys of the Patriarchal blessings upon the heads of all my people, that whoever he blesses shall be blessed and

---

[26] Joseph Sr. had pronounced Patriarchal blessings upon his children and their spouses approximately six years earlier on December 9, 1834.

[27] Smith, Lucy Mack (1845). *Joseph Smith the Prophet and His Progenitors*, pp. 337-338. Reprinted in 1912 by the Reorganized Church of Jesus Christ of Latter Day Saints. Lamoni, Iowa: Herald Publishing House.

whoever he curses shall be cursed, that whatever he shall bind on the earth shall be bound in Heaven, and that whatever he shall loose on earth shall be loosed in Heaven. And from this time forth I appoint unto him that he may be a prophet, and a seer, and a revelator unto my church, as well as my servant Joseph, that he may act in concert also with my servant Joseph, and that he shall receive counsel from my servant Joseph, who shall show unto him the keys whereby he may ask and receive, and be crowned with the same blessings.[28]

Like Joseph, Hyrum became blessed of the Lord. These two brothers rose up to a higher level, or practice, of true religion, stirring the Heavens to take notice and connect with them. In the entire history of this creation there have been few men whom the Lord trusts enough to ordain with sealing authority and power.[29] Hyrum was a man who was loved and trusted by the Lord "because of the integrity of his heart and because he love[d] that which [was] right before [Him]."[30]

Hyrum was ordained by the Lord a Holy Spirit of Promise. Honoring the birthright pattern established in the beginning, the Lord placed Hyrum first in His Priesthood.[31]

There were other disciples in the early Restoration Church who labored and sacrificed much for the cause of Zion but were unable to rise up to the level of faith required to obtain the rights of the Fathers as Hyrum and Joseph had done. Joseph saw a vision of "the twelve apostles . . . standing together in a

---

[28] T&C 141:32.
[29] While the Lord forgives whom He will forgive, very few have proven that He can trust them.
[30] T&C 141:5.
[31] See T&C 141:32, and 41.

circle much fatigued, with their clothes tattered and feet swollen, with their eyes cast downward, **and Jesus in their midst, and they did not behold him.** The Savior looked upon them and wept."[32]

The Lord stands knocking at our door, ready and waiting to extend His great mercy unto all — we are the ones who refuse to bid Him enter.

There were among the saints those who had more zeal than knowledge, running ahead of and in some cases entirely disregarding the commandments of God. Hyrum preached:

> We are told by some that circumstances alter the revelations of God-tell me what circumstances would alter the ten commandments? they were given by revelation-given as a law to the children of Israel;-who has a right to alter that law? Some think that they are too small for us to notice, they are not too small for God to notice, and have we got so high, so bloated out, that we cannot condescend to notice things that God has ordained for our benefit? . . . I know that nothing but an unwavering, undeviating course can save a man in the kingdom of God. . . . Let the saints be wise; let us lay aside our folly and abide by the commandments of God; so shall we be blessed of the great Jehovah in time and in eternity.[33]

Hyrum was a valiant protector of women and children and had little tolerance for men who did not care for their families. He believed in, lived, and taught the principle in the scripture, "If any provide not for his own, and especially for those of his own house, he has denied the faith and is worse

---

[32] T&C 122:7.
[33] *Times and Seasons* Vol. 3, No. 15 (June 1, 1842), pp. 799-801.

than an unbeliever."[34] This is evidenced in the great care Hyrum demonstrated for his parents, his own wife and children, his sisters, Sophronia and Catherine who were living in difficult marriages, and for others who were in need.[35]

Hyrum employed the use of Church courts and legal courts to try to persuade men to step up to their duties as fathers and husbands. In a letter to his cousin Harriet in 1843, Hyrum expressed his strong opinions and the determined actions he took toward men who shirk their responsibilities to their families:

> Respected Cousin, . . .You no doubt recollect the girl that was Fanny Dort;[36] the one that married Matthew G. Casto, she lies now at the point of death, and we do not think she will ever be any better. She had a young child a few days ago, and it was dead. Her husband is a nefarious villain, he turned her out of doors about the first of last January naked and destitute; because it

---

[34] NC NT—1 Timothy 1:13.

[35] In 1836 Hyrum testified before the Kirtland High Council against his brother-in-law Jenkins Salisbury who had left Catharine and their small children with little wood and no provisions, never intending to return. See "Minutes, 16 May 1836," pp. 205-206, The Joseph Smith Papers, accessed on July 20, 2022, https://www.josephsmithpapers.org/paper-summary/minutes-16-may-1836/1. There were at times upwards of 20 people living in his household, from young, orphaned children to widows and elderly men.

[36] Fanny Dort (1823-about 1850) daughter of David Dort and Mary Mack. Mary Mack was a first cousin to Hyrum Smith. Fanny was most likely one of the children that Mary Fielding taught while living as a private tutor in the home of Mr. and Mrs. Dort in Kirtland, Ohio in October 1837. Matthew G. Casto abused Fanny and her family, including Hyrum, helped her get away from him. She had two children with Casto: Joseph and Hyrum, who died as a newborn baby. Fanny's son Joseph became blind as a young boy. He lived on his own until his death at 68 years of age, making his living selling trinkets to local towns people, and known as "Blind Joe."

happens to be her misfortune to be weakly and unable to work, when she is in the family way; and the poor girl, would have suffered death, by cold and hunger, had it not been for her two brothers and the rest of her friends here, long before this time. I have rendered her what assistance I could, and have taken up the case in the name of her nearest, or best friend and prosecuted the rascal, and got a judgement against him of forty or fifty dollars, towards her support, and intend to sue him every month, until he will take care of her, if she lives; or until . . . her divorce from him.[37]

Hyrum consistently demonstrated through word and action that he valued marriage and family and held the relationships formed within that union in the highest regard. He encouraged husbands and wives to seek to redeem each other and to keep their families together if possible.[38]

Hyrum was well-respected as a steadfast man of honor and integrity, even so, the saints struggled to pay him any heed or attention as a Prophet. On October 31, 1841, Hyrum read a letter he had prepared for saints still living in Kirtland. An extract of that inspired letter was printed in the *Times and Seasons* and *Millenial Star* "because it contain[ed] instructions of vital importance to all the children of God."[39] That letter contained "thus saith the Lord" revelation and prophecy, yet it has never been included in any book of scripture.[40]

---

[37] Hyrum Smith letter to Harriet Whittemore, April 9, 1843.
[38] T&C 149:8.
[39] *The Latter-day Saint Millenial Star*, Vol. 2, No. 8, (December 1, 1841), p. 125.
[40] Despite the efforts of an independent scripture committee to add revelations from Hyrum post his appointment as prophet in January 1841 when they produced the Restoration Edition scriptures in 2017, this

Joseph understated the things of God that he had seen and heard. Hyrum was even more circumspect and private than Joseph. His testimony of the risen Lord is so unpretentious that it is easily passed over. Of his great suffering while imprisoned in Liberty Jail, Hyrum stated,

> I had been abused and thrust into a dungeon, and confined for months on account of my faith, and the 'testimony of Jesus Christ.' However I thank God that I felt a determination to die, rather than deny the things which my eyes had seen, which my hands had handled, and which I had borne testimony to, wherever my lot had been cast; and I can assure my beloved brethren that I was enabled to bear as strong a testimony, when nothing but death presented itself, as ever I did in my life. My confidence in God, was likewise unshaken.[41]

After Hyrum and Joseph were murdered, the Restoration fractured into dozens of branches. Today, not one of those churches understands or practices God's pattern of birthright heir, including Patriarchal Priesthood, in the manner prescribed by the Lord.

Churches today that claim the keys of Priesthood power and authority were given to them by Joseph, including the power to seal on earth and in Heaven, fail to acknowledge that once he became qualified Hyrum was placed first, ahead of Joseph, in the Lord's Priesthood. Hyrum held the rights of Patriarchal Priesthood and the right and authority to seal. There are no records or claims of anyone receiving keys from

---

revelation from him was missed. We must repent of our negligence of Hyrum by acknowledging his appointment as prophet, seer, and revelator.

[41] *Times and Seasons*, Vol. 1, No. 2, (December 1839), pp. 20-24.

Hyrum.

Four years ago today, my father was buried on his birthday. As I stood at the cemetery and watched his remains returned to the dust from whence he came, a quiet thought entered my mind that I should write a book that could help others come to know the real Joseph as I had done and get a glimpse into his heart. It is, therefore, appropriate and fitting that the publication of my book about Hyrum Smith be announced today.[42]

Two book ends of the Restoration. One brother's name had for both good and evil throughout the world. The other brother overlooked, dismissed, and unappreciated. Many in this world think they know Joseph Smith, but few know much, if anything, about his older brother Hyrum. Not one church claiming succession from Joseph Smith recognizes Hyrum in their list of prophets or presidents.

After years of research, study, and reflection, my admiration for Hyrum Smith has swelled into a deep and profound gratitude for the man who in quiet, solemn meekness stood as a pillar of love, strength, and support for the entire Smith family, striving to follow Christ in very deed, and for my God, who willingly works with anyone who desires to follow His path of progression and redemption.[43]

When Hyrum and Joseph were murdered, the Restoration was not yet complete. To fulfill His promises to the Fathers, the Lord has begun His work anew in our day. Those who desire to join together in the great cause of God must

---

[42] *Hyrum Smith A Prophet Unsung.*
[43] See 1 Corinthians 1:43.

understand what behaviors the Lord requires for a people to be His and what it takes to qualify to become His sons and daughters. On August 16, 1842, Joseph recorded Hyrum's name in the Book of the Law of the Lord "for those who come after . . . to look upon that they may pattern after [his] works."[44] The Lord promised Hyrum that his name would be had in honorable remembrance from generation to generation for ever and ever, yet, he remains a Prophet unsung.

---

[44] Joseph Smith, Reflections and Blessings, August 16, 1842, Nauvoo, Hancock Co., Illinois. "The Book of the Law of the Lord," p. 164, The Joseph Smith Papers, accessed August 13, 2022, https://www.josephsmithpapers.org/paper-summary/the-book-of-the-law-of-the-lord/180.

Death and the World of Spirits

Whitney N. Horning
©April 2024

My father called me on a Friday, a little after 5 p.m., to tell me that my mother had died. She was 71 years old. My father was in his home office down the hallway from their bedroom when he heard her loudly gasp. When he arrived by her side, he knew she was gone. He attempted administering CPR, but the height of their bed along with his advanced Parkinson's prevented him from being able to do so effectively. By the time the emergency responders arrived there was nothing to be gained through resuscitative efforts.

Five days prior to this event my mother had been affected by contortions and spasms throughout her body. My father gave her a blessing, in faith, using the priesthood authority that he believed he had been ordained unto. During the blessing he heard a voice tell him to release my mother from this life. My dad could not do it. I am not sure that many people who have loved a spouse for as long as my dad has loved my mother could have either. Five days later, God took that decision out of the hands of my father; He reached out and brought my mother from this world of care and sorrow into the World of Spirits.

> To everything there is a season and a time to every purpose under heaven; a time to be born, and a time to die; a time to plant, and a time to pluck up that which is planted . . . a time to heal . . . a time to build

up; a time to weep, and a time to laugh; a time to mourn, and a time to dance.[1]

As an active and believing Latter-day Saint, I had held great comfort and a carnal security in the fact that my mother had received her temple endowments, been sealed to her parents, and later to my father in the Salt Lake Temple.[2] According to LDS theology, I had been taught that upon death her spirit would reside in Spirit Paradise and eventually, after the resurrection, the Celestial Kingdom. Upon her death, I began to seriously reflect upon all I thought I knew about life after death. For some reason, I did not feel secure in the assurances I had once held concerning my mother. I lost sleep in the weeks following her death, worrying, praying, and asking the Lord to give me comfort regarding the state of her soul. I did not know if God judged her righteous and that she was in a paradisiacal state resting from all troubles, care, and sorrow. I hoped this was the case, because above all else she craved peace.

My mother's death was the first of five close family members who died over a two year period. My paternal grandmother died soon after my mother. She was followed by my father who died one year and one week after my mother. He was followed by my husband's grandmother. The final death was that of my brother-in-law who had young children. Our family had barely begun recovering from one death when another wave of loss and mourning would be upon us. So much death in such a short window of time deepened the craving

---

[1] OC Ecclesiastes 1:10.
[2] See 2 Nephi 12:4.

within me to understand the World of Spirits. I longed to find solace for my grieving soul.

As I searched and studied, I came to realize that I know far less than I had supposed and have far more to learn. I believe that all truth may be circumscribed into one great whole. In the beginning there was one true gospel, taught by God to Father Adam and Mother Eve. Through time, and because truth is difficult to hold onto, the original gospel shattered into millions of pieces. Remnants remain today found within all nations, kindreds, tongues, and peoples. Those who desire to labor alongside God's chosen servants as they reconstruct, or restore, Adam's gospel, can and should search and study the various religious beliefs. Doing so requires the spirit to manifest truth, "and whoever is enlightened by the spirit shall obtain benefit therefrom, and whoever receives not the spirit cannot be benefited."[3] With this understanding, let us consider some of the major beliefs regarding the World of Spirits.

The Books of Breathing are several ancient Egyptian funerary texts dating as early as 350 B.C. and are a simplified form of the Book of the Dead. They are intended to enable deceased persons to continue existing in the afterlife.[4] The word breathing in the titles is a metaphorical term for all aspects of life that the deceased hope to experience in the

---

[3] T&C 91:1.

[4] The Books of Breathing were originally named *The Letter for Breathing Which Isis Made for Her Brother Osiris*, *The First Letter for Breathing*, and *The Second Letter for Breathing*.

afterlife.[5] Some of the papyri that Joseph Smith used to translate the Book of Abraham are parts of the Books of Breathing.[6] The Book of the Dead is one of the most famous aspects of ancient Egyptian culture. It was written as a necessary guide for the dead to use on their perilous and confusing journeys to the afterlife and describes tests which deceased persons must pass in their progression to earn eternal life among the gods.[7] The texts were written by multiple authors with their own variations. However, the narrative is generally the same and is divided into four main sections: the deceased enters the underworld where they regain the physical abilities of the living, the deceased is resurrected and joins Ra to rise as the sun each day, the deceased travels across the sky before judgment by a panel of gods, and finally, if the deceased has not been destroyed by failing the tests, they will join the gods.[8]

---

[5] See Hornung, Erik (1999). *The Ancient Egyptian Books of the Afterlife* (in German). David Lorton (translator), pp. 23-25. Cornell University Press and Smith, Mark (2009). *Traversing Eternity: Texts for the Afterlife from Ptolemaic and Roman Egypt*, pp. 462, 466, 499-500, 503, 514,517-518, and 521. Oxford University Press.

[6] See Ritner, R. K. (2013). *The Joseph Smith Egyptian papyri: A complete edition*, P. JS 1-4 and the hypocephalus of Sheshonq, p. 74. Salt Lake City: Signature Books.

[7] One of the more familiar tests from the Book of the Dead is the scale that weighs the heart of the deceased against a feather. The Book of the Dead also included spells, names the dead must speak correctly, and answers they must respond with to the gods' questions. See Warren, Kellie. Book of the Dead: A Guidebook to the Afterlife. ARCE: American Research Center in Egypt. Retrieved from https://arce.org/resource/book-dead-guidebook-afterlife/#:~:text=Although%20the%20text%20itself%20varies,travels%20across%20the%20sky%20before; accessed on April 2, 2024.

[8] Warren, Kellie. "Book of the Dead: A Guidebook to the Afterlife." ARCE: American Research Center in Egypt. Retrieved from

Judaism offers a range of views on the afterlife. Some of these parallel familiar concepts of heaven and hell found in Christian teachings. There are several biblical references to a place called Sheol which generally represents "the place of the dead" inhabited by both the righteous and the unrighteous. In ancient Hebrew thought, this "place of the dead" was divided into two sections: a place of suffering and a holding place for the righteous.[9] The term Sheol is sprinkled across the Tanakh. The phrase "going down to Sheol" has been used synonymously with dying. According to a Chassidic tradition, heaven and hell are really the same place, for one person it is paradise, and for the other, it is hell.[10] Sheol is described as a "dark and deep" region, the "Pit," and "the Land of

---

https://arce.org/resource/book-dead-guidebook-afterlife/#:~:text=Although%20the%20text%20itself%20varies,travels%20a cross%20the%20sky%20before; accessed on April 2, 2024. Ra's name came from a combination of Re and Amun. The name Re was from Upper Egypt and the name Amun came from Lower Egypt. When the two came together the name was changed to Amun-Re. Over thousands of years the name Amun-Re evolved into Amun-Ra and then just Ra.

[9] We find this idea in the teaching of Jesus in Luke 16:19-31, where Jesus speaks of a wicked rich man and a righteous poor beggar named Lazarus. Upon their deaths, the wicked man, who had "everything in life," went to the place of torment, Hades, which is the closest thing to a Greek equivalent of the Hebrew *sheol*, whereas the poor man, Lazarus, went to paradise. They are both in the same "place of the dead," but separated by a "great chasm" as verse 26 calls it. The place of the righteous is called "the bosom of Abraham," while the place of torment is called "Hades." Staples, Tim (November 8, 2021). "What is Hell?" Catholic Answers Magazine. https://www.catholic.com/magazine/online-edition/what-is-hell, accessed on April 2, 2024.

[10] See Exploring Judaism, "What is the Jewish Afterlife?" retrieved from https://www.exploringjudaism.org/living/lifecycles/death-and-dying/what-is-the-jewish-afterlife/#:~:text=Sheol%20%2F%20Hades,is%20used%20synonymously%2 0with%20dying. Accessed on April 2, 2024.

Forgetfulness," where the spirit of human beings descend after death. Cut off from God's presence and humankind they live on in some shadowy state of existence.[11]

Most Hindus believe that humans are in a cycle of death and resurrection, rebirth, or reincarnation called samsara. They believe that when a person dies, their soul (atman) is reborn into a different body. Some believe that rebirth happens directly at death, others believe that a soul may exist in other realms, either a heavenly one (swarg) or a hellish one (narak) for a period of time before it is resurrected or reborn.[12]

Muslims refer to life after death as Akhirah. They believe that when a person dies, their soul is taken by the Angel of Death (Azra'il) to a state of waiting called Barzakh. There two angels, sent by God, come to question the waiting soul. If the questions are answered correctly, the soul enters a state of sleep until the resurrection. If answered incorrectly, the soul is tormented. Muslims believe that God will hold them accountable for their actions in this life. If they were obedient to Allah (God) they will inherit Paradise, but if disobedient they will be sent to hell.[13] Muslims believe in a Day of Resurrection

---

[11] See Rabbi Or N. Rose, (2022-2024), "Afterlife: Heaven and Hell in Jewish Tradition," My Jewish Learning, retrieved from https://www.myjewishlearning.com/article/heaven-and-hell-in-jewish-tradition; accessed on April 2, 2024.

[12] See "Belief in Reincarnation," retrieved from https://www.bbc.co.uk/bitesize/guides/zddbqp3/revision/6#:~:text=Most%20Hindus%20believe%20that%20humans,may%20exist%20in%20other%20realms; accessed on April 2, 2024.

[13] Muslims believe that there are seven levels to Heaven, which may also be interpreted as "many levels." This is similar to the Christian understanding, "In my father's house are many mansions," which may also be interpreted as "many levels" or "many stages with temporary abodes." See NC John 9:6,

also known as the Day of Judgement or the Last Hour.[14]

Catholics believe that when a member of their faith dies, their soul is immediately judged on how they lived their life and sent to one of three states: Heaven, Purgatory, or Hell. The most pious are delivered safely to the eternal paradise of Heaven. Purgatory is the state for those "who die in God's grace and friendship, but still imperfectly purified." [15] These spirits undergo a process of purification after death "so as to achieve the holiness necessary to enter the joy of heaven."[16] The faithful who are still alive on earth can help the souls in Purgatory by offering prayers in suffrage for them, by almsgiving, indulgences, works of penance, and the Eucharist sacrifice.[17] The unrepentant who have perpetrated the gravest sins descend into Hell. The damned are eternally deprived of the beatific vision, which is the immediate knowledge of God that the angelic spirits and the souls of the just enjoy in

---

T&C 98:3, and T&C 171—The Testimony of St. John 10:9. See Key beliefs in Islam, retrieved from https://www.bbc.co.uk/bitesize/guides/zdxdqhv/revision/5#:~:text=The%20afterlife,to%20question%20the%20waiting%20soul; accessed on April 2, 2024.

[14] See Resurrection, judgement and life after death, retrieved from https://www.bbc.co.uk/bitesize/guides/zvm96v4/revision/5#:~:text=On%20this%20day%2C%20all%20the,Judgement%20(yawm%20ad%2Ddin); accessed on April 2, 2024.

[15] Catechism of the Catholic Church 1030-1031.

[16] Ibid.

[17] The Eucharist is that which is offered to God in the Holy Communion, the loving surrender of our wills and our lives to God. When Catholics receive the Holy Communion, they are strengthened by Christ real presence so that they can do the Father's will.

Heaven.[18] They will not receive any consolation in hell, escape from the pain of hellfire, or have any company except for the demons that tempted them.[19] The Final Judgement will come at the end of time, when all of humanity will be raised from the dead and the body and soul will be reunited to be judged by Christ who will have returned in all His glory.

Christian religious beliefs regarding an afterlife vary. Some denominations believe that they are judged by God immediately upon death for the deeds they have done during their lifetime and then sent directly to Heaven or to Hell. Others believe that those who die in a state of grace are immediately, or after a period of purification, admitted to the bliss of heaven, where they become like God and see God face to face. The Eastern Orthodox church believes in an intermediate state after death and before the final judgement, and consequently offer prayers for the dead. These denominations believe that their "prayers for the departed can help them in [the] process of healing and purification. . . . Prayer for the departed also gives [the living believer] another way to continue in the awesome privilege of participating in God's ongoing work of the salvation, sanctification, and glorification of every soul."[20] The theological doctrine of glorification is the final step in the application of redemption

---

[18] See Catholic Answers Encyclopedia, Beatific Vision. Retrieved from https://www.catholic.com/encyclopedia/beatific-vision; accessed on April 2, 2024.

[19] See Master Nazareth Catechism, Catechism of the Council of Trent: Sentence of the Wicked.

[20] Ford, David C. "Prayer and the Departed Saints." St. Stephen Antiochian Orthodox Church. Retrieved from https://www.protomartyr.org/our-faith/prayer-and-the-departed-saints/; accessed on April 2, 2024. This is believed in Reformed Christian Churches.

and refers to the resurrection of the believer who will be given a new body that has a degree of continuity with their mortal selves.[21]

The current belief in the Church of Jesus Christ of Latter-day Saints (LDS) is that the World of Spirits is divided into two separate places: Paradise and Prison.[22] The LDS Church teaches that the spirits of members who had been baptized and remained faithful, including, if old enough and previously endowed, a current temple recommend, go to Spirit Paradise soon after death.[23] Those who were not faithful members, and those who were never baptized into the LDS faith, will find themselves in Spirit Prison. The spirits of deceased, faithful members serve missions to those in Spirit Prison. If those in prison accept the gospel, repent of their sins, receive the ordinance of baptism, and their temple work is done for them by proxy, they may leave Prison and enter Paradise.[24] All of this is now believed to take place before the resurrection.

The majority of religious denominations agree that there is a world of spirits where those who have died wait until the resurrection. There is truth to be discovered in each of

---

[21] See Wayne, Grudem (1994). *Systematic Theology*, pp. 828–839. Nottingham: Inter-Varsity Press.

[22] See "Paradise" under Topics and Questions on The Church of Jesus Christ of Latter-day Saints website; https://www.churchofjesuschrist.org/study/manual/gospel-topics/paradise?lang=eng#title1; accessed on March 20, 2024.

[23] See "Paradise" under Topics and Questions on The Church of Jesus Christ of Latter-day Saints website; https://www.churchofjesuschrist.org/study/manual/gospel-topics/paradise?lang=eng#title1; accessed March 20, 2024).

[24] Ibid.

these various religious traditions and beliefs. Yet, they have all gone astray. Even LDS theology has shifted and changed over time and is no longer consistent with the truths it was founded upon. The LDS Church originated with the teachings and revelations of Joseph Smith Jr. who was one of this world's most singular and brilliant theologians. Through his connection to God, he held the keys of revelation and seership. He defined these as the ability to ask God and receive an answer.[25] As he labored to correct the Biblical text, Joseph revealed new truths and cleared up long-held mistranslations which had introduced confusion into Christianity. One of those regarded Christ's comments to the thief who hung by his side during the crucifixion. Of this event, Joseph taught:

> There has been much said about the sayings of Jesus on the Cross to the thief saying this day thou shalt be with me in paradise. The commentators or translators make it out to say Paradise but what is Paradise it is a modern word it does not answer at all to the original that Jesus made use of . . . but it was this day I will be with thee in the World of Spirits and will teach thee or answer thy inquiries. The thief on the cross was to be with Jesus Christ in the World of Spirits, he did not say Paradise or heaven. . . Hades, Sheol, paradise, spirits in prison, are all one; it is a world of spirits, the righteous and the wicked all go to the same world of spirits.[26]

In 1976, LDS Apostle Bruce R. McConkie reiterated

---

[25] See T&C A Glossary of Gospel Terms, "Key(s)."

[26] Ehat, Andrew F. & Cook, Lyndon W. (1980). *The Words of Joseph Smith*, pp. 213-214. Provo, UT: Religious Studies Center Brigham Young University. See also NC Luke 13:22 RE.

Joseph's teaching when he stated, "It is clearly set forth that the whole Spirit World, and not only that portion designated as hell, is considered to be a spirit prison."[27] At what point these teachings became modified into modern LDS doctrine is not certain.

Regarding the afterlife, there is a great comfort and a carnal security in the LDS Church's interpretation of the vision of the Spirit World, canonized in Doctrine and Covenants as section 138. A close examination seems to give the idea that at least a portion of it is an accurate account, in alignment with Joseph Smith Jr.'s teachings on the subject. However, it is possible that interpretations and conflations were made to the text. While this vision does not give a fulsome account of what one can expect in the afterlife, between death and the resurrection, it does give important insights that can assist in discovering the truths contained within the various religious beliefs as they are currently understood.

On October 3, 1918, LDS Church President Joseph F. Smith received a vision regarding the World of Spirits. His son, Hyrum, and Hyrum's wife, Ida, had recently died.[28] President Smith had been suffering from illness for many months. These difficulties, and perhaps anxiety over his own fate, led him to ponder deeply upon the scriptures. During the October 4, 1918, LDS General Conference, 79 year old President Smith spoke:

---

[27] Bruce R. McConkie, "A New Commandment: Save Thyself and Thy Kindred," *Ensign*, August 1976, p. 11. The Ensign (Salt Lake City); 1971-1980; 1976; 1976 August; Church History Library, https://catalog.churchofjesuschrist.org/assets/a67fe553-eb2f-40c7-9a1b-73df02569b0c/0/12?lang=eng; accessed: March 19, 2024.

[28] Hyrum Mack Smith March 21, 1872 - January 23, 1918; Ida Elizabeth Bowman Smith April 19, 1872 - September 24, 1918.

Although somewhat weakened in body, my mind is clear . . . I will not, I dare not, attempt to enter upon many things that are resting upon my mind this morning, and I shall postpone until some future time, the Lord being willing, my attempt to tell you some of the things that are on my mind, and that dwell in my heart. I have not lived alone these five months, I have dwelt in the spirit of prayer, of supplication, of faith and of determination; and I have had my communication with the Spirit of the Lord continuously. [29]

The next day, President Smith dictated the vision to his son, Joseph Fielding Smith. President Smith recalled that on the evening in question, he had been alone in his room,

[R]eflecting upon the great atoning sacrifice that was made by the Son of God, for the redemption of the world; and the great and wonderful love made manifest by the Father and the Son in the coming of the Redeemer into the world; that through his atonement, and by obedience to the principles of the gospel, mankind might be saved. [30]

He opened the Bible and read 1 Peter chapters 3 and 4 concerning Christ preaching to the spirits in prison. [31] As he pondered over these chapters, the "eyes of [his] understanding were opened, and the Spirit of the Lord rested upon [him], and

---

[29] Conference reports of The Church of Jesus Christ of Latter-day Saints; 1910-1919; 1918 October; Church History Library, https://catalog.churchofjesuschrist.org/assets/649a3c7a-743b-4c5a-a5c9-abc2baf1497e/0/3?lang=eng; accessed on March 12, 2024.

[30] LDS D&C 138:2-5.

[31] President Smith was reading from the King James Version of the Bible. The corresponding chapters in the Restoration Edition are NC 1 Peter 1:10-18.

[he] saw the hosts of the dead, both great and small" in the World of Spirits.[32]

President Smith saw assembled together in one place:

[A]n innumerable company of the spirits of the just, who had been faithful in the testimony of Jesus while they lived in mortality; and who had offered sacrifice in the similitude of the great sacrifice of the Son of God, and had suffered tribulation in their Redeemer's name. All these had departed the mortal life, firm in the hope of a glorious resurrection . . . [they] were filled with joy and gladness, and were rejoicing together because the day of their deliverance was at hand.[33]

To this righteous congregation, who were waiting for the advent of the Son of God into the Spirit World to declare their redemption from the bands of death, Christ appeared, "declaring liberty to the captives who had been faithful; and there he preached to them the everlasting gospel, the doctrine of the resurrection and the redemption of mankind from the fall, and from individual sins on conditions of repentance."[34]

President Smith perceived that to the wicked, who were in the same World of Spirits, Christ did not go, "and among the ungodly and the unrepentant who had defiled themselves while in the flesh, his voice was not raised."[35] These were in darkness, having rejected God, and the testimonies and

---

[32] See Doctrine and Covenants 138; this vision was later canonized and added to the LDS Doctrine and Covenants in 1976 https://rsc.byu.edu/archived/you-shall-have-my-word/obscurity-scripture-joseph-f-smiths-vision-redemption-dead.

[33] D&C 138:14-15.

[34] D&C 138:18-19.

[35] D&C 138:20.

warnings of the ancient prophets, choosing rebellion rather than righteousness.[36] President Smith wondered at the words of Peter, "wherein he said that the Son of God preached unto the spirits in prison, who sometime were disobedient . . . and how it was possible for him to preach to those spirits and perform the necessary labor among them in so short a time."[37] His eyes were again opened, his understanding quickened, and he perceived that the Lord did no go in person unto the wicked and disobedient who had rejected the truth. Rather, from among the righteous, he organized and appointed messengers, clothed them with power and authority, and commissioned them to "go forth and carry the light of the gospel to them that were in darkness, even to all the spirits of men; and thus was the gospel preached to the dead."[38]

President Smith saw among the congregation of the righteous, Father Adam and Mother Eve, and many of their faithful sons and daughters, including the prophets who lived among the Nephites.[39] It was this congregation of those who had testified of Him while in the flesh that the Lord instructed and prepared to take the message of redemption unto all the dead.[40] These the Lord taught, and "gave them power to come forth, after his resurrection from the dead, to enter into his Father's kingdom, there to be crowned with immortality and eternal life, and continue thenceforth their labor as had been promised by the Lord, and be partakers of all blessings which

---

[36] D&C 138:21-22.
[37] D&C 138:28.
[38] D&C 138:30.
[39] D&C 138:49.
[40] D&C 138:36-37.

were held in reserve for them that love him."[41] It is of importance to note that those who came forth in this first resurrection were the faithful who had died previous to the Lord's ascension from the tomb.

President Smith's description of the World of Spirits resembles the revelation Joseph Smith Jr. gave of the Telestial world, or the world in which we presently reside.[42] As it is here upon the earth, so it is in the World of Spirits: A mingling of various spiritual levels of progression. Just as the Lord sends messengers to bear testimony of Him, to teach His gospel, and to call mankind to repent in the mortal realm, so He does in the spiritual realm. The Lord does not leave the proud and rebellious in darkness, He continuously seeks to reclaim them, in all spheres of existence. His servants' message is the same: faith in the Lord, Jesus Christ, repentance, and baptism. Whether in this life or in the next the only way to be free from the bondage of sin and unbelief is to *seek* the Savior, to *hear* him, to *see* him, and to come to *know* him.

President Smith's vision is an important one. It was found worthy of inclusion and canonization in the LDS Church's standard works.[43] It is, however, frustrating and concerning that the original transcript no longer exists. Brigham Young's daughter, Susa Young Gates, was one who was shown a transcript, possibly the original one, within a month of its dictation. She wrote about the experience in her journal on November 5, 1918, and in a letter to her friend,

---

[41] D&C 138:51-52.
[42] See T&C 69:24-28 and the LDS Temple Endowment.
[43] President Joseph F. Smith's Vision of the Spirit World was added to the Doctrine and Covenants in 1981 as section 138.

Elizabeth McCune, on November 14, 1918. Of this singular event, Susa's description of the vision contained a glaring omission compared to the version that was printed for the first time in various Church periodicals beginning in December 1918, a month after Joseph F. Smith's death.[44]

In the version first printed in December 1918, there is a list of those in the Spirit World who are described as the "choice spirits who were reserved to come forth in the fulness of times to take part in laying the foundations of the great latter-day work."[45] The list includes the Prophet Joseph Smith, Hyrum Smith, Brigham Young, John Taylor, and Wilford Woodruff.[46] In Susa's journal, however, she recorded the following:

> President Smith sent for me . . . he told Julina to bring a "paper." Jacob and others came in, and he had me read a marvellous vision and revelation which he received on Oct. 3d, 1918 . . . In it he tells of his view of Eternity; the Savior when He visited the spirits in prison — how His servants minister to them; he saw the Prophet [Joseph Smith] and all his associate Brethren laboring in the Prison Houses; Mother Eve their noble daughters engaged in the same holy cause! O, it was a comfort to me! . . . to have Eve and her

---

[44] See "Vision of the Redemption of the Dead," *Improvement Era,* vol. 22, no. 2 (Dec. 1918), pp. 166–70; see also the November 30, 1918, *Deseret News,* the January 1919 *Relief Society Magazine,* the *Young Woman's Journal,* and the *Millennial Star.* It was also included in John A. Widtsoe, ed. (1919) *Gospel Doctrine: Selections from the Sermons and Writings of Joseph F. Smith, Sixth President of the Church of Jesus Christ of Latter-day Saints,* pp. 596-601, Salt Lake City: Deseret News.
[45] D&C 138:53.
[46] D&C 138:53.

daughters remembered.[47]

In the letter written to her friend, Elizabeth, nine days later, Susa stated:

> The vision was concerned mostly with the labors of the Savior Himself, the ancient and modern prophets and apostles from Adam down to the Prophet Joseph Smith in laboring to convert and redeem the spirits in prison behind the veil. He also saw Mother Eve and her noble daughters laboring in the same cause. This is the first time that any revelation, that I know of, speaks in this way of women and presents them on the same plane with their husbands and fathers.[48]

As the daughter of Brigham Young, it is curious that Susa did not mention reading about her father, John Taylor, or Wilford Woodruff in the vision. This omission is relevant. President Smith's dictation of the vision was passed through the filter of his son, Joseph Fielding Smith, as he acted as scribe, as well as the first presidency and Quorum of the Twelve, who voted to accept and endorse it as "the Word of the Lord."[49] While a typescript copy was read to President Smith

---

[47] Susa Young Gates papers, circa 1870-1933; JOURNALS, NOTEBOOKS AND SCRAPBOOKS; SUSA YOUNG GATES JOURNALS; 1915-1925; Church History Library, https://catalog.churchofjesuschrist.org/assets/c3e88c30-e0ab-4368-bea0-791ecf68c7e2/0/126?lang=eng; accessed: March 24, 2024.

[48] Susa Young Gates letter to Elizabeth C. McCune, November 14, 1918. Susa Young Gates papers, circa 1870-1933; GENERAL CORRESPONDENCE; ALPHABETICAL SUBJECT FILES; McCune, Elizabeth Claridge, 1912-1932; McCune, Elizabeth Claridge, 1912-1919; Susa Young Gates letter to Elizabeth C. McCune; Church History Library, https://catalog.churchofjesuschrist.org/assets/4e7a7d1a-2466-4e5e-8fb4-678988793ca0/0/0?lang=eng; accessed: March 24, 2024.

[49] James E. Talmage, journal, October 31, 1918. Harold B. Lee Library, Special Collections, MSS 229 Series 1 box 5 folder 6; p. 499;

and signed by him, without the original transcript, we may never know if additions or deletions were made to his vision.

Therefore, it is not clear whether the totality of D&C 138 is a correct interpretation of what God was trying to teach Joseph F. Smith. It would be understandable if what was seen and understood by him was interpreted and flavored by his beliefs at the time of the vision, or those of his son and other members of the Quorum of the Twelve. It is a common human frailty that when God sheds upon us light and knowledge, we invariably interpret it based upon our current understanding and long-held beliefs. The scriptures warn us often that we are blinded by the false traditions of our fathers. Furthermore, mankind tends to be impatient and quick to rush to judgement. This inevitably can lead us to interpret the things of God partially, as well as to arrive at incorrect conclusions.

The things of God are of great import, and time, and experience, and careful and ponderous and solemn thoughts can only find them out.[50] Consider that Joseph Smith Jr. studied the Bible, investigated various religious denominations, and sought wisdom for a few years before God answered his prayer.[51] Nephi commented that it was his constant meditation to think upon the things which he had both seen and heard from Heaven.[52] He did not "compose what he composed, until about 40 years after the event. Because it was time and distance and reflection that gave him the ability to put into

---

https://contentdm.lib.byu.edu/digital/collection/p15999coll20/id/54779/rec/1; accessed: March 24, 2024.

[50] See T&C 138:18.

[51] See T&C 1 — Joseph Smith History Part 1 and Part 2.

[52] See NC 2 Nephi 3:6.

words the truth of what it was he had experienced."[53] Joseph F. Smith died a few weeks after receiving the vision of the Spirit World.[54] If he had lived longer, he would have had the opportunity to reflect, to ponder, to pray, and to seek a fuller, more dynamic understanding of what he both saw and heard.

The scriptures teach that the spirits of all men and women, whether they are good or evil, are taken back to a world of spirits, after their mortal body dies. In this state, they continue to have the opportunity to learn about the Savior, to repent of their sins, and to choose to believe in His name. The World of Spirits is much like the world in which we now live; for the same sociality which exists among us here, will exist among us there.[55] The spirits of those who strove while in their mortal state to be valiant in their testimony of Jesus, harkened to His voice, repented, and were baptized, find themselves in the light, or in other words, paradise. Those who refused to hear the Savior, who rejected His messengers, and were rebellious during their mortal sojourn find themselves in darkness, or in other words, prison. For the same spirit you hearken to obey while living in the flesh will, upon your death, have the same power to influence you to hearken unto that spirit in the next life.[56]

Alma, a Book of Mormon prophet who inquired diligently of the Lord that he might know concerning what

---

[53] Snuffer, Denver (September 10, 2013). "Be of Good Cheer, Be of Good Courage," *40 Years in Mormonism*, p. 5.

[54] Joseph F. Smith died November 19, 1918.

[55] Ehat, Andrew F. & Cook, Lyndon W. (1980). *The Words of Joseph Smith*, pp. 169 and 171. Provo, UT: Religious Studies Center Brigham Young University.

[56] NC Alma 16:37.

becomes of the souls of mankind after this life, revealed the following:

> And now I would inquire what becometh of the souls of men from this time of death to the time appointed for the resurrection? Now whether there is more than one time appointed for men to rise it mattereth not; for all do not die at once, and this mattereth not; all is as one day with God, and time only is measured unto men. Therefore, there is a time appointed unto men that they shall rise from the dead; and there is a space between the time of death and the resurrection. And now, concerning this space of time, what becometh of the souls of men is the thing which I have inquired diligently of the Lord to know; and this is the thing of which I do know. And when the time cometh when all shall rise, then shall they know that God knoweth all the times which are appointed unto man. Now, concerning the state of the soul between death and the resurrection, behold, it has been made known unto me by an angel, that the spirits of all men, as soon as they are departed from this mortal body, yea, the spirits of all men, whether they be good or evil, are taken home to that God who gave them life. And then shall it come to pass, that the spirits of those who are righteous are received into a state of happiness, which is called paradise — a state of rest, a state of peace, where they shall rest from all their troubles and from all care, and sorrow, etc. And then shall it come to pass that the spirits of the wicked, yea, who are evil — for behold, they have no part nor portion of the spirit of the Lord; for behold, they chose evil works rather than good, therefore the spirit of the Devil did enter into them and take possession of their house — and these shall be cast out into outer darkness. There shall be weeping, and wailing, and gnashing of teeth, and this

because of their own iniquity, being led captive by the will of the Devil. Now this is the state of the souls of the wicked, yea, in darkness and a state of awful, fearful looking for, of the fiery indignation of the wrath of God upon them. Thus they remain in this state, as well as the righteous in paradise, until the time of their resurrection. . . . there is a space between death and the resurrection of the body, and a state of the soul, in happiness or in misery, until the time which is appointed of God that the dead shall come forth and be reunited, both soul and body, and be brought to stand before God and be judged according to their works.[57]

Alma's heed and diligence resulted in more light and truth about the World of Spirits, or the state of the spirits of mankind between death and the resurrection. When Adam and Eve fell from the presence of God, they brought both spiritual and physical death into the world: "Death and hell are the devil's domain. He's the god of that world, and since we have death and suffering here, he calls himself the god of this world. . . . While captive here, [we] endure the insults of the flesh and the difficulties of trying to find [our] way back to God."[58] This is what is meant by the gates of hell.

Christ taught mankind the way to overcome the gates of hell which were brought upon the world through the Fall:

Verily, verily I say unto you that this is my doctrine, and I bear record of it from the Father. And whoso believeth in me believeth in the Father also, and unto him will the Father bear record of me, for he will visit

---

[57] NC Alma 19:5-6, 8.
[58] T&C A Glossary of Gospel Terms, "Hell."

him with fire and with the holy ghost. And thus will the Father bear record of me, and the holy ghost will bear record unto him of the Father and me, for the Father and I and the holy ghost are one. And again I say unto you, ye must repent, and become as a little child, and be baptized in my name, or ye can in nowise receive these things. And again I say unto you, ye must repent, and be baptized in my name, and become as a little child, or ye can in nowise inherit the kingdom of God. Verily, verily I say unto you that this is my doctrine. And whoso buildeth upon this buildeth upon my rock, and the gates of hell shall not prevail against them. And whoso shall declare more or less than this, and establisheth it for my doctrine, the same cometh of evil and is not built upon my rock, but he buildeth upon a sandy foundation, and the gates of hell standeth open to receive such when the floods come and the winds beat upon them.[59]

Christ's doctrine will "allow those who accept and follow it to endure against all enemies. It will allow them to prevail. Even the 'gates of hell shall not prevail against them.' Meaning that death and hell can have no claim upon them. They will not be taken captive either in this world or when they leave this world."[60] This has been true for every living soul since the days of Adam. Adam and Eve had to overcome this world through faith, repentance, and baptism until they were redeemed from the Fall and entered back into God's presence. However, their redemption did not and could not open the gates of hell.

---

[59] NC 3 Nephi 5:9.

[60] Snuffer, Denver (September 30, 2010). "3 Nephi 11:39," DenverSnuffer.com; retrieved from https://denversnuffer.com/2010/09/3-nephi-11-39/; accessed on April 14, 2024. See also NC Alma 9:3 and 16.

According to what Joseph F. Smith learned in his vision, all the spirits of the dead look upon the separation of their spirits from their bodies as a bondage.[61] This is because going to the Spirit World means a lengthy tenure there, awaiting the resurrection when the spirit and body are reunited.[62] This concept was understood by Jesus' apostles in the old world as well as His disciples in the new world who desired to come speedily unto His kingdom rather than remain either living upon this earth or waiting in the World of Spirits.[63] It was their desire to "rise quickly from the dead and resume the journey as those who had arisen from the dead with Christ."[64] When Christ broke the bands of death and attained unto the Resurrection, He freed not only Himself, but all mankind.

The gates of hell could only be opened by "someone upon whom death and hell could have no claim."[65] This is why Adam and Eve were gathered with the faithful waiting for the advent of Christ into the World of Spirits to declare their redemption from the bands of death.[66] When Christ suffered the wrath of the guilty and vile, fully assumed their punishment and abuse, and bore their penalty of death itself; when the fury relented and the wrath ended, He reclaimed life:

---

[61] D&C 138:50.

[62] Snuffer, Denver (March 27, 2015). "A Clarifying Question," DenverSnuffer.com; retrieved from https://denversnuffer.com/2015/03/a-clarifying-question/; accessed on March 27, 2024.

[63] See NC 3 Nephi 13:3, T&C 31:4, and 171 – Testimony of St. John 12:14-22.

[64] Snuffer, Denver (March 27, 2015). "A Clarifying Question," DenverSnuffer.com; retrieved from https://denversnuffer.com/2015/03/a-clarifying-question/; accessed on March 27, 2024.

[65] T&C A Glossary of Gospel Terms, "Hell."

[66] See D&C 138:12-19.

His captivity ended the captivity for all. Having then returned to life, because it was just for Him to do so, He acquired the keys of death and hell. Now He can open those gates for any and all because it was unjust for Him to have been put through either. He can now advocate for others by virtue of what He suffered and the injustice of that suffering.[67]

On April 16, 1843, in an attempt to provide comfort and reassurance to the saints who had lost loved ones, Joseph Smith related a small portion of a vision he had experienced which placed great importance on the subject of resurrection:

> For the great Elohim will deliver you and, if not before the resurrection, will set you eternally free from all these things: from pain, sorrow, and death. I have labored hard and sought every way to try to prepare this people to comprehend the things that God is unfolding to me. In speaking of the resurrection I would say that God hath shown unto me a vision of the resurrection of the dead and I saw the graves open and the saints as they arose, took each other by the hand, even before they got up or while getting up, and great joy and glory rested upon them.[68]
>
> Those who have died in Jesus Christ, may expect to enter in to all that fruition of Joy when they come forth, which they have pursued here. So plain was the vision I actually saw men, before they had ascended from the tomb, as though they were getting up slowly, they took each other by the hand. And it was my father and my son, my mother and my daughter, my brother

---

[67] T&C A Glossary of Gospel Terms, "Hell."

[68] Ehat, Andrew F. & Cook, Lyndon W. (1980). *The Words of Joseph Smith*, p. 198. Provo, UT: Religious Studies Center Brigham Young University, and T&C A Glossary of Gospel Terms, "Resurrection/Burial."

and my sister. When the voice calls, suppose I am laid by the side of my father. What would be the first joy of my heart? Where is my father, my mother, my sister? They are by my side. I embrace them and they me. . . . I am glad I have the privilege of communicating to you some things, which if grasped closely will be a help to you when the clouds are gathering and the storms are ready to burst upon you like peals of thunder, lay hold of these things and let not your knees tremble, nor your hearts faint . . . all your losses will be made up to you in the resurrection provided you continue faithful, by the vision of the almighty I have seen it. More painful to me [is] the thought of annihilation than death. If I had no expectation of seeing my mother, brother, and sisters, and friends again, my heart would burst in a moment and I should go down to my grave. The expectation of seeing my friends in the morning of the resurrection cheers my soul and make[s] me bear up against the evils of life. It is like their taking a long journey and on their return we meet them with increased joy. God has revealed His Son from the Heavens and the doctrine of the resurrection also. And we have a knowledge that these we bury here, God bring[s] them up again, clothed upon and quickened by the spirit of the great God.[69]

It is my sincerest hope that my loved ones who have passed from this mortal estate into the World of Spirits are waiting in anticipation of a glorious resurrection with others who have found the peace and joy that can only come through our Lord and Savior, Jesus Christ. If, however, they are

---

[69] Ehat, Andrew F. & Cook, Lyndon W. (1980). *The Words of Joseph Smith*, p. 196. Provo, UT: Religious Studies Center Brigham Young University, and T&C A Glossary of Gospel Terms, "Resurrection/Burial."

mingling with those who were and are deceived by false spirits and false religions, it is my prayer that they will "seek this Jesus of whom the prophets and apostles have written, that the grace of God the Father, and also the Lord Jesus Christ, and the Holy Ghost, which beareth record of them, may be and abide in [them] for ever. Amen."[70]

---

[70] NC Ether 5:8.

Essay 7

Malachi 3[1]

Whitney N. Horning

©2016[2]

Unlike so many, we do not peddle the word of God for profit. On the contrary, in Christ we speak before God with sincerity, as those sent from God.[3]

Experience supplies painful proof that traditions once called into being are first called useful, then they become necessary. At last they are too often made idols, and all must bow down to them or be punished.[4]

All truth passes through three stages. First, it is ridiculed. Second, it is violently opposed. Third, it is accepted as self-evident.[5]

Malachi 3 is one of the most quoted yet one of the most misunderstood chapters in the Old Testament. It is popular scripture repeated numerous Sundays each year in various congregations all over the world to encourage congregants to give generously, in financial dollars which are called "tithes," in order to support and sustain their church leaders, agendas, and properties. This is a chapter rich in meaning, rich in

---

[1] This essay was written before the Restoration Edition of the scriptures was published. All scriptural references, unless otherwise noted, are based upon The Church of Jesus Christ of Latter-day Saints 1981 edition, including the King James Version of the Holy Bible.

[2] Minor edits in 2017 to add pertinent information regarding the salaries of LDS General Authorities, minor edits and updated URL links in 2024 to prepare for publication in this volume.

[3] 2 Corinthians 2:17 (NIV).

[4] John Charles (J.C.) Ryle, 19th Century English Writer and Minister.

[5] Arthur Schopenhauer, 19th century German Philosopher.

warning and rich in blessings and promises. It is unfortunate that only a small segment is quoted repeatedly, and that wrongly, when this chapter teaches and expounds upon some of the greatest blessings the Lord offers to mankind.

> Malachi 3:1 Behold, I will send my messenger, and he shall prepare the way before me: and the Lord, whom ye seek, shall suddenly come to his temple, even the messenger of the covenant, whom ye delight in: behold, he shall come, saith the Lord of hosts.

What qualifies an individual to act as the Lord's messenger? What would the message sound like? How can you test the message and the messenger to know that they have been sent from the presence of the Lord?[6] God has given us a litmus test: "By their fruits ye shall know them."[7] What are the fruits messengers need to bear? There have always been and will continue to be both true and false messengers. It is up to us to study their messages and decide for ourselves if they are true. This is worth careful study, pondering, and prayer. It is our responsibility to choose between truth and error.

God has made Himself directly known to prophets of old. He did so with Abraham as seen in Genesis 15:1; Jacob/Israel as seen in Genesis 46:2; and Moses in Numbers 12:6. He has promised that He will do so with any authentic

---

[6] See Sonntag, Robert (2014), *What is a Prophet?*, retrieved from https://salemthoughts.com/Topics/What_Is_A_Prophet.pdf; accessed on date updated on January 10, 2024.

[7] Matthew 7:16, 20 (KJV). Unless otherwise noted, scriptural references are from the 1981 edition of The Church of Jesus Christ of Latter-day Saints scriptures.

prophet.[8] God does not abandon His children, therefore, He has either already sent or He will send us the messenger spoken of in this verse. One of the tests this messenger must pass is that of preparing the way for Christ's return. He will accomplish this in the same way John the Baptist did: through preaching repentance and baptism, restoring light and truth that will help those who pay heed to their message turn away from worshipping false idols to follow Christ.

The verse continues, "The Lord, whom ye seek, shall suddenly come to His temple, even the messenger of the covenant." Christ suddenly coming to His temple can be fulfilled in one of two ways. "Know ye not that ye are the temple of God, and that the Spirit of God dwelleth in you?" His personal appearance to an individual is one way.[9] Another is through participation in sacred ordinances and rites found within a holy temple, commanded, built, and sanctified by the Lord.[10] When searching for this true messenger and testing their message one of the signs will be that this messenger has had the Lord appear to him. The Lord has promised that through this messenger His covenant with be re-established. The message will bear the weight of scrutiny. It will be a message that will brush away darkness and replace it with light.

Malachi 3:2 But who may abide the day of his coming?

---

[8] See Snuffer, D. (August 25, 2015), "Baptism is Mandatory." DenverSnuffer.com.

[9] 1 Corinthians 3:16. See also 1 Corinthians 6:19 "What? know ye not that your body is the temple of the Holy Ghost which is in you, which ye have of God, and ye are not your own?" See also D&C 93:1.

[10] See Snuffer, Denver. (April 29, 2016). Why A Temple? Retrieved from https://denversnuffer.com/2016/04/why-a-temple/; accessed on May 22, 2016.

and who shall stand when he appeareth? for he is like a refiner's fire, and like fullers' soap: 3 And he shall sit as a refiner and purifier of silver: and he shall purify the sons of Levi, and purge them as gold and silver, that they may offer unto the Lord an offering in righteousness.

This refers to Christ's second coming. This verse tells us that when Christ appears He shall be like a refiner's fire and like fuller's soap; the refiner (Christ) will use fire to burn off the dross and purify the precious metal (His children). Similarly, the fuller (Christ) will use soap to clean the wool and remove the impurities so that what is left is pure. These are purifying processes. During the second coming of Christ all that do wickedly shall be burned as stubble while those who have humbled themselves, repented, and been baptized will be spared.[11]

Who in modern churches is Christ referring to when He states that He will "purify the sons of Levi?" If this is referring to the purification of all church leaders in all denominations who claim to have a portion of Christ's priesthood, what will the purification look like and why does it need to be done? Is it possible that church leaders of various and sundry denominations have strayed from the ordinances of God and polluted His holy church thereby requiring purification and purging so that an acceptable offering done in righteousness can be performed?[12]

---

[11] Matthew 3:12; 13:30; Luke 3:17; and JST Matthew 3:39 (KJV).

[12] Isaiah 24: 5-6 "The earth also is defiled under the inhabitants thereof; because they have transgressed the laws, changed the ordinance, broken the everlasting covenant." Doctrine and Covenants 13: 1 "Upon you my

Malachi 3:4 Then shall the offering of Judah and Jerusalem be pleasant unto the Lord, as in the days of old, and as in former years. 5 And I will come near to you to judgment; and I will be a swift witness against the sorcerers,[13] and against the adulterers,[14] and

fellow servants, in the name of Messiah I confer the Priesthood of Aaron, which holds the keys of the ministering of angels, and of the gospel of repentance, and of baptism by immersion for the remission of sins; and this shall never be taken again from the earth, until the sons of Levi do offer again an offering unto the Lord in righteousness." Burton, Alma P *Discourses of the Prophet Joseph Smith* 1977 " These sacrifices, as well as every ordinance belonging to the Priesthood, will, when the Temple of the Lord shall be built, and the sons of Levi be purified, be fully restored and attended to in all their powers, ramifications, and blessings. This ever did and ever will exist when the powers of the Melchizedek Priesthood are sufficiently manifest; else how can the restitution of all things spoken of by the Holy Prophets be brought to pass. It is not to be understood that the law of Moses will be established again with all its rites and variety of ceremonies; this has never been spoken of by the prophets; but those things which existed prior to Moses' day, namely, sacrifice, will be continued."

[13] Blank, Wayne (2012) "What is Sorcery?" The word "sorcery" originated from the Latin word, sortiarius, which meant one who sorts, as in casts lots with the assistance of evil spirits. The King James Version uses "sorcery," "sorcerer," or "sorceress" to translate a number of Hebrew and Greek words, some of which apply as much to pseudo-sciences (e.g. astrology, alchemy) as to other heathen religions. The Hebrew word, pronounced kaw-shawf, means to whisper, or to enchant (to "cast a spell over someone or something; to put a hex on someone or something"), the Hebrew word, pronounced kawsh-shawf, or kheh-shef means a magician or magic, the Hebrew word, pronounced awn-nawn, means to cover, or to cloud over, as in to behave in a hidden manner i.e. occult, from which the word cult originated, the Greek word pronounced far-mak-yoos, means to drug; the present-day respectable words pharmacy and pharmacist originated from that Greek word, which originally referred to people who used drugs or narcotics to poison or control people.

[14] Jesus extended the definition of adultery to include sexual relations between a married man and a woman other than his wife (Mark 10:11-12, Luke 16:18). Other New Testament teachings also understand it that way (1 Corinthians 6:15-16, 1 Corinthians 7:2). Jesus enlarged the concept when he taught, "whosoever looketh on a woman to lust after her hath committed adultery with her already in his heart." Matthew 5:28 (KJV).

against false swearers,[15] and against those that oppress the hireling in his wages, the widow, and the fatherless, and that turn aside the stranger from his right,[16] and fear not me, saith the Lord of hosts.

This list of behaviors for which we will be judged bears deep consideration.[17] Christ alone will be the judge of all mankind. Christ is the keeper of the gate; no man enters into His Father's kingdom but by Him![18] He alone will judge us. He will be swift in his witness against those who have not repented of the evil they have done in His sight. He alone knows the desires of our hearts. By our words and our deeds, we demonstrate what it is we truly desire. In this world of darkness, chaos, and confusion it is difficult to remain pure. But there are three things that can remain pure: "the truth, which is fixed and cannot be touched by us. God's love, which is free

---

[15] Willfully and knowingly giving a false statement; this may also refer to taking the name of the Lord in vain which, in part, means to claim to speak for God when He has given you no such errand.

[16] This condemnation is to ANYONE, church leader or lay member who "fares sumptuously" while poor Lazarus starves (Luke 16:19-31, KJV); taking advantage of another in any way in order to obtain more for themselves; any church or church leader who oppresses the poor through the collection of tithes; Alma taught that those who have not (the poor) do not need to give but instead that they should be given (Mosiah 18:27).

[17] Doctrine and Covenants 76:98-106 includes a part of this list in the definition of who will inherit a telestial kingdom.

[18] 2 Nephi 9:41 "O then, my beloved brethren, come unto the Lord, the Holy One. Remember that his paths are righteous. Behold, the way for man is narrow, but it lieth in a straight course before him, and the keeper of the gate is the Holy One of Israel; and he employeth no servant there; and there is none other way save it be by the gate; for he cannot be deceived, for the Lord God is his name." John 14: 6 "Jesus saith unto him, I am the way, the truth, and the life; no man cometh unto the Father, but by me."

and available to all. . . . and our desires."[19] One of the ways by which the Lord, and others, may come to know what is hidden within the recesses of our hearts is given in the book of Matthew, "And the King shall answer and say unto them, verily I say unto you, inasmuch as ye have done it unto one of the least of these my brethren, ye have done it unto me."[20]

> Malachi 3:6 For I am the Lord, I change not; therefore ye sons of Jacob are not consumed. 7 Even from the days of your fathers ye are gone away from mine ordinances, and have not kept them. Return unto me, and I will return unto you, saith the Lord of hosts. But ye said, Wherein shall we return?

God is an unchangeable being; if He were changeable, He would cease to be God.[21] Therefore, what He commanded, taught, expounded, and required at one time is true still today.[22] Covenants, blessings, and promises He extended in one time-period He will extend in ours. To obtain these promises requires qualification. We should be watchful and preparing in order to be ready for the day when the covenants and ordinances are re-established. The sons of Jacob are literal descendants of Jacob, son of Isaac, grandson of Abraham. As such they have a right to the blessings, as well as the curses that

---

[19] Snuffer, Denver (September 9, 2014), "Preserving the Restoration," *40 Years in Mormonism*, p. 13.

[20] Matthew 25:41 (Holy Scriptures, Inspired Version).

[21] Jehovah — The covenant or proper name of the God of Israel. It denotes the "Unchangeable One," "the eternal I Am" (Exodus 6:3; Psalms 83:18; Isaiah 12:2; 26:4).

[22] Doctrine and Covenants 20:17 "By these things we know that there is a God in heaven, who is infinite and eternal, from everlasting to everlasting the same unchangeable God, the framer of heaven and earth, and all things which are in them."

follow disobedience, which stem from the covenant God established with Abraham.

The phrase sons of Jacob also refers to the world's population today. Abraham was promised that his posterity would fill the earth. Over the centuries intermarriage and migration have spread the blood of Israel into all nations. Within these verses Christ is giving a warning to all mankind that they have ALL gone astray from His ordinances, even from the days of their fathers: Abraham, Isaac, and Jacob/Israel. Yet, Christ continues to extend mercy unto all; He promises that those who repent and return to Him will not be consumed.[23]

The way we qualify to be spared is through repentance and baptism. We must then continue to press on, to endure to the end, and to seek to be a greater follower of righteousness. The baptism of fire and the Holy Ghost as seen in 2 Nephi 31:17 is given without man's involvement, comes from heaven, and is promised by both the Father and the Son. It is a signal of

---

[23] Snuffer, Denver "Abraham's Sons" April 15, 2014: "Last night I was awakened by this: Did not Ishmael and Isaac mourn together and bury their father Abraham? Was not their father's blood precious unto them both? Does not the blood of Abraham run in both Isaac and Ishmael? Does not the blood of Abraham run in both Esau and Jacob? Let Ishmael today find the blood of his father, Abraham, precious still. Let Isaac likewise today find the blood of his father, Abraham, precious again. For Abraham's sake, let all the brothers who descend from Abraham now mourn when Abraham's blood is spilled by any of his descendants. If Abraham's sons do not find his blood to be precious still, there remains nothing between them but the shedding of Abraham's blood. For all his sons who fail to find Abraham's blood to be precious will be held to account by God, who will judge between the sons of Isaac and the sons of Ishmael, the sons of Esau and the sons of Jacob for father Abraham's sake, with whom God covenanted. The sons of Abraham will not be permitted to continue this disregard of their common father's blood without provoking God, who will soon judge between Abraham's sons."

redemption, purification, and holiness. It is included in the "gate" for entering into God's presence, for God is a "consuming fire" and those who enter into that presence must be able to endure that fire.[24] Without the capacity to do so, a person would be consumed by the flames.[25]

Jesus Christ wants us to repent and turn and face him. In Malachi 3, the Lord is speaking to all of us, but primarily to the leaders of the churches that profess to know his name, those who have transgressed the laws and changed His everlasting ordinances.[26] By changing the ordinances the leaders have led people away from Christ. Christ knows that in our world it is difficult to hold onto truth. Yet, He constantly and consistently extends the invitation to return to Him. His promise is that once we do so He will return to us. This means coming back into the literal presence of the Savior and is not limited to feeling His presence in your heart![27]

How can we return unto Him?

Is it possible to know, understand, and observe, in the correct manner as far as is revealed, the laws and ordinances contained in the scriptures so that we might return unto the

---

[24] See Hebrews 12:29 and Deuteronomy 4:24.

[25] See Snuffer, Denver "2 Nephi 31:17," August 28, 2010, and Leviticus 10: 1-2.

[26] Isaiah 24:5-6 The earth also is defiled under the inhabitants thereof; because they have transgressed the laws, changed the ordinance, broken the everlasting covenant. Therefore hath the curse devoured the earth, and they that dwell therein are desolate: therefore the inhabitants of the earth are burned, and few men left. (KJV)

[27] John 14:23 (KJV) and Doctrine and Covenants 130:3 The appearing of the Father and the Son, in that verse, is a personal appearance; and the idea that the Father and the Son dwell in a man's heart is an old sectarian notion, and is false.

Lord in order that He might return unto us?

Can we do so as an individual, outside of an organized religious institution?

Does doing so require courage?

Does doing so require that we may have to choose between the Lord and the leaders of our churches?

LDS Doctrine and Covenants 93:1 promises, "Verily, thus saith the Lord: It shall come to pass that every soul who forsaketh his sins and cometh unto me, and calleth on my name, and obeyeth my voice, and keepeth my commandments, shall see my face and know that I am." This invitation extends to **every soul** as God is no respecter of persons.[28]

In Malachi 3:6-7 Christ explains that when this invitation is extended to church leaders they will reply, "Wherein shall we return?" In their pride and loftiness, church leaders presume that they are observing all the laws, rites, and ordinances necessary for salvation. They presume that by right of their position, they have returned to Him. Christ answers their query with the following statement:

> Malachi 3: 8 Will a man rob God? Yet ye have robbed me. But ye say, Wherein have we robbed thee? In tithes and offerings. 9 Ye are cursed with a curse: for ye have robbed me, even this whole nation.

Verse 8 is often used by church leaders to manipulate and guilt their followers into paying tithes and offerings to

---

[28] Acts 10:34-35: "Then Peter opened his mouth, and said, of a truth I perceive that God is no respecter of persons; but in every nation he that feareth him, and worketh righteousness, is accepted with him."

them and their organization rather than to the poor. What if it is to the leaders of the various denominations that Christ is speaking and not to the members? What if it is the leaders that Christ is condemning? If this is true, then this verse now takes on a whole new meaning. It is the leaders who have robbed the Lord, as well as their own people, "even this whole nation." Then this means that this scripture is speaking to the priests concerning their negligence in their holy positions and their robbing of the tithes and offerings, using these funds for themselves, that were meant to provide for the widows, and the orphans, and the strangers who found themselves within their gates.

The leaders respond to the Lord's query, "Wherein have we robbed thee?" They appear to be genuinely confused at the Lord's condemnation of them. They have been laboring and preaching about the payment of tithes and offerings to their congregants to the point of ad nauseam. Yet the Lord accuses them, not their parishioners, of being guilty of theft with this simple statement: "In tithes and offerings." The very scripture that church leaders use to guilt and pressure their followers into giving money to fund their extravagant living is the very same scripture that God will use to condemn them for their sin.

What, then, is the Law of the Tithe? When translating the Hebrew word מַעֲשֵׂר into Greek it translates as δέκατο which in English means decade. A decade is 10 years; therefore, the meaning of the word Tithe has come to be defined as a tenth. The first recorded instance in the Bible regarding the tithe is found in Genesis 14: 36-39:

And this Melchizedek, having thus established righteousness, was called the king of heaven by his people, or, in other words, the King of peace. And he lifted up his voice, and he blessed Abram, being the high priest, and the keeper of the storehouse of God; Him whom God had appointed to receive tithes for the poor. Wherefore, Abram paid unto him tithes of all that he had, of all the riches which he possessed, which God had given him more than that which he had need.[29]

Lot, Abraham's nephew, had been kidnapped by a group of kings who had waged war against the King of Sodom. Abraham "armed his trained men and they who were born in his own house" and went in pursuit.[30] He was victorious in rescuing Lot, regaining all his goods, and the women also, and the people.[31] Hebrews 7:4 suggests the idea that the tithes Abraham paid were a tenth of what he had taken in the battle, "Now consider how great this man was [Melchizedek], unto whom even the patriarch Abraham gave the tenth of the spoils." [32]

Melchizedek, King of Salem, was a great High Priest, and had been appointed by God to receive tithes for the poor. Abraham's tithe was a tenth of all he possessed, above that which he had need, and went to the storehouse of God. This City of Salem was a Zion community much like the City of

---

[29] Holy Scriptures Inspired Version, 1867.
[30] Genesis 14:1-13.
[31] See ibid.
[32] Holy Scriptures, Inspired Version, 1867; and the KJV. The Book of Mormon says this in Alma 13:15: "And it was this same Melchizedek to whom Abraham paid tithes: yea, even our father Abraham paid tithes of one-tenth part of all he possessed."

Enoch. One of the key characteristics of a Zion community is that there are no poor among them.[33] Abraham was one who "sought for the blessings of the fathers," therefore, this means that the payment of tithes to care for the poor, the widow, the fatherless, and the stranger had been observed by the righteous from the days of Adam.[34]

The next instance that tithes are mentioned in the Bible is found in Genesis 28. Jacob was traveling to Haran to find himself a wife. During his travels he lay down to sleep and had a dream or vision of a ladder extending from earth into Heaven.[35] Because of that vision, Jacob anointed and set apart the land as the House of God and then he covenanted with God, "All that thou shalt give me I will surely give the tenth unto thee."[36]

Many historical Christian scholars believe that the Law of the Tithe was only voluntarily observed by Abraham and Jacob but was not given as a law until it was given unto the house of Israel upon Mount Sinai through Moses. Under the Law of Moses, the preferred payment of tithes was in produce and animals.[37] Provisions were made for persons who had long

---

[33] Alma, in the Book of Mormon, taught his people the law of tithing, in this way: The people of the church should impart of their substance, every one according to that which he had; if he have more abundantly he should impart more abundantly; and of him that had but little, but little should be required; and to him that had not should be given. And thus they should impart of their substance of their own free will and good desires towards God, and to those priests that stood in need, yea, and to every needy, naked soul. See Mosiah 18: 27-28.

[34] Abraham 1:2, Pearl of Great Price.

[35] Genesis 28:11-22 (Holy Scriptures, Inspired Version, 1867).

[36] Genesis 28:22.

[37] Leviticus 27:30-34; Deuteronomy 14:22-23, 28-29; 2 Chronicles 31:5-6, 12; Nehemiah 10:37-38 (Holy Scriptures, Inspired Version)

distances to travel to exchange their produce for money. Under this law tithes were to be given to the poor, the widow, the fatherless, and the stranger.[38] A portion was to be given to the Levites as they had no land inheritance and were unable to grow their own produce or raise their own flocks. From this portion the Levites were allowed to give some to the priests for their care.[39]

When Jesus Christ came to renew, re-establish, reset, reconnect and, above all else, to redeem fallen man with God, all of the ordinances, as well as the Law of Moses, had become corrupted.[40] One of those ways was in the observance of the payment of tithes. Christ has taught that we should do all in our power to take care of the poor. When the rich young man approached Christ asking what more he could do to follow him, the reply was, "go, sell that thou hast, and give to the poor."[41] When Christ chastised the Jewish leaders for the widow casting in her mite, He was not only praising her in her faithfulness, but He was also condemning them for extorting money from the poor in order that they might fare sumptuously.[42]

Considering that scripture establishes that the law of the tithe is for taking care of the poor, how do we balance caring

---

[38] Deuteronomy 26:12.

[39] Deuteronomy 14:29; Nehemiah 12: 44; Nehemiah 13:5 (Holy Scriptures, Inspired Version). Almas also instructed his people, "And thus they should impart of their substance of their own free will and good desires towards God, to those priests that stood in need, yea, and to every needy, naked soul." See Mosiah 18:28-29.

[40] Isaiah 24:5 The earth also is defiled under the inhabitants thereof; because they have transgressed the laws, changed the ordinance, broken the everlasting covenant.

[41] Matthew 19:21 (Holy Scriptures, Inspired Version); Mark 10: 21.

[42] See Mark 12:38-44, Luke 16:19-31, Luke 16: 24-36 (Holy Scriptures, Inspired Version); and Luke 21:1-4.

for the needs of our own family, children, spouse, etc. with looking after the poor among us?[43] The first covenants that a member of the LDS Church[44] makes in their temples are that of obedience and sacrifice.

> The order places the obligation for obedience before the obligation for sacrifice. They belong in that order. Obedience requires men to support their wives (D&C 83:2) and parents to care for their children (D&C 83:4). [The first verse of the *Book of Mormon* informs us Nephi was supported by his goodly parents, including receiving a good education. (1 Ne. 1:1.)] This principle to care for family must happen before any sacrifices can be considered. In other words, before any sacrifice is made to help the poor, build a temple, support a community, or any other good and charitable thing obedience to the commandment to care for your family members must be satisfied. Those who fail to provide for their families are no better than the faithless. (1 Tim. 5:8.) Those who disobey the obligation to support and care for their families bring the faith of Christ into disrepute and cause scorn for His church.[45]

If you hail from the LDS Church, paying 10% tithing on your income is considered mandatory for salvation. In order to be "worthy" of the highest ordinances the LDS Church offers

---

[43] See also 1 Timothy 5:8 "If any provide not for his own, and especially for those of his own house, he has denied the faith and is worse than an unbeliever."

[44] LDS will refer throughout this paper to the Church of Jesus Christ of Latter-Day Saints, also known as the Mormons.

[45] Snuffer, Denver (December 17, 2015), "Obedience and Sacrifice." Retrieved from https://denversnuffer.com/2015/12/obedience-and-sacrifice/, accessed on date updated on January 12, 2024.

in their temples, one must pay an "honest and full tithe," as defined by LDS Church leaders, and you must pay those tithes directly to the Church.[46]   Tithe payers are rewarded with temple recommends and higher leadership positions, while non-tithers are barred from the temple, from performing certain ordinances, and are disqualified from higher callings.[47]

Unfortunately, this false tradition is also present in other Christian churches. It is understandable that paying 10% of one's income takes the guess work out of the decision. However, it gives a false sense of security before God, it allows men in leadership to have power over their congregants, and in many cases, it causes individuals and families who are struggling financially to become even poorer. In their book *Pagan Christianity* Frank Viola and George Barna make this observation:

> God's people are persuaded to give one-tenth of their income every week. When they do, they feel they have made God happy. And they can expect Him to bless them financially. When they fail, they feel they are being disobedient, and they worry that a financial curse looms over them . . . tithing today is sometimes presented as the equivalent of a Christian stock investment. Pay the tithe, and God will give you more money in return. Refuse to tithe, and God will punish

---

[46]   LDS   Temple   Recommend   Questions; https://www.lds.org/manual/preparing-to-enter-the-holy-temple/preparing-to-enter-the-holy-temple?lang=eng; accessed on date updated on January 12, 2024.

[47] Though not a creed it is nevertheless true that in many instances in the LDS Church callings for both men and women are contingent upon holding a current temple recommend and in order to hold a temple recommend one must pay a full tithe to the LDS Church.

you.

[I]n our day, mandatory tithing equals oppression to the poor. Not a few poor Christians have been thrown into deeper poverty because they have felt obligated to give beyond their means . . . In such cases, the gospel is no longer good news to the poor. Rather, it becomes a heavy burden. Instead of liberty, it becomes oppression . . . the original tithe that God established for Israel was to benefit the poor, not hurt them! Conversely . . . it is good news to the rich. To a high earner, 10 percent is a paltry sum. Tithing, therefore, appeases the consciences of the prosperous without impacting their lifestyles. Not a few wealthy Christians are deluded into thinking they are "obeying God" because they throw 10% of their income into the offering plate.[48]

The New Testament disciples understood that taking care of the poor and the needy was paramount to establishing a Zion community and a unity of belief. Christ taught, "For inasmuch as ye do it unto the least of these, ye do it unto me." [49] The City of Enoch was a Zion community and is described as a community of equals, "And the Lord called his people ZION, because they were of one heart and one mind, and dwelt in righteousness; and there was no poor among them."[50] Early Christians were very generous to the poor and the needy, they gave freely, out of a cheerful heart, without guilt, obligation, or

---

[48] Viola and Barna (2012) *Pagan Christianity: Exploring the Roots of our Church Practices,* pp. 172 and 179-180, Carol Stream, IL: Tyndale House Publishers.
[49] Doctrine and Covenants 42:38.
[50] Moses 7:18.

manipulation.[51]

Isaiah warns:

[W]o unto them that decree unrighteous decrees, and that write grievousness which they have prescribed; to turn away the needy from judgment, and to take away the right from the poor of my people, that widows may be their prey, and that they may rob the fatherless! And what will ye do in the day of visitation, and in the desolation which shall come from far? To whom will ye flee for help? And where will ye leave your glory? Without me they shall bow down under the prisoners, and they shall fall under the slain. For all this his anger is not turned away, but his hand is stretched out still.[52]

In 2 Nephi 28:12-13 God warns:

Because of pride, and because of false teachers, and false doctrine, their churches have become corrupted, and their churches are lifted up; because of pride they are puffed up. They rob the poor because of their fine sanctuaries; they rob the poor because of their fine clothing; and they persecute the meek and the poor in heart, because in their pride they are puffed up.

Taking care of the poor and the needy is paramount to being a disciple of Christ. In the Book of Mormon, King Benjamin admonished his people:

And also, ye yourselves will succor those that stand in need of your succor; ye will administer of your

---

[51]Viola and Barna (2012) *Pagan Christianity: Exploring the Roots of our Church Practices,* p. 183, Carol Stream, IL: Tyndale House Publishers; see 2 Corinthians 8:1-4, 9:6-7. For an in-depth historical account of early Christianity and their generosity see Kreider's 2010 book *Worship and Evangelism in Pre-Christendom.*
[52] 2 Nephi 20:1-4 1.

substance unto him that standeth in need; and ye will not suffer that the beggar putteth up his petition to you in vain, and turn him out to perish. Perhaps thou shalt say: The man has brought upon himself his misery; therefore I will stay my hand, and will not give unto him of my food, nor impart unto him of my substance that he may not suffer, for his punishments are just— But I say unto you, O man, whosoever doeth this the same hath great cause to repent; and except he repenteth of that which he hath done he perisheth forever, and hath no interest in the kingdom of God. For behold, are we not all beggars? Do we not all depend upon the same Being, even God, for all the substance which we have, for both food and raiment, and for gold, and for silver, and for all the riches which we have of every kind? And behold, even at this time, ye have been calling on his name, and begging for a remission of your sins. And has he suffered that ye have begged in vain? Nay; he has poured out his Spirit upon you, and has caused that your hearts should be filled with joy, and has caused that your mouths should be stopped that ye could not find utterance, so exceedingly great was your joy. And now, if God, who has created you, on whom you are dependent for your lives and for all that ye have and are, doth grant unto you whatsoever ye ask that is right, in faith, believing that ye shall receive, O then, how ye ought to impart of the substance that ye have one to another. And if ye judge the man who putteth up his petition to you for your substance that he perish not, and condemn him, how much more just will be your condemnation for withholding your substance, which doth not belong to you but to God, to whom also your life belongeth; and yet ye put up no petition, nor repent of the thing which thou hast done. I say unto you, wo be unto that man, for his substance shall perish with him; and now, I say these things unto those who are rich as pertaining to the things of this world. And again, I say unto the poor, ye who have not and yet have sufficient, that ye remain from day to day; I mean all you who deny the beggar, because ye have not; I would that ye say in your hearts that: I give not because I have not, but if I had I would give. And now, if ye say this in your hearts ye remain guiltless, otherwise ye are condemned; and your condemnation is just for ye covet that which ye have not received. And now, for the sake of these things which I have spoken unto you—that is, for the sake of retaining a remission of your sins from day to day, that ye may walk guiltless before God—I would that ye should impart of your substance to the poor, every man according to that which he hath, such as feeding the hungry, clothing the naked, visiting the sick and administering to their relief, both spiritually and temporally, according to their wants. And see that all these things are done in wisdom and order; for it is not requisite that a man should run faster than he has strength. And again, it is expedient that he should be diligent, that thereby he might win the prize; therefore, all things must be done in order.[53]

Alma, another Book of Mormon prophet-servant, taught his people that they should impart of their substance according to what they had: if they had abundance they should impart abundantly; if they had little, little should be required, and if they had none, they should receive. He taught the people that they should impart of their substance of their own free will and good desires toward God. He allowed for the imparting of their substance to a priest, but only if he stood in need, and as

---

[53] Mosiah 4:16-27.

long as the people also imparted to every needy, naked soul:[54]

> And thus, in their prosperous circumstances, they did not send away any who were naked, or that were hungry, or that were athirst, or that were sick, or that had not been nourished; and they did not set their hearts upon riches; therefore they were liberal to all, both old and young, both bond and free, both male and female, whether out of the church or in the church, having no respect to persons as to those who stood in need.[55]

In the New Testament churches, as well as in some instances in the Book of Mormon, the people practiced what is known as the Law of Consecration. Individuals covenanted to share property, goods, and profits, receiving these things according to their wants and needs.[56] During the Restoration, the Latter Day Saints attempted to live the Law of Consecration in both Kirtland and Missouri. After the LDS experiences in the early common-stock companies, and in community efforts in Kirtland, Ohio, Independence, and Far West, Missouri, Joseph Smith ended any attempts at consecration. In a council meeting on March 6, 1840, in Montrose, Iowa Territory, he announced to the church that the Lord had rescinded consecration: "He said that the Law of consecration could not be kept here, & that **it was the will of the Lord that we should desist from trying to keep it**, & if persisted in it would produce a perfect abortion, & that he assumed the whole responsibility of not keeping it untill

---

[54] Mosiah 18:27-29.
[55] Alma 1: 30.
[56] D&C 51:3; 78:1–15; 104; https://www.lds.org/scriptures/gs/united-order?lang=eng; accessed on date updated on January 12, 2024.

proposed by himself."[57]

Despite this revelation from the Lord, the LDS Church under Brigham Young reintroduced the law of consecration, calling it the United Order. James E. Talmage, an apostle for the Church from 1911-1933, in his book *Articles of Faith*, published in 1917, did not acknowledge that the Lord had rescinded the law and as such perpetuated confusion for the LDS members:

> Consecration and Stewardship-The law of tithing, as accepted and professedly observed by the Church today, is after all but a lesser law, given by the Lord in consequence of the human weaknesses, selfishness, covetousness, and greed, which prevented the Saints from accepting the higher principles, according to which the Father would have His children live. Specific requirement regarding the payment of tithes were made through revelation in 1838; but seven years prior to that time, the voice of the Lord had been heard on the subject of consecration, or the dedication of all one's property, together with his time, talents, and natural endowments, to the service of God to be used as occasion may require. This again is not new; to the present dispensation the law of consecration is given as a re-enactment.[58]

Doctrine and Covenants Section 119 is known as the "law of tithing" for the LDS Church. In this revelation the Lord states that all surplus property should be put into the hands of the bishops of the church for the building of a temple, laying

---

[57] *JS Papers, Documents Vol. 7,* (2018), p. 215, emphasis added, all spelling as in original.
[58] Talmage, James E. (1917), *Articles of Faith,* pp. 449-450, Salt Lake City, UT: Deseret News publishing.

the foundation for Zion, and for relieving the current debts of the presidency of the church. After that initial, one time obligation was met, the people were then to pay one-tenth of all their interest once each year.[59] In Joseph's day, tithing was taken from surplus, meaning unnecessary excess property, and increase, meaning what remains after all costs of the household have been paid. It was meant to be drawn out of the giver's abundance, not from property required for their necessities. The Lord has never revoked this law nor is there any revelation changing it into what the LDS Church practices today.

The scriptures teach that the Lord's foremost intention for the distribution of tithes is that of caring for the poor, the needy, the widow, the fatherless, and the stranger. Tithes are not to be used for buildings, shopping malls, land acquisitions, private hunting compounds, private jets, lavish lifestyles, not even for a professional or "non" professional clergy. Once our obligation to take care of the poor among us is fulfilled, if there are tithes left over the Lord will allow the surplus to be used for the building of a temple.

In the New Testament, Paul testified that he had labored alongside his brethren for his own support and did not rely on money from his fellow members. He said, "I have coveted no man's silver, or gold, or apparel. Yea, ye yourselves know, that these hands have ministered unto my necessities,

---

[59] Doctrine and Covenants 119. Because of Doctrine and Covenants 64:23, tithing is often referred to as "fire insurance:" Behold, now it is called today until the coming of the Son of Man, and verily it is a day of sacrifice, and a day for the tithing of my people; for he that is tithed shall not be burned at his coming.

and to them that were with me. I have shewed you all things, how that so labouring ye ought to support the weak, and to remember the words of the Lord Jesus, how he said, It is more blessed to give than to receive."[60] In the Book of Mormon the example of King Benjamin as well as the teachings of Alma demonstrated to the people that the priests were not to depend on the people for their living but were to labor for their own support.[61]

If God's desire for the use of tithing is so clear in the scriptures where did the tradition of a paid clergy originate?

Elders and Ministers were unsalaried for the first 3 centuries after Christ. They were men with an earthly vocation, laboring alongside their flock for their own necessities. In 200 AD a Christian writer named Cyprian of Carthage argued the practice of financially supporting the clergy based on the fact that Ancient Israel supported the Levite tribe according to the Law of Moses.[62] His petition was not agreeable to the Christian people en masse until much later. Around 300 AD other Christian leaders began to advocate paying tithes to support the clergy. Emperor Constantine of Rome instituted the practice of paying clergy a salary from church funds as well as from the municipal and imperial treasuries during the 4th century.

The widespread use of tithes to support churches financially began between 600 and 700 AD. During this time

---

[60] Acts 20: 33-35, Holy Scriptures, Inspired Version.

[61] Mosiah 18:26.

[62] The landed tribes were expected to support the Levites with a tithe, particularly the tithe known as the First tithe, ma'aser rishon. The kohanim, a subset of Levites, were the priests who performed the work of holiness in the temple. See Numbers 18:21-25.

leasing land was a common practice in Europe. The "tenth" was used to calculate rent payments to landlords. As the institutional church began to purchase and own more and more land, the rent charges which were originally paid to secular landlords began to be paid to ecclesiastical ones. Essentially, the tithe became the ecclesiastical tax. The leaders creatively rebranded this rent tax as the Old Testament Law of Tithing.[63]

The earliest positive legislation on the subject seems to be contained in the letter of the bishops assembled at Tours in 567 and the canons of the Council of Mâçon in 585. In the course of time, the payment of tithes was made obligatory by ecclesiastical enactments in all the countries of Christendom. As to the civil power, the Christian Roman emperors granted the right to churches to retain a portion of the produce of certain lands. But the earliest instance of the enforcement of the payment of ecclesiastical tithes by civil law is found in the capitularies of Charlemagne, at the end of the eighth century.[64]

The use of tithes to pay clergy, as well as to financially support churches, has allowed mischief and priestcraft to enter the realms of religion.[65] When a person's livelihood is attached

---

[63] Viola and Barna (2012), *Pagan Christianity: Exploring the Roots of our Church Practices,* 2012, pp. 176-177, Carol Stream, IL: Tyndale House Publishing.

[64] Knight, Kevin, *New Advent*, Catholic Encyclopedia; retrieved from https://www.newadvent.org/cathen/14741b.htm; accessed on date updated on January 15, 2024.

[65] According to the Merriam-Webster dictionary the definition of priestcraft is a professional knowledge and skill in respect to the exercise of priestly functions; the scheming and machinations of priests; 2 Nephi 26:29 defines it this way, "He commandeth that there shall be no priestcrafts; for, behold,

to how popular he or she is with their congregation it encourages leaders to be "people pleasers" and slaves of men. Viola and Barna postulate that "giving a salary to pastors elevates them above the rest of God's people. It creates a clerical caste that turns the living body of Christ into a business. Since the pastor and his staff are compensated for ministry, they are paid professionals. The rest of the church lapses into a state of passive dependence."[66]

Nephi, the son of Helaman, expounded the concept in this manner:

> But behold, if a man shall come among you and shall say: Do this, and there is no iniquity; do that and ye shall not suffer; yea, he will say: Walk after the pride of your own hearts; yea, walk after the pride of your eyes, and do whatsoever your heart desireth—and if a man shall come among you and say this, ye will receive him, and say that he is a prophet. Yea, ye will lift him up, and ye will give unto him of your substance; ye will give unto him of your gold, and of your silver, and ye will clothe him with costly apparel; and because he speaketh flattering words unto you, and he saith that all is well, then ye will not find fault with him.[67]

A paid, professional clergy goes against the grain of Zion. In Mosiah 2:12 and 14, King Benjamin gave himself as an example to his people:

---

priestcrafts are that men preach and set themselves up for a light unto the world, that they may get gain and praise of the world; but they seek not the welfare of Zion."

[66] Viola and Barna (2012), *Pagan Christianity: Exploring the Roots of our Church Practices,* pp. 180-181, Carol Stream, IL: Tyndale House Publishing.
[67] Helaman 13:27-28.

I say unto you that as I have been suffered to spend my days in your service, even up to this time, and have not sought gold nor silver nor any manner of riches of you; . . . And even I, myself, have labored with mine own hands that I might serve you, and that ye should not be laden with taxes, and that there should nothing come upon you which was grievous to be borne—and of all these things which I have spoken, ye yourselves are witnesses this day.

A common fallacy perpetuated by the LDS Church is that they have no paid clergy. While this is true for what is known as the local level of leadership, this is not true on the General level. Members of the LDS Church are divided into congregations based on geographic location. The smallest congregations are known as branches and consist anywhere from a few members up to a hundred or so. The priesthood leader of a branch is called a branch president. Once a congregation grows large enough in size it is termed a ward. The priesthood leader of a ward is given the title of bishop. Groups of branches and wards are organized into stakes. The priesthood leader of a stake is called a stake president. These are known as local leaders and all are unpaid, non-professional clergy who must provide their own living while sacrificing their time to serve their congregations.

The LDS Church's General level of leadership is over large, or general geographic areas of the Church, and are called General Authorities. General Authorities are organized into the First Presidency, the Quorum of the Twelve Apostles, the First and Second Quorums of the Seventy, and the Presiding Bishopric. A document leaked in 2014 noted that the "base living allowance" for all Mormon general authorities was being raised from \$116,400 to \$120,000 per year.[68] These men also enjoy additional perks such as health care benefits, free cars, and book royalties. LDS Mission Presidents also benefit from tithing funds.[69] Because the LDS Church refuses to be transparent, accountable, and open with their collected donations no one can say with certainty how much the general leaders benefit from the tithes of their people. What is known, is that the LDS Church reimburses these leaders with anywhere from a meager to an extremely generous living allowance and pays many of their expenses.[70] Apparently, if you call a salary a living allowance then you can claim that your church has an unpaid clergy.

Nephi warns that there will be "many which shall teach after this manner, false and vain and foolish doctrines, and

---

[68] See Fletcher, Peggy (February 2, 2017), How Much do top Mormon leaders make? Leaked pay stubs may surprise you. Retrieved from https://www.sltrib.com/news/mormon/2017/02/02/how-much-do-top-mormon-leaders-make-leaked-pay-stubs-may-surprise-you/ , accessed on May 05, 2016. In August 1844, the Twelve Apostles voted to exempt themselves from paying tithes. It is unclear if that is still followed today.

[69] LDS Mission Presidents are not paid a salary or living stipend, but their expenses are paid by the Church, some of which are extravagant. The full LDS Church's Handbook for Mission Presidents was leaked to the internet, in the handbook it was revealed what types of things Mission Presidents and their families could be reimbursed for above and beyond what was needed to sustain life (food, shelter, transportation, medical/dental, etc.); some of these extras include a maid, a babysitter, gardener, private schooling, orthodontics, Christmas/birthday/anniversary gifts, etc. See the leaked Mission President's Handbook at https://mormonleaks.io/wiki/documents/0/03/Mission_Presidents_Handbook_2006.pdf, accessed on date updated on January 12, 2024.

[70] See The Church of Jesus Christ of Latter-day Saints answer to "Do General Authorities get paid?" found at https://faq.churchofjesuschrist.org/do-general-authorities-get-paid; accessed on date updated on January 12, 2024.

shall be puffed up in their hearts, and shall seek deep to hide their counsels from the Lord."[71] How might one better hide their counsels from the Lord, than to conceal the details of the money that is gathered from the tithes of His people? How might one better hide their counsel than to hide from view all the revenues paid to the authorities of the church, and even admonish the paid mission presidents that they must never disclose the revenue benefits that they are receiving? How might one better hide their counsel, than to conceal it from the very sheep that are being shorn?

The rebuke Malachi gives in chapter 3 is to the leaders of all churches who squander the gifts of their people upon themselves and who offer unclean sacrifices to God. The ideal is to never have a professional class of clergyman. The ideal is for every one of us to be equals. We are all equally accountable before God. In a revelation given through the prophet Joseph Smith in 1831, it states: "Let the residue of the elders watch over the churches, and declare the word in the regions round about them; and let them labor with their own hands that there be no idolatry nor wickedness practiced."[72]

To labor with their own hands means that a minister, missionary, pastor, bishop, general authority, etc. are not professional clergy receiving compensation for preaching, teaching, ministering, and so forth because as soon as you turn them into a professional clergy people begin to idolize them. The object is to avoid idolatry, to avoid the professional class of clergy to whom people look for blessings at their compensated

---

[71] 2 Nephi 28:9.
[72] Doctrine and Covenants 52:39.

hands. "That there be no idolatry nor wickedness practiced."[73] "Wickedness" because when you have people elevated so as to have control over others, almost invariably the existence of control tends to lead inexorably to abuse.[74]

Viola and Barna recognize this truth, "If all Christians got in touch with the call that lies upon them to be functioning priests in the Lord's house (and they were permitted to exercise that call), the question would immediately arise: 'What on earth are we paying our pastor for!?'"[75] The prophet Nephi gave a warning for our day:

> For the time speedily shall come that all churches which are built up to get gain, and all those who are built up to get power over the flesh, and those who are built up to become popular in the eyes of the world, and those who seek the lusts of the flesh and the things of the world, and to do all manner of iniquity; yea, in fine, all those who belong to the kingdom of the devil are they who need fear, and tremble, and quake; they are those who must be brought low in the dust; they are those who must be consumed as stubble; and this is according to the words of the prophet.[76]

Jesus clearly taught how it is we "give to God." The giving He spoke of had nothing to do with financing a church organization. In as much as we give to others who are in need (the poor, the sick, the imprisoned, the hungry, even the lost),

---

[73] Ibid.

[74] See Snuffer, Denver (September 9, 2014), "Preserving the Restoration," *40 Years in Mormonism*, p. 2.

[75] Viola and Barna (2012) *Pagan Christianity: Exploring the Roots of our Church Practices,* pp. 180-181, Carol Stream, IL: Tyndale House Publishing.

[76] 1 Nephi 22:23.

we are ministering directly to Him.[77] This ministry of giving entails far more than finances. It embodies the commandment to love others.[78] This does not mean washing our hands of them, thereby alleviating our consciences, by sending in our money to some organization so that someone else can do the work. It means we listen to the voice of our Lord and go ourselves to each one He sends us to. If we see our neighbor with a need we have in our power to meet, we bring forth the fruit of love and meet it. God has made each of us who know Him priests and priestesses unto Him, we fulfill this responsibility as we serve our fellowman. This means that no one else can mediate His work for us. We can hear His voice and obey it to the best of our ability.

In his lecture series titled *40 Years in Mormonism,* Denver Snuffer, Jr. taught:

> Tithing is for the poor. It is not designed to pay for a professional clergy class. If we have no buildings more money can go to assist with the needs of people. In this day, and in this economy, anything that can be done to assist with the poor is a good thing.[79]
>
> There is nothing divine in neglecting the poor. The primary purpose of collecting the tithes . . . is to bless and benefit the lives of those who are in need. So, given the fact that you are commanded to pay tithing, . . . I would suggest one small thing you could begin is to collect your own tithing in a group. You manage it among yourselves. You assist the poor among you. If you disagree with what your churches are doing but

---

[77] See Matthew 25:37-40.
[78] See Matthew 5:43-48 and John 13:34-35.
[79] Snuffer, Denver (September 9, 2014), "Preserving the Restoration," *40 Years in Mormonism,* p. 30.

recognize the obligation to pay, then take control over the funds to do what you believe God would have done to help others. As groups of common believers, pay tithing into a common fund. Then by the voice of your own group, dispose of it by common consent so that everyone in your group knows everything that comes in and everything that goes out. Then you begin to have no poor among your group. You provide for those who need housing, food, clothing, healthcare, education, and transportation. Do it without a leader. Do it by the voice of your own common consent, by your own unanimous approval. Do it by united agreement.[80]

In each of your churches there are lots of people who get benefited in lots of ways. But that doesn't excuse the money that those "Strongmen" spend on themselves. The highest-paid clergies in the world manage the various denominations of the various Mormon movements. The top LDS Church leaders have access to private hunting preserves, fenced vacation compounds, a private jet, and, in comparison with poor Lazarus, "fare sumptuously." . . . [T]he institutions stemming from Joseph Smith's efforts are almost entirely led by rather well-paid professional clergy. Take the money the Lord intended for the poor and administer it for the poor among you. If you try this experiment, there will be some among you who receive rather than give because they have not. Let me remind those who receive of another statement made in the revelations of this dispensation in Doctrine and Covenants 42:42 *"Thou shalt not be idle; for he that is idle shall not eat the bread nor wear the garments of the*

---

[80] Snuffer, Denver (April 12, 2014), "Zion," *40 Years in Mormonism*, p. 14.

laborer."[81]

Malachi 3: 10 Bring ye all the tithes into the storehouse, that there may be meat in mine house, and prove me now herewith, saith the Lord of hosts, if I will not open you the windows of heaven, and pour you out a blessing, that there shall not be room enough to receive it.

What does the Lord mean by the statement, "I will open you the windows of heaven, and pour you out a blessing, that there shall not be room enough to receive it?"

When a window is opened, one can see inside to what was previously closed off and hidden. Could it be that the phrase "the windows of heaven" is symbolic for the "veil" that separates us from heaven and the presence of God? Could the opening of heaven's windows be the actuality of the veil parting and allowing an individual to see Angels, the Lord, Jesus Christ, God the Father, and the hosts of Heaven?[82] Joseph Smith taught: "Could you gaze into heaven five minutes, you would know more than you would by reading all that ever was written on the subject."[83] If the windows of heaven were opened to you, would you describe the experience as not having "room enough to receive it?" Joseph Smith also taught

[81] Snuffer, Denver (April 12, 2014), "Zion," *40 Years in Mormonism*, pp. 15. Italics in original.

[82] Since the New Testament scores of others have seen God and the Heavenly Hosts; the following is a sampling and is not an exhaustive list: numerous individuals written about in the Book of Mormon, Joan of Arc, St. Francis of Asisi, Joseph Smith, Jr., Oliver Cowdery, Hyrum Smith, Sidney Rigdon, Denver Snuffer, Jr., and others we know not of.

[83] Smith, Joseph Fielding (1938), *Teachings of the Prophet Joseph Smith*, p. 324; Salt Lake City: Deseret Book Co. and Ehat & Cook (1980) *The Words of Joseph Smith,* 9 October 1843, p. 254, Salt Lake City: Bookcraft.

that if we live up to our privileges the angels cannot be restrained from being our associates.[84] There are people who have had the windows of heaven opened unto them who have stated that for weeks afterward they were filled to overflowing with love and peace toward all mankind. Joseph Smith recorded in his own hand the following account relative to his first vision experience:

> I cried unto the Lord for mercy for there was none else to whom I could go and obtain mercy and the Lord heard my cry in the wilderness and while in the attitude of calling upon the Lord, in the 16th year of my age, a pillar of light above the brightness of the sun at noon day came down from above and rested upon me and I was filled with the Spirit of god, *and the Lord opened the heavens upon me and I saw the Lord* and he spake unto me saying Joseph, my son, thy sins are forgiven thee. Go thy way, walk in my statutes and keep my commandments behold I am the Lord of glory I was crucified for the world, that all those who believe on my name may have Eternal life, behold, the world lieth in sin at this time and none doeth good, no not one, they have turned aside from the gospel and keep not my commandments, they draw near to me with their lips while their hearts are far from me and mine anger is kindling against the inhabitants of the earth to visit them according to their ungodliness and to bring to pass that which hath been spoken by the mouth of the prophets and Apostles, behold and lo I come quickly as it was written of me in the cloud,

---

[84] Joseph Smith, in Relief Society Minute Book, Nauvoo, Illinois, Apr. 28, 1842, 38–39. Nauvoo Relief Society Minute Book, p. 38, The Joseph Smith Papers, accessed on date updated on January 15, 2024, https://www.josephsmithpapers.org/paper-summary/nauvoo-relief-society-minute-book/61.

clothed in the glory of my Father. *And my soul was filled with love and for many days I could rejoice with great Joy and the Lord was with me* but could find none that would believe the heavenly vision, nevertheless, I pondered these things in my heart.[85]

Malachi 3:10 is a continuation of the verses before which relate to tithing. It seems clear that one of the Lord's tests that determines whether or not an individual is one to whom He can open the windows of heaven and reveal heavenly things is that they care about and care for the poor, the needy, and the downtrodden. Tithes are to be used for the needs of our own families and the needs of those with whom we associate and fellowship. It is in the way we treat our families and our fellowman that we reveal what is truly in our hearts. By this, then, the Lord learns whom He can trust with greater knowledge because with greater knowledge comes greater responsibility to serve others on His behalf.[86]

> Malachi 3:11 And I will rebuke the devourer for your sakes, and he shall not destroy the fruits of your ground; neither shall your vine cast her fruit before the time in the field, saith the Lord of hosts. 12 And all nations shall call you blessed: for ye shall be a delightsome land, saith the Lord of hosts.

This is Zion, a place which will be delightsome,

---

[85] Smith, Joseph, Jr. historical account of his first of many visions of the Lord, Jesus Christ, written circa 1832; History, circa Summer 1832, p. 1, The Joseph Smith Papers, accessed on date updated on January 12, 2024, https://www.josephsmithpapers.org/paper-summary/history-circa-summer-1832/1?p=1#!/paperSummary/history-circa-summer-1832&p=3; spelling and grammar modernized; italicized and bold added for emphasis.
[86] See Mosiah 2:17.

productive, plentiful, and blessed. The people will be of one heart and one mind, they will dwell in righteousness, and there will be no poor among them.[87] Zion will be a place of refuge for those who refuse to take up arms against their neighbors. Those who qualify to live in Zion will be people who have prepared themselves, not only spiritually and physically, but emotionally and mentally as well. They will be those who have learned to govern themselves within the bounds the Lord has set.[88] They will be harmless to themselves and others and for this reason they will need to reside in a community of likeminded, like behaving, individuals who will provide safety and refuge for each other. They will be people who have learned to bind within themselves the accusatory nature of mankind which mimics that of Satan, the great accuser.[89] Through their heed and diligence to the laws and principles of the Gospel, they will be able to live in peace. The residents of Zion will be blessed because "they shall teach no more every man his neighbour, and every man his brother, saying, Know the LORD: for they shall all know me, from the least of them unto the greatest of them, saith the LORD: for I will forgive

---

[87] Moses 7:18.

[88] When God placed Adam and Eve in the Garden, He placed "walls" around it which were the boundaries, or commandments, set by Him. Likewise, the ten commandments are boundaries by which we should learn to govern ourselves. As we master these skills, the Lord encourages us to strive to continue to refine and govern not just our actions but also our desires, appetites, and passions still further as delineated in the Sermon on the Mount and the Sermon at the Temple in Bountiful.

[89] See Revelation 12:10-12.

their iniquity, and I will remember their sin no more."[90]

> Malachi 3:13 Your words have been stout against me, saith the Lord. Yet ye say, What have we spoken so much against thee? 14 Ye have said, It is vain to serve God: and what profit is it that we have kept his ordinance, and that we have walked mournfully before the Lord of hosts? 15 And now we call the proud happy; yea, they that work wickedness are set up; yea, they that tempt God are even delivered.

The leaders of various institutional churches believe that through their ordinances, their rites, and their traditions they are preaching faith in Jesus Christ and salvation through Him. Teachings have crept into modern religion which tell us there is no hell, and not to worry because "odds are everyone is going to be exalted."[91] One of the most destructive teachings is that mankind cannot and does not need to see the face of Christ in mortality, to have the windows of heaven opened, individually and personally. Many members of the LDS Church believe that most, if not all, of their Apostles have seen Christ and been ministered to by Him. In a talk given in Boise,

---

[90] Jeremiah 31: 34; Joseph Smith taught that "the ancient prophets (Jeremiah, for one) foretold it - "when no man need say to his neighbor, Know ye the Lord; for all shall know Him ... from the least to the greatest" (History of the Church, 3:380). The Prophet Joseph Smith said that this promise has reference to personal revelation, to a visitation of the Lord to an individual (see History of the Church, 3:381).

[91] 2 Nephi 28:8 "And there shall also be many which shall say: Eat, drink, and be merry; nevertheless, fear God—he will justify in committing a little sin; yea, lie a little, take the advantage of one because of his words, dig a pit for thy neighbor; there is no harm in this; and do all these things, for tomorrow we die; and if it so be that we are guilty, God will beat us with a few stripes, and at last we shall be saved in the kingdom of God." See also Alonzo L. Gaskill's book, 2008, *Odds are You're Going to be Exalted, Evidence that the Plan of Salvation Works,* Salt Lake City: Deseret Book Company.

Idaho in 2015, Elder Dallin H. Oaks of the Quorum of Twelve Apostles admitted that the apostles' testimonies are like that of any other member of the church. He added that all of the righteous desire to see the face of the Savior, but the suggestion that this must happen in mortality is a familiar tactic of the adversary.[92]

Christ decried against church leaders who teach that it is not necessary to see Him in this life, "But woe unto you, scribes and Pharisees, hypocrites! for ye shut up the kingdom of heaven against men: for ye neither go in yourselves, neither suffer ye them that are entering to go in."[93] And again, Christ exclaimed, "Woe unto you, lawyers! For ye have taken away the key of knowledge: ye entered not in yourselves, and them that were entering in ye hindered."[94] Christ called this type of leader "blind," and warned, "they be blind leaders of the blind. And if the blind lead the blind, both shall fall into the ditch."[95] Can it be said today, just as it was in Joseph Smith's day, "They draw near to me with their lips, but their hearts are far from me, they teach for doctrines the commandments of men, having a form of godliness, but they deny the power thereof?"[96]

It seems a paradoxical concept that individuals who claim to have a deep faith in the Lord Jesus Christ believe that

---

[92] To hear Elder Oaks talk in its entirety see: http://mormonstories.org/boise-rescue-oaks-turley/; this quote begins just after the 1 hour mark, accessed on date updated on January 12, 2024.

[93] Matthew 23:13; Matthew 23: 10 (Holy Scriptures, Inspired Version).

[94] Luke 11:52.

[95] Matthew 15:14.

[96] Joseph Smith History 1:19; Matthew 15:7-8 (Holy Scriptures Inspired Version); Matthew 15:7-9; see also the book written by Viola and Barna (2012) *Pagan Christianity: Exploring the Roots of our Church Practices,* Carol Stream, IL: Tyndale House Publishing.

they cannot and do not need to seek to enter His presence in mortality. The Lord has said, "Behold, I stand at the door, and knock: if any man hear my voice, and open the door, I will come in to him, and will sup with him, and he with me."[97] Furthermore, He has promised that all those who qualify will see His face and know that He lives.[98]

What is a seeker of Truth to do then?[99]

How can one open the Windows of Heaven and see the Christ?

Evidence demonstrates that perspectives, expectations, assumptions, practices, traditions, and creeds often serve as barriers which keep us from encountering the living God.[100] In the *Lectures on Faith* 3:2-5, Joseph Smith taught:

> 2 Let us here observe, that three things are necessary, in order that any rational and intelligent being may exercise faith in God unto life and salvation.
> 3 First, The idea that he actually exists.
> 4 Secondly, A correct idea of his character, perfections and attributes.
> 5 Thirdly, An actual knowledge that the course of life which he is pursuing, is according to his will.—For without an acquaintance with these three important facts, the faith of every rational being must be imperfect and unproductive; but with this understanding, it can become perfect and fruitful,

---

[97] Revelation 3:20.
[98] See D&C 93:1.
[99] Jesus Christ is the TRUTH: John 14:16 6 Jesus saith unto him, I am the way, the truth, and the life: no man cometh unto the Father, but by me.
[100] Viola and Barna (2012) *Pagan Christianity: Exploring the Roots of our Church Practices*, pp. xxxii-xxxiii, Carol Stream, IL: Tyndale House Publishing.

abounding in righteousness unto the praise and glory of God the Father, and the Lord Jesus Christ.

It matters how we practice our faith. We can begin by opening our eyes to false traditions, leaders, ideas, and idols; learning and understanding the true nature of God; developing a belief in Him, acting on that belief to grow it into a faith in Him, supplicating Him, and then waiting patiently upon Him.[101]

> Malachi 3:16 Then they that feared the Lord spake often one to another: and the Lord hearkened, and heard it, and a book of remembrance was written before him for them that feared the Lord, and that thought upon his name.

The Lord wants us to gather together often, in order that we might "mourn with those that mourn; yea, and comfort those that stand in need of comfort, and to stand as witnesses of God at all times and in all things, and in all places that [we] may be in, even until death."[102] The Lord has promised, "For where two or three are gathered together in my name, there am I in the midst of them."[103]

A book of remembrance is referenced several times throughout scripture. Adam and his righteous posterity wrote the first records of God's dealings with mankind. These records were called a book of remembrance and were passed down

---

[101] Denver Snuffer, Jr. wrote a first -hand, modern account as a guidebook to aid those seeking to come back into the presence of the Lord. It is titled *The Second Comforter: Conversing with the Lord through the Veil*, published in 2006.
[102] Mosiah 18:9.
[103] Matthew 18:20 (Holy Scriptures, Inspired Version); Matthew 18:20.

until they came into Abraham's hands.[104] Books of remembrance may also be known as the Lamb's Book of Life.[105] Scripture cautions that in order to withstand the coming judgements our name must be written in this book.[106] Joseph Smith taught,

> Whatsoever you record on earth shall be recorded in heaven, and whatsoever you do not record on earth shall not be recorded in heaven; for out of the books shall your dead be judged, according to their own works, whether they themselves have attended to the ordinances in their own propria persona, or by the means of their own agents, according to the ordinance which God has prepared for their salvation from before the foundation of the world.[107]

The apparent question then becomes, how does one's name get written in this book?

Baptism has been and will always be the sign required be demonstrated by those who claim they are repentant, the way a person can be washed clean of their sins and reconnect with Christ.[108] In Matthew 3 we learn that John was baptizing in

---

[104] See Abraham 1:29-31.

[105] See Revelation 13:8, 21:22-27, LoF 5:Q&A on pp. 56-57.

[106] Exodus 32:33; Psalms 69:28; Malachi 3:16; Luke 10:20; Philippians 4:3; Revelation 3:1-6; Revelation 13:8; Revelation 17:8; Revelation 20: 11-15; Revelation 21:27; Alma 5:58; Doctrine and Covenants 88:2; Doctrine and Covenants 128:6-9.

[107] Doctrine and Covenants 128:8.

[108] Baptism as the sign of repentance is taught throughout the Book of Mormon. See the following as one example: 3 Nephi 7:24-26 "Now I would have you to remember also, that there were none who were brought unto repentance who were not baptized with water. 25 Therefore, there were ordained of Nephi, men unto this ministry, that all such as should come unto them should be baptized with water, and this as a witness and a testimony

the river Jordan all who had come to him confessing their sins. Jesus Christ came to John to be baptized in order to fulfill all righteousness. Nephi taught, "Do the things which I have told you I have seen that your Lord and your Redeemer should do; for, for this cause have they been shown unto me, that ye might know the gate by which ye should enter."[109] Christ taught, "[T]he Gentiles, if they will not harden their hearts, that they may *repent,* and come unto me, and *be baptized in my name,* and know of the true points of my doctrine, that they may be numbered among my people, O house of Israel."[110] One who desires to turn away from sin and face God, to reconnect with Him, should be baptized by immersion, by one who has authority from God.

Baptism as an infant is not baptism unto repentance as all children are innocent before God until the age of accountability. Mormon taught, "Listen to the words of Christ, your Redeemer, your Lord and your God. I came into the world not to call the righteous but sinners to repentance; the whole need no physician, but they that are sick; wherefore, little children are whole, for they are not capable of committing sin; wherefore the curse of Adam is taken from them in me."[111] While correcting the Bible, Joseph Smith made this important addition, "And I will establish a covenant of circumcision with you, and it shall be my covenant between me and you and your

---

before God, and unto the people, that they had repented and received a remission of their sins. 26 And there were many in the commencement of this year that were baptized unto repentance; and thus the more part of the year did pass away."

[109] 2 Nephi 31:17.

[110] 3 Nephi 21:6; emphasis added.

[111] Moroni 8: 8.

seed after you in their generations, that you may know for ever that children are not accountable before me till eight years old."[112] The Doctrine and Covenants reaffirms this truth, children should be baptized for the remission of sins at the age of eight years old.[113]

Viola and Barna propose that in the first century water baptism was the outward confession of a person's faith and was the way someone came to the Lord. Baptism marked a complete break with the past and a full entrance to Christ; it was simultaneously an act of faith as well as an expression of faith.[114] Those who survived the mass destruction of their civilization in 3rd Nephi were told by a voice from Heaven that they were spared because they had received the prophets and been baptized.[115] It is interesting to note that one of the very first things Christ taught these people was the correct ordinance of baptism and commanded them all to be baptized

---

[112] See Genesis 17:11-12 (Holy Inspired Version).

[113] See Doctrine and Covenants 68:27. See also Doctrine and Covenants 18:42; 20:71; and 137:10.

[114] Viola and Barna (2012) *Pagan Christianity: Exploring the Roots of our Church Practices,* pp. 188-189, Carol Stream, IL: Tyndale House Publishing.

[115] 3 Nephi 10:12-13, 24-26 "And it was the more righteous part of the people who were saved, and it was they who received the prophets and stoned them not; and it was they who had not shed the blood of the saints, who were spared. . . 24 Now I would have you to remember also, that there were none who were brought unto repentance who were not baptized with water. 25 Therefore, there were ordained of Nephi, men unto this ministry, that all such as should come unto them should be baptized with water, and this as a witness and a testimony before God, and unto the people, that they had repented and received a remission of their sins. 26 And there were many in the commencement of this year that were baptized unto repentance; and thus the more part of the year did pass away."

again.[116] Later on in the narrative, Jesus showed Himself again to the disciples who were gathered together, united in mighty prayer and fasting, and taught them many things pertaining to His gospel which they were to preach to the people, one of which was, "Now this is the commandment: Repent, all ye ends of the earth, and come unto me and be baptized in my name, that ye may be sanctified by the reception of the Holy Ghost, that ye may stand spotless before me at the last day."[117] The invitation to be baptized, immersed in living waters, by one who has authority from Jesus Christ is extended to all, "Repent all ye ends of the earth, and come unto me, and be baptized in my name, and have faith in me, that ye may be

---

[116] 3 Nephi 11: 18-28 "And it came to pass that he spake unto Nephi (for Nephi was among the multitude) and he commanded him that he should come forth. . . 21 And the Lord said unto him: I give unto you power that ye shall baptize this people when I am again ascended into heaven. 22 And again the Lord called others, and said unto them likewise; and he gave unto them power to baptize. And he said unto them: On this wise shall ye baptize; and there shall be no disputations among you. 23 Verily I say unto you, that whoso repenteth of his sins through your words, and desireth to be baptized in my name, on this wise shall ye baptize them—Behold, ye shall go down and stand in the water, and in my name shall ye baptize them. 24 And now behold, these are the words which ye shall say, calling them by name, saying: 25 Having authority given me of Jesus Christ, I baptize you in the name of the Father, and of the Son, and of the Holy Ghost. Amen. 26 And then shall ye immerse them in the water, and come forth again out of the water. 27 And after this manner shall ye baptize in my name; for behold, verily I say unto you, that the Father, and the Son, and the Holy Ghost are one; and I am in the Father, and the Father in me, and the Father and I are one. 28 And according as I have commanded you thus shall ye baptize. And there shall be no disputations among you, as there have hitherto been; neither shall there be disputations among you concerning the points of my doctrine, as there have hitherto been."
[117] 3 Nephi 27:20.

saved."[118]

Some common arguments against baptism by immersion are: one who has accepted Jesus in their heart does not need baptism; one who was baptized as an infant or a young child does not need baptism later in life; or one's previous baptism in another church is sufficient.[119] Baptism is a gift that God has extended to us which can be, and should be, accepted and acted upon throughout our lives, whenever we feel the necessity of turning from our old selves and facing Him, repenting of our sins, and reconnecting with the Lord we can be baptized. Baptism is the fruit of repentance.

It is often argued that there is only one Lord, one faith, and one baptism, therefore the necessity of being baptized more than once is a false concept.[120] What if "one baptism" is referring to only one **mode** of baptism which is acceptable to the Lord? The Lord taught by example as well as by word that baptism must be by immersion.[121] Baptism symbolizes the death of the old man or woman of sin as they are laid down under the water, and the resurrection as they are brought up out of the water into a new life in Christ.[122]

---

[118] Moroni 7:34. See also Denver Snuffer's writings on Baptism and Rebaptism at this link: http://denversnuffer.com/?s=baptism, accessed on date updated on January 12, 2024. This is a website where you can learn more and submit a request for baptism: https://bornofwater.org/, accessed on date updated on January 12, 2024.

[119] See the Sinner's Prayer; see https://en.wikipedia.org/wiki/Sinner%27s_prayer, accessed on date updated on January 12, 2024.

[120] Ephesians 4:5.

[121] Matthew 3:13-1, "And Jesus, when he was baptized, went up straightway out of the water," and 3 Nephi 11:26: "Then shall ye immerse them in the water, and come forth again out of the water."

[122] See Romans 6:1-7.

Due to the Fall of Adam and Eve, and the conditions placed upon the world at that time by God, men are responsible for performing outward ordinances such as baptism and the sacrament.[123] In order to baptize, a man must be given authority from Heaven. This is evident in the baptismal prayer required by Christ to be recited when performing the ordinance: "These are the words which ye shall say, calling them by name, saying: **Having authority** given me of Jesus Christ, I baptize you in the name of the Father, and of the Son, and of the Holy Ghost. Amen."[124] Ordination to the priesthood does not fully qualify a man to claim he is one "having authority." This requires another step. Any ordained man should go to the Lord in prayer, asking for His authority, and obtain His voice on the matter.[125]

The baptism of children before the age of accountability, and baptism by any mode other than by immersion by one having authority, are not accepted by the Lord as His because they do not comply with His required pattern. If all denominations are presently astray, this means they do not have authority to baptize and therefore are not accepted as the Lord's.[126] The Church of Jesus Christ of Latter

---

[123] When the earth is returned to its paradisiacal state in the millennium, things will return to the way they were in the Garden.

[124] 3 Nephi 11:24-25.

[125] Alma exemplified this when he went down into the water with Helam and before baptizing him, Alma cried out, "O Lord, pour out thy spirit upon thy servant, that he may do this work with holiness of heart. And when he had said these words, the spirit of the Lord was upon him." Mosiah 18:12-13.

[126] Joseph Smith History 1:19; and Smith, Joseph, Jr. historical account of his first of many visions of the Lord, Jesus Christ, written circa 1832; History,

Day Saints in Joseph Smith's day offered a baptism that was acceptable to the Lord. But since Joseph's death they have added to and taken away from the doctrine of Christ.[127] If the baptism offered by the LDS Church today is an adulteration of Christ's doctrine, it might be wise to consider if it is effective to produce faith unto salvation and is still accepted by Christ as His.[128]

---

circa Summer 1832, p. 1, The Joseph Smith Papers, https://www.josephsmithpapers.org/paper-summary/history-circa-summer-1832/1?p=1#!/paperSummary/history-circa-summer-1832&p=3, accessed on date updated on January 12, 2024.

[127] The Doctrine of Christ is found in 3 Nephi 11.

[128] 3 Nephi 11:40 "And whoso shall declare more or less than this, and establish it for my doctrine, the same cometh of evil, and is not built upon my rock; but he buildeth upon a sandy foundation, and the gates of hell stand open to receive such when the floods come and the winds beat upon them." Today, the LDS Church requires a list of Baptismal Interview Questions to be "passed" before a candidate may be baptized. The following is from the missionary manual Preach My Gospel, page 206 (as of 2016):

The Missionary Will Ask the Following Questions:

1. Do you believe that God is our Eternal Father? Do you believe that Jesus Christ is the Son of God, the Savior and Redeemer of the world?

2. Do you believe the Church and gospel of Jesus Christ have been restored through the Prophet Joseph Smith? Do you believe that [current Church President] is a prophet of God? What does this mean to you?

3. What does it mean to you to repent? Do you feel that you have repented of your past transgressions?

4. Have you ever committed a serious crime? If so, are you now on probation or parole? Have you ever participated in an abortion? a homosexual relationship?

5. You have been taught that membership in The Church of Jesus Christ of Latter-day Saints includes living gospel standards. What do you understand of the following standards? Are you willing to obey them?

a. The law of chastity, which prohibits any sexual relationship outside the bonds of a legal marriage between a man and a woman?

b. The law of tithing.

c. The Word of Wisdom.

The Lord requires baptism. It is an essential part of repentance and is the sign to the Lord that you have accepted His doctrine. Baptism should be offered freely, without obligation, and without requirement to follow anyone other than Christ. The only condition for baptism is to accept the Doctrine of Christ.[129] Christ commanded it be done. It remains the way whereby we may demonstrate faith in Him, as well as our acceptance of His work whenever a new dispensation of the gospel is underway.

The Lord requires the names of those baptized to be recorded.[130] No other information, personal or otherwise, needs to be collected. Baptism was never intended to link a person to a specific religious institution. The Lord desires that we are baptized in the way that He has set forth and allows us the privilege of worshiping Him according to the dictates of our own conscience. We should allow all men the same privilege, let them worship how, where, or what they may.[131]

Malachi 3:17 And they shall be mine, saith the Lord of

---

d. The Sabbath day, including partaking of the sacrament weekly and rendering service to fellow members.

6. When you are baptized, you covenant with God that you are willing to take upon yourself the name of Christ and keep His commandments throughout your life. Are you ready to make this covenant and strive to be faithful to it?

*If you answer yes to any of the questions entailed in point four, the missionary conducting the interview will refer you to the mission president to determine if you qualify for baptism.

[129] The doctrine of Christ is set forth by the Lord's own words in 3 Nephi 11.

[130] We must record our names in the Lamb's Book of Life. See Doctrine and Covenants 128:8; and http://www.recordersclearinghouse.com/, accessed on date updated on January 12, 2024.

[131] "Article of Faith 11" retrieved from https://www.churchofjesuschrist.org/study/scriptures/pgp/a-of-f/1?lang=eng; accessed on date updated on January 12, 2024.

hosts, in that day when I make up my jewels; and I will spare them, as a man spareth his own son that serveth him.[132] 18 Then shall ye return, and discern between the righteous and the wicked, between him that serveth God and him that serveth him not.

What great love and mercy the Lord extends if we but do His will. Those who repent and come unto Him, obey His voice, and accept His work now underway, will be numbered among His jewels. They will be counted among His people who are a treasured possession to Him. The Lord is at work again today. He is extending an invitation to come and labor with Him in His vineyard, for the "time draweth near and the end soon cometh. Wherefore, [the Lord] must lay up fruit against the season unto [His] own self."[133] The day will come when the season has ended, and the Lord will cause His vineyard to be burned with fire.[134] The Lord has promised that in that day, His jewels will be spared.

As the world groans under darkness and is covered by thick clouds of deception, the Lord wants us to rise above it all and to have joy. He has overcome the world and has promised that He will return again in glory. Before this long awaited event can be fulfilled there must be a place prepared to receive Him. For those who succeed, the Lord's promises are great indeed:

And the bow shall be in the cloud; and I will look upon it, that I may remember the everlasting covenant, which I made unto thy father Enoch: that, when men

---

[132] See also Luke 17:34-40 (Holy Scriptures, Inspired Version).
[133] Jacob 5:29.
[134] Jacob 5:77.

should keep all my commandments, Zion should again come on the earth, the city of Enoch which I have caught up unto myself. And this is my everlasting covenant that I establish with you: that when your posterity shall embrace the truth and look upward, then shall Zion look downward, and all the heavens shall shake with gladness and the earth shall tremble with joy. And the general assembly of the church of the Firstborn shall come down out of Heaven and possess the earth, and shall have place until the end come. And this is mine everlasting covenant which I made with thy father Enoch.[135]

---

[135] Genesis 9:21-23 (Holy Scriptures, Inspired Version); Joseph Smith Translation Genesis 9:21-23.

Essay 8

An Examination on
Women and the Priesthood

Whitney N. Horning

©March 2024

Many women throughout the religious history of this world have questioned their place in God's kingdom precisely due to mankind's interpretation of the priesthood claims of their chosen religion. In the world's largest religion, Christianity, the major denominations such as Catholic and Orthodox traditions do not permit women to be ordained to their priesthood.[1] The second largest religion in the world is Islam. In ancient Islamic tradition, women were seen as equal to men and were allowed to serve as Imams, or the person who leads prayers in a mosque. That began to change during the sexism of medieval times when women became barred from leading congregations. This ban on women leaders has continued to our day but is slowly changing. Today, a small number of schools of Islamic thought are beginning to recognize that the spirit of true Islam teaches that women are equal to men and are once again allowing women to lead prayer.[2] The smallest population of the major religions of the

---

[1] More Christian denominations today are allowing women to be ordained to the priesthood than ever before; however, these churches do not understand that they are violating the conditions God established on this earth when Adam and Eve fell from His presence.

[2] See Answers to Frequently Asked Questions About Islam and Muslims; retrieved from https://ing.org/resources/answers-to-frequently-asked-questions-about-islam-and-muslims/; accessed on February 19, 2024.

world is Judaism. Orthodox Jews do not ordain or allow women to act in priesthood roles which are reserved solely for men.

There has been much confusion and much debate over the roles of men and women from the beginning of time. Many of the debates in Judeo-Christian traditions stem from interpretations of the Adam and Eve story in the Christian Bible and the Jewish Tanakh.[3] Eve is often portrayed by these religions in a negative light, as the temptress and deceiver who caused Adam, and all of creation, to sin and fall from God's presence, thereby bringing death into this world.[4] This image of Eve has resulted in an extremely negative impact on women. It was, and in too many churches today, is still believed and taught that menstruation, pregnancy, and childbirth were assigned to Eve as her punishment.

Some of the most influential ancient Jewish and Christian writers perpetuated the idea that women are untrustworthy, morally inferior, and wicked precisely because they inherited these traits from Eve. Since all women after her have inherited the same traits, along with the ability to bear children, it has been assumed that all must be like her in nature and temperament.[5] In the book of Ecclesiasticus it states, "All wickedness is but little to the wickedness of a woman: let the portion of a sinner fall upon her. . . . Of the woman came the

---

[3] The Jewish scriptures are called the Tanakh after the first letters of the three parts in the Jewish tradition: T for Torah, the Teachings of Moses, or the first five books; N for Nevi'im, the books of the prophets; and Kh for Ketuvim, for the Writings, which include the psalms and wisdom literature.

[4] Satan, the Great Accuser, is the God of death and therefore, when Eve succumbed to his temptation to partake of the fruit, she brought him into the world—even death, decay, chaos, and confusion.

[5] See a few examples at NC Ecclesiastes 1:32, and (Catholic Bible) Ecclesiasticus 25:19,24.

beginning of sin, and through her we all die."[6] The Apostle Paul wrote to Timothy,

> Let the woman learn in silence with all subjection, for I suffer not a woman to teach, nor to usurp authority over the man, but to be in silence. For Adam was first formed, then Eve. And Adam was not deceived, but the woman being deceived was in the transgression. Notwithstanding, they shall be saved in childbearing if they continue in faith, and charity, and holiness, with sobriety.[7]

The Jewish Talmud asserts that ten curses, including those associated with childbearing, desiring her husband, and death were inflicted upon Eve as punishment for her sin.[8]

Adam, on the other hand, is portrayed by the Judeo-Christian traditions as a faithful, just man who withstood the serpent's attempts to lead him astray, only partaking of the forbidden fruit when his wife seduced him. This belief, coupled with the idea that because Adam was created before Eve she was obviously inferior to him, has often led men to believe they are superior to women and to behave in such a manner.

In the Islamic Qur'an the story of Adam and Eve is told in such a way that the couple share the responsibility for eating the fruit and falling from God's presence.[9] There is evidence

---

[6] Catholic Bible, Ecclesiasticus 25:19, 24.

[7] NC 1 Timothy 1:7.

[8] See The Shalvi/Hyman Encyclopedia of Jewish Women, *Eve: Midrash and Aggadah* by Tamar Kadari. Retrieved from https://jwa.org/encyclopedia/article/eve-midrash-and-aggadah, accessed on February 19, 2024.

[9] Qur'an 7:19-23.

that the ancient Islamic faith honored women as equal to men. Today's mistreatment of women is seen by progressive Muslims, who are striving to get back to ancient practices, as stemming from sexism, misinterpretations, and misapplications of the Qur'an.[10]

What we do know for certain is that God knew that jealousies, envies, and strifes would exist in this world between men and women and, therefore, has consistently reminded humankind that "he inviteth all to come unto him and partake of his goodness, and he denieth none that come unto him, black and white, bond and free, male and female; and he remembereth the heathen, and all are alike unto God, both Jew and gentile."[11]

This world is in a constant state of entropy. Holding onto truth can prove difficult. Cycles of apostasy from light and truth and restoration are seen throughout the scriptural record. One of the consequences of apostasy is the confounding of language, or a confusion of terms, definitions, beliefs, and ideas.[12] One of those, which is found at the very core of the long-standing false tradition that men are superior to women is confusion regarding the woman's role in connection to priesthood.

To begin to grasp a portion of understanding concerning women and the priesthood requires that we go back to the very beginning, to the very place and scene wherein

---

[10] See Azeem, Dr. Sherif Abdel (1995). *Women in Islam versus Women in the Judeo-Christian Tradition.* Retrieved from https://www.iium.edu.my/deed/articles/womeninjud_chr.html#_Toc3355 66654. Accessed on February 19, 2024.

[11] NC 2 Nephi 11:17.

[12] See OC Genesis 6:6, NC introduction to Book of Mormon, and T&C 146:10.

so much mischief and false belief is founded: The Garden of Eden and the key actors, Adam, Eve, and the serpent. We must necessarily begin with the creation of Adam and Eve, and perhaps we must go even further back to a place and time before the creation of this world in which we now live.

In a prior estate, Adam and Eve had progressed, united as one, to become living souls with both bodies and spirits. In that estate, they were sealed by the Holy Spirit of Promise and proved true and faithful. At one time, they had sat upon a throne in God the Father's kingdom, equal and joined eternally together. Eve sat beside Adam and was a necessary part of his enthronement for he could not be there if not for her covenant with him.[13] Together, they had obtained the Melchizedek Priesthood, or the Holy Order after the Order of the Son of God. With this was included the right to preside over all the human family.[14]

When Adam was chosen to come down to this world as the first man, he was created in God's image.[15] Yet, he was not complete, for it was not good for him to be alone.[16] It was necessary for him to have a helpmeet, therefore, the woman, with whom he was one, joined him.[17] While Adam had been created from the dust of the earth, Eve was created from an already existing part of the man—his rib, signifying that she

---

[13] See T&C 157:42 and A Glossary of Gospel Terms, "Eve."

[14] See T&C A Glossary of Gospel Terms, "Holy Order."

[15] See OC Genesis 2:8.

[16] See T&C 145—Abraham 7:11.

[17] Helpmeet has many meanings and definitions: to rescue, to save, to be strong, to help, one who helps, but the Greek translation appears to capture the meaning God intended the best: an advocate, and intercessor, a counselor, and a helper.

was formed from something equal to him, able to stand beside him in all things.[18] Adam and Eve were joined in marriage by God who walked with them in the Garden in the cool of the day.[19] Eve was Adam's equal in every way, she completed him and the two, together, cleaved unto each other and were one flesh.[20]

To understand Priesthood necessitates that one must forget all one believes they know about the meaning of the word, about keys, authority, and the roles of men and women. Priesthood, in its simplest terms, is an association or fellowship between mankind and the Powers of Heaven, or angels who are on the other side of the veil.[21] The purpose of priesthood is to have valid ordinances and to obtain answers or direction from Heaven. The first can be accomplished through the lesser portion of priesthood, the Aaronic which can be passed, or conferred, from man to man. The second purpose comes through the Holy Priesthood after the Order of the son of God. Priesthood, in this highest form, is a call to serve and bless others. This power cannot be controlled by men. It comes by the voice of God who alone confers it upon a man.[22] In short,

---

[18] See OC Genesis 2:14, and T&C A Glossary of Gospel Terms, "Eve."

[19] See OC Genesis 2:17 and T&C 157:34-43.

[20] See T&C 145—Abraham 7:11. Definition of cleaved: Attached, held onto, embraced, clung, entwined, and adhered.

[21] See T&C A Glossary of Gospel Terms, "Priesthood."

[22] A man can be ordained to the Holy Order; however, God alone confirms the ordination. For example, Joseph Smith Sr. ordained his son, Hyrum Smith, to this higher priesthood in September 1840. On January 19, 1841, the voice of the Lord confirmed the ordination, "[T]hat my servant Hyrum may take the office of Priesthood and Patriarch, which was appointed unto him by his father by blessing, and also by right." See T&C 141:32. For Hyrum Smith to be ordained to the Holy Order, it was necessary that he have a wife.

"men do not make priests; God does. Men do not make prophets. God has reserved that right for Himself."[23]

The higher portion of Priesthood, or the Holy Order, includes men and women, as husband and wife. When a man and woman marry and the woman takes upon herself the name of her husband, they become one in name. This is to symbolize that they are together a new creation. The marriage is more than the two separate individuals. It becomes a living, breathing entity. In the scriptures, God calls the unity of a man and his wife by the name of the man. Therefore, whenever one reads the name of a servant of God in the scriptures, one should recognize that there are two individuals being spoken of, the man and his wife. For instance, when the scriptures speak only the name of Adam, it should be understood Eve is often included in that title.

Because Adam and Eve obtained Priesthood jointly before the foundation of this world and had subsequently been chosen to be the first man and woman, as such they had priestly responsibilities and stewardships placed upon them in Eden. When Eve succumbed to the serpent's temptation to "be as gods, knowing good and evil," she partook of the fruit of the Tree of Knowledge of Good and Evil and gave it also to Adam. When asked by God if they had eaten the fruit which He had commanded them "you shall not eat it, neither shall you touch it," Adam admitted that faced with the choice between obeying

---

It is interesting to note that he was not sealed to Jerusha until May 29, 1843, over two years after he was ordained and called by God to the Holy Order. Jerusha had died in 1837 and Hyrum was remarried to Mary Fielding, however, she chose to stand as proxy on Jerusha's behalf in order that Hyrum could be sealed to his first wife.

[23] T&C A Glossary of Gospel Terms, "Priesthood," and OC Numbers 7:22.

the command not to partake versus the command to remain with his wife, he chose to leave his father and mother and cling unto Eve.[24]

The breaking of God's command not to partake brought death, both physical and spiritual, into the world. The consequence of which was that Eve, and all women after her, lost Priesthood authority to perform public ordinances.[25] In the Millennium, when the earth has returned to a paradisiacal state, all things will be returned to their proper order. This necessarily includes Priesthood, which will be a mirror image of what was in the beginning.[26] The Lord's conditions for this fallen world surrounding women, the Priesthood, and public ordinances, or rites, does not refer to "those rites and performances the public are excluded from knowing. The Holy Order conveys blessings and information that is withheld from the world. . . . men and women jointly obtain the Holy Order."[27]

After the fall, God revealed information to the man, Adam, and the woman, Eve, which would help them, and all men and women after them, understand their eternal roles. Adam was primarily and specifically created "in the image of my Only Begotten," Jesus Christ.[28] As Christ's progeny, coupled with the possession of the Holy Order, Adam was given the right to preside over the human family. Joseph Smith taught:

---

[24] See OC Genesis 2:14-17, T&C 110—LoF 2:10, and T&C 145 Abraham 7:10-11.

[25] Public ordinances are rites such as baptism by immersion, blessing the sacrament of bread and wine, and bestowing the Covenant.

[26] See T&C 167.

[27] See T&C A Glossary of Gospel Terms, "Public Rites (Ordinances)."

[28] See OC Genesis 2:8.

[B]ecause he was the first and father of all, not only by progeny, but he was the first to hold the spiritual blessings, to whom was made known the plan of ordinances for the salvation of his posterity unto the end, and to whom Christ was first revealed, and through whom Christ has been revealed from Heaven and will continue to be revealed from henceforth. Adam holds the keys of the dispensation of the fullness of times; i.e., the dispensation of all the times have been and will be revealed through him, from the beginning to Christ, and from Christ to the end of all the dispensations that are to be revealed.[29]

As such, Adam inherited the role of knowledge. It is by his authority that the keys of the Holy Order are brought from Heaven whenever the Gospel is sent.[30] He is the father of the human family and as such one of his responsibilities is to watch over the ordinances, which are to be the same for ever and ever, and to "watch over them, to reveal them from Heaven to man or to send angels to reveal them."[31] This is a heavy burden, it is service, not aggrandizement. Due to the fall and the conditions placed upon the world at that time by God, outward, public ordinances such as baptism and sacramental rites are to be performed by men who have received God's authority to do so. This is in part because these ordinances and rites are directly linked to the Savior and His atonement.

The word authority today conveys the idea of the "power or right to give orders, make decisions, and enforce obedience."[32] Authority, by God's definition, is His approval to

---

[29] T&C 140:3.
[30] See T&C A Glossary of Gospel Terms, "Adam."
[31] T&C 140:6.
[32] See Oxford dictionary, "Authority."

act in some capacity for the benefit of mankind and is binding upon man. God has warned us that "it is the nature and disposition of almost all men, as soon as they get a little authority, as they suppose, they will immediately begin to exercise unrighteous dominion. Hence many are called, but few are chosen."[33] Joseph taught the following on this subject:

> [T]he rights of the Priesthood are inseparably connected with the Powers of Heaven and that the Powers of Heaven cannot be controlled nor handled, only upon the principles of righteousness. That they may be conferred upon us, it is true, but when we undertake to cover our sins or to gratify our pride, our vain ambition, or to exercise control, or dominion, or compulsion, upon the souls of the children of men in any degree of unrighteousness, behold, the Heavens withdraw themselves, the spirit of the Lord is grieved, and when it is withdrawn, Amen to the priesthood or the authority of that man.[34]

Other words, in relation to Adam's role, have also been twisted and corrupted by mankind. Adam was given dominion. The definition of dominion today is "sovereignty or control."[35] God's definition, as conveyed to Adam, should be more accurately understood as that of a caretaker, or a gardener who is "responsible for making the garden thrive, grow, and bear fruit." Adam "taught and pled and instructed, but he did not abridge the agency of his children, even when one of his sons killed another of his sons. . . . [he] held dominion, but he exercised it like our Lord, pleading for the

---

[33] T&C 139:5.
[34] Ibid.
[35] Oxford dictionary, Dominion.

best interest of others. [He] invited and solicited all to obey God, hoping for their best interests."[36]

In addition, Adam was set, by God, as a ruler over Eve, and by extension, her daughters. The word ruler today connotates the idea of a person who exercises government power or control.[37] God's definition is one who teaches truth, one who is accountable and responsible for instructing others.[38] It is Adam, and his sons, eternal role to become, obtain, and keep knowledge of, and instruct their posterity on, the correct character, perfections, and attributes of God.[39] Men will be accountable for how they fulfill their role. It was imperative that Eve be placed under Adam's rule in order that his redemption from the fall would become her redemption.[40] This was not done by God to minimize the woman, to hold her down, to subjugate her. Rather, because Adam, and all men after him, are the progeny of Jesus Christ, this allows all mankind to be rescued through Christ's atonement.[41]

Eve was likewise created in God's image. She was specifically created in the image of God the Mother. This was imperative in order that Eve, and all women after her, would inherit from the Mother the ability to create new life within the womb and bring it forth into the world. It is within the womb that the veil, the body of flesh and blood, is woven together for

---

[36] T&C A Glossary of Gospel Terms, "Dominion."
[37] See Oxford dictionary, Ruler.
[38] See NC Hebrews 1:59, 61, 64, NC Jacob 1:2, and T&C A Glossary of Gospel Terms, "Ruler."
[39] T&C 110—LoF 3:1-5 and T&C A Glossary of Gospel Terms, "Knowledge."
[40] See T&C A Glossary of Gospel Terms, "Ruler."
[41] Ibid.

the spirit to inhabit.[42] It is through the power of creation that the woman works in tandem with God. This is something only women can do. It is their responsibility, and they will be held accountable for how they fulfill this God-given authority.

In partnership with the man's eternal role to become knowledge, the woman's eternal role is to become wisdom, "because creation will only move forward if guided by wise counsel and prudent adaptations."[43]

> Only together do [the man and the woman] become complete and therefore *one*. Alone they are barren and unfruitful but joined they are infinite, because they continue. Knowledge alone may provide the spark of creation, but it is potentially dangerous when merely energetic. Creation must be wisely assisted to avoid peril. Wisdom alone is not an agent of action. Knowledge can initiate action, but wisdom is necessary to guide and counsel. The physical is a mirror of the spiritual. The seed of man provides the spark of life, but it is the womb of women where life develops. Likewise, the role of the woman in nurturing new life here is akin to the role of wisdom in eternity. Together, man and woman become whole, capable of creating and then nurturing a new creation.[44]

The partnership between the man and the woman is interwoven in perfect symmetry. Man can only come into this world through the woman, the woman can only get out of this world by the redemption of the man. Paul the Apostle taught this truth in this way:

---

[42] See T&C A Glossary of Gospel Terms, "Veil."

[43] T&C A Glossary of Gospel Terms, "Wisdom." Wisdom is a feminine noun in the scriptures (see OC Proverbs 1, NC Mosiah 5:14 for examples).

[44] Ibid.

But the woman is the glory of the man, for the man is not of the woman but the woman of the man, neither was the man created for the woman but the woman for the man. For this cause ought the woman to have a covering on her head: because of the angels. Nevertheless, neither is the man without the woman, neither the woman without the man, in the Lord. For as the woman is of the man, even so is the man also by the woman; but all things of God.[45]

This verse contains another misunderstood concept regarding women. The idea that a woman should cover her head, or her hair, is of ancient origin, but the reason for doing so has not been well preserved. Many women of various religious denominations wear head coverings. The reasons for doing so vary, and in far too many instances, the meaning has become corrupted and, in many instances, has been used as a tool to demean and demoralize women.

Some denominations believe that a head covering demonstrates modesty, others believe that it is an outward expression of the woman's faith in God, while still others believe that it is worn to remind mankind that the woman (Eve) sinned and should hide her head in shame, and still others that the woman's body is a temptation to men and as such must be covered.[46] Scholars of the Qur'an have interpreted the verses

---

[45] NC 1 Corinthians 1:44.

[46] The Talmud asserts that the woman is garbed like a mourner, covering her head in shame; Rabbi Joshua asked, "Why does a man go forth [sometimes] with uncovered head, while the woman goes forth with her head covered?" He replied: "This is like someone who committed a transgression and is embarrassed before other people, therefore the woman goes forth covered [for she sinned and is ashamed]." See The Shalvi/Hyman Encyclopedia of

which speak of a head covering as a curtain separating one part of Muhammad's house from another. Other scholars interpret these verses as the seclusion of women from men in the public sphere. Another interpretation, which is the most accurate of them all, refers to the head covering as "the veil which separates man or the world from God. In particular, it can mean the illusory aspect of creation."[47]

In The Church of Jesus Christ of Latter-day Saints (LDS), women wear a veil while serving in certain areas of the temple. The LDS Church has lost the significance of what this symbolizes. Women wear veils, not because they need to hide their heads in shame, nor is it done because they are temptresses, or are lesser than and subject to their husbands as too many religions claim. Rather, the wearing of a veil is a glorious reminder to all mankind that the great creative force is housed within the woman:

> [The] woman is veiled in temple ceremony to show that in a fallen world, trapped by decay and death, creation continues through her. Life springs anew, and what is sacred and pure is born into mortal life. It is not proper to remove the ceremonial veiling from the woman [in the LDS temples] unless the intention is to abort the symbol of new life and creation. [Removing it from ceremonial dress] destroys the symbol of the sacred power given to woman.[48]

Jewish Women, *Eve: Midrash and Aggadah* by Tamar Kadari. Retrieved from https://jwa.org/encyclopedia/article/eve-midrash-and-aggadah, accessed on February 19, 2024. See also Bereshit Rabbah Ch. 17(*Gen. Rabbah* 17:8).
[47] Glasse, Cyril (2001). "Hijab." *The New Encyclopedia of Islam*, pp. 179-180. Walnut Creek: Alta Mira Press.
[48] See T&C A Glossary of Gospel Terms, "Veil."

Now that we have a more correct understanding regarding Eve and all women after her, let us climb higher and examine what the scriptures say regarding the Mother: "A great deal can be learned about Heavenly Mother by searching for the word 'wisdom' in scripture. Very often the reference to 'wisdom' is to Her distinctly, not merely an abstract attribute, Wisdom refers almost exclusively to the Mother."[49] It is unfortunate that many religious denominations do not believe in a pre-earth existence. Yet, even for those that do, far too few have contemplated who Mary, the Mother of Christ, was before she came into this world. Nephi, a Book of Mormon prophet, was shown a vision wherein he beheld "a virgin most beautiful and fair above all other virgins." The angel said unto Nephi, "Knowest thou the condescension of God?"[50]

> [S]he, like all mankind, existed before this world. If God the Father obeys the same commandments He imposes upon His children, then for Him to father a child with any woman other than His Wife would violate His decrees about adultery and chastity. Before this creation, the Mother in Heaven was with the Father, she was beside Him when His work began, She was there when the plan was laid, the boundaries established, and the compass applied to establish order for the creation. All the Father knows, the Mother knows. . . . They are One.[51]

One of the dangers of revealing the existence of the

---

[49] See T&C A Glossary of Gospel Terms, "Mary, the Mother of Christ."
[50] NC 1 Nephi 3:8.
[51] See T&C A Glossary of Gospel Terms, "Mary, the Mother of Christ."

Mother is that too often once mankind learns of Her they begin to worship Her. Looking at the angel's question to Nephi to guide us, if "the condescension of God" referred to both the Mother of God as well as Her Son, then She was also a critical participant for providing the sacrificial lamb required for our redemption. Jesus Christ is the Savior and Redeemer whose atoning sacrifice is the means whereby we are rescued from sin and death. The moon symbolizes Her, a Mother watching over Her children throughout the night while reflecting the light of the Sun. From our perspective on earth, the moon and the sun are of equal size, the quintessential symbol of the union of a man and his wife. It is appropriate to regard God as both male and female, the original image of God, our Father and Mother.

Now that we have cleared away the dust and debris caused by generations of apostasy and laid a firm foundation in truth, let us move to the time of the Restoration of the Gospel with the Prophet, Joseph Smith. Joseph was a religious revolutionary, not only in the truth and knowledge he restored, but also in his regard toward women. Joseph treated his wife, Emma, with respect and admiration. He looked to her for prudent guidance and wise counsel. She was his equal, his partner, and his truest love. Joseph called Emma his "choice in preference to any other woman [he had] ever seen."[52] She was his confidant, his greatest support, and his closest friend. He was loyal and faithful to her and to their marriage in word and in deed.

Joseph believed that women could behold the face of

---

[52] Smith, Lucy Mack (1845) *Joseph Smith the Prophet and His Progenitors,* p. 105. Reprinted in 1912 by the Reorganized Church of Jesus Christ of Latter Day Saints. Lamoni, Iowa: Herald Publishing House.

God. In a time and era where men were the ecclesiastical leaders, revered by their congregations as the intercessor between themselves and God, the idea that women, who were not ordained to priesthood offices, could stand in God's presence was radical. Joseph taught the women of the Nauvoo Relief Society:

> [I]t is natural for females to have feelings of charity, you are now placed in a situation where you can act according to those sympathies which God has planted in your bosoms. If you live up to these principles how great and glorious! If you live up to your privilege, the angels cannot be restrained from being your associates, females, if they are pure and innocent can come into the presence of God; for what is more pleasing to God than innocence; you must be innocent or you cannot come up before God.[53]

Men and women have too often equated priesthood with authority and power, specifically authority and power over others. This distortion of truth takes the focus off what may be more important: Faith. It was by faith that the worlds were formed.[54] It was by faith that Melchizedek, as a child, "stopped the mouths of lions and quenched the violence of fire."[55] Faith is not limited to a specific gender, it is a principle of action and is available to all who act on their beliefs. In that same talk, Joseph taught the women:

> [S]igns, such as healing the sick, casting out devils &c.

---

[53] Nauvoo Relief Society Minute Book, p. 38, The Joseph Smith Papers, accessed March 9, 2024, https://www.josephsmithpapers.org/paper-summary/nauvoo-relief-society-minute-book/61.
[54] See T&C 110—LoF 1:14-17.
[55] OC Genesis 7:18.

should follow all that believe whether male or female ... if the sisters should have faith to heal the sick, let all hold their tongues, and let everything roll on. ... [R]especting the female laying on hands ... there could be no devil in it if God gave his sanction by healing — that there could be no more sin in any female laying hands on the sick than in wetting the face with water — that it is no sin for any body to do that [who] has faith, or if the sick has faith to be healed by the administration.[56]

What if all we think we know about priesthood is inaccurate and incomplete? What if we have confused priestly service for our fellowman with gender, rank, position, and institutional authority? Joseph Smith taught that all Priesthood is Melchizedek, or in other words, the Holy Order after the Order of the Son of God, but there are different degrees or portions of it.[57] If Priesthood is an association, consider, then, that the Aaronic priesthood is a fellowship with angels and the Telestial world. The Melchizedek is a fellowship with Jesus Christ and the Terrestrial World. And the Patriarchal and Matriarchal portion of Priesthood is an association with God, the Father and Mother, and the Celestial World.

This, then would be why one who uses the priesthood in the name of Jesus Christ, or God the Father, to serve and bless mankind, would need Their authority to act on Their behalf. Not every man or woman who claims authority to act on God's behalf is acknowledged by God. This is why God

---

[56] Nauvoo Relief Society Minute Book, p. 36, The Joseph Smith Papers, accessed March 9, 2024, https://www.josephsmithpapers.org/paper-summary/nauvoo-relief-society-minute-book/59.

[57] Ehat, Andrew F. & Cook, Lyndon W. (1980). *The Words of Joseph Smith*, p. 59. Provo, UT: Religious Studies Center Brigham Young University.

advises us to test the fruits of all who profess to say, "Lord, Lord, have we not prophesied in your name, and in your name have cast out devils, and in your name done many wonderful works?"[58]

One who has connected with heaven itself, and been sent on an errand by Them, has not only authority but also power in the Priesthood. Doing so does not set the person above any other, rather it gives them the opportunity to serve and bless others, reaching out to lift mankind to greater heights. Whenever a woman serves and blesses those within her sphere of influence, she is acting the part of a priestess:

> Mothers who minister to their children in patience and love will undoubtedly be among those whom the Lord will remember in the final day.... [It is] little acts through which one finds their Lord....[The] enduring power of a mother's love . . . like the Lord's own sacrifice . . . this often underappreciated calling has been and continues to be a lifetime of service. Mothers oftentimes do not take time to study because they are too busily engaged in the *actual work* of charity, love, and service. Some may not be able to construct a scripture-based explanation or exposition, but they recognize truth by the light that has been acquired within them by their fidelity to the Lord's system of conferring light and truth.[59]

Mankind can repent of the false traditions of their fathers which has caused the enmity that exists between the sexes. The Gods know that in our fallen world, mankind is susceptible to envy, strife, ambition, selfishness, and

---

[58] NC Matthew 3:47.
[59] T&C A Glossary of Gospel Terms, "Mothers."

contention. They challenge and encourage us to ascend above the natural man, to honor, respect, value, and love one other.

It is time to cease clamoring and coveting each other's eternal responsibilities. It is time to trust the Gods: They are no respecter of persons, every soul in every nation has an equal privilege to lay hold upon truth, to work righteousness, and to be accepted of Them.[60] We have a Father and a Mother who do all things together in unity, harmony, and divine partnership to bring to pass the immortality and eternal life of all mankind.[61] They are the pattern we should strive to follow. Women can rise up to their privileges, and embrace, rejoice, celebrate, and cultivate their divinely appointed role as Wisdom.

---

[60] See NC Acts 6:7, NC Moroni 8:3, T&C 22:6, 54:6, 80:4, 110—LoF 3:11, 17, 23, 38, 47, and 159:33.
[61] See OC Genesis 1:7.

Essay 9

H. O. P. E.
For a Better World

Whitney N. Horning

©2023

This world is a juxtaposition of opposites: good and evil, joy and sorrow, peace and conflict, faith and disbelief, creation and entropy, order and chaos, to name a few. We are surrounded by a cacophony of voices and a tumult of opinions which can make discerning and holding onto truth challenging. The struggles and great sufferings we experience in this life can cause even the naturally cheerful and optimistic to cry out, "O God, where are you?"[1] Most likely because Jesus Christ's ministry was filled with miraculous healings, Christians today have an idea that if one believes in and has

---

[1] See Joseph Smith letter to the Church, Liberty Jail, March 20, 1839. Found in Teachings & Commandments (T&C) 138:4-5: "O God, where are you? And where is the pavilion that covers your hiding place? How long shall your hand be stayed and your eye, yea, your pure eye, behold from the eternal Heavens the wrongs of your people and of your servants, and your ear be penetrated with their cries? Yea, O Lord, how long shall they suffer these wrongs and unlawful oppressions before your heart shall be softened towards them, and your bowels be moved with compassion towards them? O Lord God Almighty, maker of heaven, earth, and seas, and of all things that in them are, and who controls and subjects the Devil, and the dark and benighted dominion of Sheol, stretch forth your hand, let your eye pierce, let your pavilion be taken up, let your hiding place no longer be covered, let your ear be inclined, let your heart be softened and your bowels moved with compassion toward us, let your anger be kindled against our enemies; and in the fury of your heart, with your sword avenge us of our wrongs. Remember your suffering saint, O our God, and your servants will rejoice in your name for ever."

216

accepted the Lord as their Savior, nothing difficult, harmful, or evil should befall them. As the sun shines and the rain falls on the righteous and the wicked alike, so, too does suffering, sorrow, and pain. The realities of this life can cause a moroseness, a gloominess, a depression. This may be one reason why the Lord reminds us often in scripture that because He has overcome the world we should be of good cheer, and that we should have hope, even a hope for a better world.[2]

Hope is an interesting word. Four letters that contain so much opportunity and possibility:

To have suffering end.

To find peace and happiness.

To end sadness and despair.

To be filled with joy and gladness.

The definition of HOPE is a desire of some good, accompanied with at least a slight expectation of obtaining it, or a belief that it is obtainable; confidence in a future event and to trust in with confident expectation of good.[3]

In the Book of Mormon, there is a record of an ancient prophet of the Lord named Ether who lived on this land. Ether wrote about a hope that makes us sure and steadfast, always abounding in good works, being led to glorify God.[4] In consideration of this scripture, let us focus on four areas of HOPE:

---

[2] See New Covenants, The New Testament (NC—NT) John 9:18: "In the world you shall have tribulation, but be of good cheer; I have overcome the world" and T&C 171—Testimony of St. John 10:29: "In this world there are difficult trials to be faced by my followers, but those who remain devoted will, like me, finish the path and experience the fullness of joy."

[3] Webster's Dictionary, Hope.

[4] New Covenants, the Book of Mormon (NC—BoM), Ether 5:1.

Happiness

Opportunity

Peace

Eternity

Attaining this type of Hope is a journey that cannot be reached in a day, a week, a month, or even a year. Hope is a lifetime pursuit, an eternal pursuit.

Happiness: The pursuit of happiness has become a popular catch phrase of much interest in our world today. It has become a mantra used to force society into supporting, even allowing, people the right to pursue whatever it is that makes them "happy." To justify the pursuit of secular beliefs and ungodly behaviors, the Declaration of Independence is invoked. In particular, the portion that reads: "We hold these truths to be self-evident, that all men are created equal, that they are endowed by their Creator with certain unalienable Rights, that among these are Life, Liberty and the pursuit of Happiness."

What people today have lost sight of, and what has become corrupted in our modern world, is what those who wrote the Declaration of Independence understood in their time when they included the words "the pursuit of happiness." In 1776, this phrase meant that all mankind had a right to live their life in conformity with the will of God. The phrase comes from Scottish moral philosophers who differentiated between "imaginary happiness" and "true happiness." These philosophers understood that it was not merely the pursuit of pleasure, property, or self-interest, but the freedom to make decisions that result in the best life possible for a human being that leads one toward true happiness.

Ancient Greek philosopher Aristotle believed that the ultimate goal in life was to achieve eudaimonia, or the highest human good.[5] He believed that eudaimonia was not simply virtue, nor pleasure, but rather the exercise of virtue. In 1689, English philosopher John Locke wrote:

> *The necessity of pursuing happiness [is] the foundation of liberty.* As therefore the highest perfection of intellectual nature lies in a careful and constant *pursuit of true and solid happiness*; so the care of ourselves, that we mistake not imaginary for real happiness, is the necessary foundation of our liberty. The stronger ties we have to an unalterable *pursuit of happiness* in general, which is our greatest good, and which, as such, our desires always follow, the more are we free from any necessary determination of our will to any particular action.[6]

Francis Hutcheson, a leading Scottish Enlightenment figure in the 18th century defined the pursuit of happiness as a battle between our reason and our passion so that we can be our best selves and serve others.[7] Joseph Smith Jr. explained the

---

[5] Eudaimonia is a Greek word which means the state or condition of "good spirit" and is commonly translated as "happiness" or "welfare." In the works of Aristotle, eudaimonia was the term for the highest human good.

[6] Locke, John (1689), *An Essay Concerning Human Understanding*, p. 348. See also Pursuit of Happiness blog retrieved from https://www.pursuit-of-happiness.org/history-of-happiness/john-locke/#:~:text=The%20pursuit%20of%20happiness%20is%20the%20foundation%20of%20individual%20liberty,experience%20of%20pleasure%20and%20pain, accessed on July 13, 2023.

[7] See Hutchison, Francis (1747), A Short Introduction to Moral Philosophy, retrieved from https://constitutioncenter.org/the-constitution/historic-document-library/detail/francis-hutchesona-short-introduction-to-moral-philosophy-1747, accessed on July 10, 2023.

concept in this way:

> Such was and always will be the situation of the saints of God: that unless they have an actual knowledge that the course that they are pursuing is according to the will of God, they will grow weary in their minds and faint, for such has been and always will be the opposition in the hearts of unbelievers and those that know not God, against the pure and unadulterated religion of Heaven (the only thing which ensures eternal life), that they will persecute to the uttermost all that worship God according to his revelations, receive the truth in the love of it, and submit themselves to be guided and directed by his will, and drive them to such extremities that nothing short of an actual knowledge of their being the favorites of Heaven, and of their having embraced that order of things which God has established for the redemption of man, will enable them to exercise that confidence in him necessary for them to overcome the world and obtain that crown of glory which is laid up for them that fear God.[8]

God explains it in this way, "Men are that they might have joy."[9]

Clinical psychologists have studied the concept of happiness in depth. Specifically, how one goes about attaining it. What they concluded surprised many in the behavioral science community. It was discovered that the feeling of happiness is fleeting and unpredictable. They found that if attaining worldly happiness becomes the meaning or purpose of life, then when the feeling of happiness leaves it brings about a feeling of emptiness, even of failure. Psychologists learned

---

[8] T&C 110—Lectures on Faith (LoF) 6:4.
[9] NC—BoM 2 Nephi 1:10.

that in order for a person to obtain a truer, more lasting form of happiness, or joy, they must pursue proper meaning.[10]

In other words, we will obtain what we aim for. If we aim at dark and corrupt things, we will become dark and corrupt. The reverse is also true. When we look up and aim at something higher, when we focus on a more noble purpose or target, when we "act right" we become purer and more filled with Light and Truth. This is how we can build proper meaning in our lives.

The Lord gives Light to everyone who comes into the world, an inborn instinct for ethics and meaning.[11] We have within us an intrinsic desire to take the highest path; to take on the challenge to do better and to be better than we were yesterday; to live a life that is pleasing to the Lord. To aid us on our journey to become a higher, more noble self, the Gods have given us bumper guards or safety nets. These are known as commandments but can also be understood to be fences, boundaries, or walls which have been set by Them and are the same throughout eternity. The Lord has said, "If you love me, stand ready, watching for every communication I will send to you . . . He that treasures my teaching, and stands ready, watching for every communication I send him, is he who shows love for me."[12] In other words, those who love the Lord will keep His commandments.[13]

---

[10] Lott, T. (2018, January 21). Jordan Peterson: 'The pursuit of happiness is a pointless goal.' *The Guardian*. Retrieved from https://www.theguardian.com/global/2018/jan/21/jordan-peterson-self-help-author-12-steps-interview, accessed on July 1, 2023.

[11] See T&C 82:18.

[12] T&C 171—Testimony of St. John 10:11–12.

[13] See NC—NT John 9:8.

As we take on the challenge of living in this fallen, mortal world, we can attain a hope of being spiritually and psychologically reborn despite the inevitable suffering that this life brings. We can look up to Heaven and to the example of our Lord, where there is no corruption, and set our sights on becoming like the Son of God. The proper joy, or happiness, we should be seeking is an emotion excited by the acquisition of good and comes from a deeper place, a connection with the Godly and divine. This type of happiness and joy, brought about by aiming for a higher, more God-like purpose, is everlasting. Having the courage to voluntarily shoulder the great burden of being, in order to move toward that meaning is what the stories of the scriptures are all about. Human beings are capable of doing very difficult things and of making great sacrifices. With God, we can be stronger than the suffering that is part of this world.[14]

The surest way to obtain an everlasting joy and happiness is through a personal relationship with the Lord, who descended below it all and by so doing redeemed all of creation from the Fall.[15] He is the "Man of Sorrows, who was acquainted with grief."[16] Precisely because the Lord sacrificed and suffered all things, He knows how to succor each of us and is able to wipe away our every tear.[17] This is why He is called the

---

[14] See NC—NT Matthew 9:23, "...But Jesus beheld their thoughts and said unto them, With men, this is impossible; but if they will forsake all things for my sake, with God, whatever things I speak are possible."

[15] See T&C 86:1, 110—LoF 5:2, 139:8, 157:50, 161:21, and 175:4.

[16] OC Isaiah 19:2.

[17] NC—NT Revelation 8:8 RE.

Second Comforter.[18] As you take on the challenge of living life according to the will of the Lord, you are pursuing happiness. In so doing, you will be afforded opportunities to come to know God.

Opportunities to Know God: This is life eternal—that we might come to know the only true God, and Jesus Christ whom He has sent.[19] We are on an eternal journey not only to come to know God but to become like Them. We are sent down to this fallen world for the purpose of being added upon. This life affords ample opportunities for each of us to come to know God. This is achieved through learning and experience. Opportunities to connect with God and to come to know Them come in a wide variety of ways, too numerous and too varied to list.

We are in a constant state of inertia. We are always moving. There is no standing still. Our choices will move us, and that movement will take us either closer to or further away from God. We are the ones who choose whether we progress or regress. Hyrum Smith compared this concept to the moon, how it "waxes and wanes."[20] In other words, like the moon, we either increase and gain light or decrease and lose light,

---

[18] See NC—NT John 9:8; T&C 171—The Testimony of St. John 10:13; and T&C—A Glossary of Gospel Terms, "Comforter, The" and "Comforter, The Second."

[19] NC—NT John 9:19.

[20] Hyrum Smith, August 1, 1843, "Those of the Terrestrial Glory either advance to the Celestial or recede to the Telestial else the moon could not be a type 'It waxes & wanes.'" CHL MS 4409 Scriptural Items, Franklin D. Richards, retrieved from, https://catalog.churchofjesuschrist.org/assets/03558fd5-b5b4-4105-90e2-6e3f555bceab/0/35?lang=eng accessed on July 17, 2024.

sometimes on a daily basis. Jacob of the Old Testament had a vision which demonstrated this concept: "And he dreamed, and behold, a ladder set up on the earth, and the top of it reached to Heaven. And behold, the angels of God ascending and descending on it. And behold, the Lord stood above it and said, I am the Lord God of Abraham your father, and the God of Isaac."[21]

The scriptures are personal accounts of individuals, couples, and families who, through learning and experience, have taken the opportunities afforded them to come to know God. In turn, they have qualified to receive the promise of eternal life. A man and his wife who have laid hold upon these promises may be called to become servants unto their families, and some even to their fellowmen. God instructs His servants to record their ministry as well as their encounters with the divine for the purpose of teaching each of us the path that we too must walk to come to know God.

In this fallen world, we are beset, not only by the appetites, passions, and desires of the natural man, but also by the temptations of the devil.[22] Joseph Smith revealed that this is part of God's plan for our learning and growth: "It must needs be that the Devil should tempt the children of men, or they could not be agents unto themselves, for if they never should have bitter, they could not know the sweet."[23] Like Father Adam and Mother Eve, each of us begin this life as pure and innocent before God. As we age, have experiences, and make choices, we either draw nearer to or more distant from God.

---

[21] OC Genesis 9:20.
[22] See NC—BoM Mosiah 1:16.
[23] T&C 9:11.

Each of us is uniquely created and as such we will relate to and connect with God in our own unique way. At times, we may feel that God is no longer speaking to us, but scripture testifies that at times such as these, it is we who have stopped listening. Consider that even after Cain murdered his brother, Abel, the Lord continued to speak to him,

> Not only was there a manifestation made unto Adam of the existence of a God, but Moses informs us ... that God condescended to talk with Cain after his great transgression in slaying his brother, and that Cain knew that it was the Lord that was talking with him, so that when he was driven out from the presence of his brethren, he carried with him the knowledge of the existence of a God.[24]

In this we see that God never moves away and never cuts us off. He stands at our door and knocks waiting for us to let Him in.[25] Furthermore, the Lord has made this promise, "[E]very soul who forsakes their sins, and comes unto me, and calls on my name, and obeys my voice, and keeps all my commandments, shall see my face and know that I am."[26] The Lord intends to fulfill His promises. We are the ones who keep Him distant and His promises from being fulfilled.

Joseph Smith Jr. is one of this world's examples of an individual who took the opportunities given to him to connect with and come to know God. Like all true servants of the Lord, he, too, spent his life in service to his fellowman, attempting to

---

[24] T&C 110—LoF 2:32.

[25] See NC—NT Revelation 1:20, T&C A Glossary of Gospel Terms, "Doctrine of Christ."

[26] T&C 93:1.

lift their eyes heavenward, and to inspire their faith to grow until they, too, could enter into and withstand God's presence. To aid in this effort, Joseph created a series of lessons titled *Lectures on Faith*. In lecture 4 he taught:

> Let us here observe that the real design which the God of Heaven had in view in making the human family acquainted with his attributes was that they, through the ideas of the existence of his attributes, might be enabled to exercise faith in him, and through the exercise of faith in him might obtain eternal life. For without the idea of the existence of the attributes which belong to God, the minds of men could not have power to exercise faith on him so as to lay hold upon eternal life. The God of Heaven, understanding most perfectly the constitution of human nature and the weakness of man, knew what was necessary to be revealed and what ideas must be planted in their minds in order that they might be enabled to exercise faith in him unto eternal life.[27]

Joseph laid out the attributes of God that are necessary to know and understand in order for any rational being of the human family to have an idea of so that they might exercise faith unto salvation. The attributes are, in order: knowledge, faith (or power), justice, judgment, mercy, and truth.[28]

Knowledge:

> [W]ithout the knowledge of all things, God would not be able to save any portion of his creatures. For it is by reason of the knowledge which he has of all things, from the beginning to the end, that enables him to give

---

[27] T&C 110—LoF 4:2.
[28] See T&C 110—LoF 4.

that understanding to his creatures, by which they are made partakers of eternal life; and if it were not for the idea existing in the minds of men that God had all knowledge, it would be impossible for them to exercise faith in him.[29]

Faith or Power:

[U]nless God had power over all things and was able, by his power, to control all things and thereby deliver his creatures who put their trust in him from the power of all beings that might seek their destruction, whether in Heaven, on earth, or in hell, men could not be saved. But with the idea of the existence of this attribute planted in the mind, men feel as though they had nothing to fear, who put their trust in God, believing that he has power to save all who come to him to the very uttermost.[30]

Justice:

[W]ithout the idea of the existence of the attribute justice in the Deity, men could not have confidence sufficiently to place themselves under his guidance and direction, for they would be filled with fear and doubt, lest the Judge of all the earth would not do right; and thus fear, or doubt, existing in the mind, would preclude the possibility of the exercise of faith in him for life and salvation. But when the idea of the existence of the attribute justice in the Deity is fairly planted in the mind, it leaves no room for doubt to get into the heart, and the mind is enabled to cast itself upon the Almighty without fear, and without doubt, and with most unshaken confidence, believing that

---

[29] T&C 110—LoF 4:11.
[30] T&C 110—LoF 4:12.

the Judge of all the earth will do right.[31]

Judgment:

But no sooner is the idea of the existence of this attribute planted in the minds of men than it gives power to the mind for the exercise of faith and confidence in God and they are enabled, by faith, to lay hold on the promises which are set before them and wade through all the tribulations and afflictions to which they are subjected by reason of the persecution from those who know not God and obey not the gospel of our Lord Jesus Christ; believing that in due time the Lord will come out in swift judgment against their enemies, and they shall be cut off from before him, and that in his own due time he will bear them off conquerors and more than conquerors in all things.[32]

Mercy:

[W]ithout the idea of the existence of this attribute in the Deity, the spirits of the saints would faint in the midst of the tribulations, afflictions, and persecutions which they have to endure for righteousness' sake. But when the idea of the existence of this attribute is once established in the mind, it gives life and energy to the spirits of the saints, believing that the mercy of God will be poured out upon them in the midst of their afflictions, and that he will compassionate them in their sufferings, and that the mercy of God will lay hold of them and secure them in the arms of his love so that they will receive a full reward for all their sufferings.[33]

---

[31] T&C 110—LoF 4:13.
[32] T&C 110—LoF 4:14.
[33] T&C 110—LoF 4:15.

Truth:

[W]ithout the idea of the existence of this attribute the mind of man could have nothing upon which it could rest with certainty; all would be confusion and doubt. But with the idea of the existence of this attribute in the Deity in the mind, all the teachings, instructions, promises, and blessings become realities, and the mind is enabled to lay hold of them with certainty and confidence, believing that these things, and all that the Lord has said, shall be fulfilled in their time, and that all the cursings, denunciations, and judgments pronounced upon the heads of the unrighteous will also be executed in due time of the Lord. And by reason of the truth and veracity of him, the mind beholds its deliverance and salvation as being certain.[34]

Those who are willing to reflect sincerely and candidly upon the idea of these attributes in God will see that they lay a sure foundation for the exercise of faith in Him for life and salvation. It is through the opportunities we have in this life by which we are able to consider God's attributes and to see those attributes in action within our own lives and the lives of those around us. As we learn and grow in belief, faith, knowledge, and wisdom, we can choose to acknowledge these attributes and incorporate them into our own self and being. As we continue on the path to come to know the Lord, one day we might be afforded the right to live in a community where no one need teach their neighbor, know the Lord, for all will know Him.[35]

---

[34] T&C 110—LoF 4:16.
[35] See NC—NT Hebrews 8:11.

Peace: What anguish, pain, and distress we suffer in this life. Some of which we bring upon ourselves by the choices we make, some of which is wrought upon us by others, and some of which are simply part of this mortal existence. When we are the cause of our own suffering, it can be difficult to process and to forgive ourselves, especially if those choices have also harmed others.

As Hyrum Smith languished in Liberty Jail, he suffered greatly in body, in mind, and in spirit. He reflected upon this thought, "Tis man's inhumanity to man that makes countless thousands to mourn."[36] We have each been endowed with the God-given ability to choose our beliefs and our actions. This life can be a dark and difficult place, and as such we stumble around, bumping into each other. Even those who have light might be blinded by it and may also cause harm to others. We each have the will and the power to make our fellowman, including ourselves, to mourn.

Some of the suffering we will experience, and is inevitable in this life, is part of being human, our spirit housed in a veil made of flesh and blood. The fragility of the flesh, and the inevitability that we will all leave this earth through death, means each of us is susceptible to ill health, genetic diseases or disorders, and injuries. All of us will be touched by death throughout our mortal sojourn: death of friends, family, and

---

[36] See Hyrum Smith poem to Mary Fielding Smith, Liberty Jail, March 23, 1839. Mary Fielding Smith collection, circa 1832-1848; Hyrum Smith letters to Mary Fielding Smith, 1839; Church History Library, https://catalog.churchofjesuschrist.org/assets/4d40e172-2d35-4d27-97a1-e7fe20287325/0/11?lang=eng (accessed on date updated on: February 3, 2024). See also, Horning, Whitney N. (2022). Hyrum Smith A Prophet Unsung, appendix, p. 429.

eventually our own. None of us can escape the suffering that comes from being human.

The abuses and trauma we suffer at the hands of others, through our own choices and actions, and by those things that well may be God-caused, God-given, or God-induced means that it is up to each of us to find peace of mind within ourselves, with our fellowman, and with God. Well might we ask, how do we do this? Is it merely the act of forgiving? Bestowing charity upon ourselves, our fellowman, and toward God? Believers in Christ have read about and been taught about His great Atonement. Knowing more about this infinite and incomprehensible act can help us through our own moments of pain and suffering.[37]

There was a man in Christ who beheld a vision of the great suffering of the Lord, Jesus Christ, in the Garden of Gethsemane:

> He saw that as the Lord knelt in prayer, His vicarious suffering began. Christ was overcome by pain and anguish. He felt within Him, not just the pains of sin, but also the illnesses men suffer as a result of the Fall and their foolish and evil choices. The suffering was long and the challenge difficult. The Lord suffered the afflictions. He was healed from the sickness. He overcame the pains, and patiently bore the infirmities until, finally, he returned to **peace of mind** and strength of body. It took an act of will and **hope** for Him to overcome the affliction which had been poured upon Him. He overcame the separation caused by these afflictions and reconciled with His Father. He was at peace with all mankind.

---

[37] See NC—BoM Alma 16:34.

He thought His sufferings were over, but to His astonishment another wave overcame Him. This one was much greater than the first. The Lord, who had been kneeling, fell forward onto His hands at the impact of the pain that was part of a greater, second wave.

This second wave was so much greater than the first that it seemed to entirely overcome the Lord. The Lord was now stricken with physical injuries as well as spiritual affliction. As he suffered anew, His flesh was torn . . . His suffering was both body and spirit, and there was anguish of thought, feeling, and soul.

The Lord overcame this second wave of suffering, and again found peace of mind and strength of body; and His heart filled with love despite what he had suffered. Indeed, it was charity or love that allowed Him to overcome. He was at **peace with His Father, and with all mankind,** but it required another, still greater act of will and charity than the first for Him to do so.

Again, the Lord thought His suffering was over. He stayed on His hands and knees for a moment to collect Himself when another wave of torment burst upon Him. This wave struck Him with such force he fell forward upon His face. He was afflicted by this greater wave. He was then healed, only to then be afflicted again as the waves of torment overflowed. Wave after wave poured out upon Him, with only moments between them. The Lord's suffering progressed from a lesser to a greater portion of affliction; for as one would be overcome by Him, the next, greater affliction would then be poured out. Each wave of suffering was only preparation for the next, greater wave.

The pains of mortality, disease, injury, and infirmity, together with the sufferings of sin, transgressions, guilt of mind, and unease of soul, the horrors of recognition of the evils men had inflicted upon others, were all poured out upon Him, with confusion and perplexity multiplied upon Him.

He longed for it to be over, and thought it would end long before it finally ended. With each wave he thought it would be the last, but then another came upon Him, and then yet another. . . .

The Lord pleaded again with the Father that "this cup may pass" from Him. But the Lord was determined to suffer the Father's will and not His own. Therefore, a final wave came upon Him with such violence as to cut Him at every pore. It seemed for a moment that he was torn apart, and that blood came out of every pore. The Lord writhed in pain upon the ground as this great final torment was poured upon Him.

All virtue was taken from Him. All the great life force in Him was stricken and afflicted. All the light turned to darkness. He was humbled, drained, and left with nothing. It is not possible for a man to bear such pains and live, but with nothing more than will, **hope in His Father**, and charity toward all men, He emerged from the final wave of torment, knowing he had suffered all this for His Father and His brethren. **By His hope and great charity, trusting in the Father, the Lord returned from this dark abyss and found grace again, His heart being filled with love toward the Father and all men.** . . .

[T]he waves of torment suffered by the Lord came in pairs which mirrored each other. The first of each wave poured upon the Lord those feelings, regrets, recriminations, and pains felt by those who injured their fellow man. Then followed a second wave, which mirrored the first, but imposed the pains suffered by the victims of the acts committed by those in the first wave. Instead of the pains of those who inflict hurt or harm, it was now the anger, bitterness, and resentments felt by those who suffered these wrongs. From each wave of suffering, . . . the Lord would overcome the evil feelings associated with these wrongs, and find His heart again **filled with peace**. . . . The greater difficulty in these paired waves of torment was always overcoming the suffering of the victim. With these waves the Lord learned to overcome the victims' resentments, to forgive, and to heal both body and spirit. . . . The victim . . . always feels it is their right to hold resentment, to judge their persecutor, and to withhold peace and love for their fellow men. The Lord was required to overcome both so that he could succor both.

In the pairing of the waves, the first torment was of the mind and spirit, and the second was torment of mind, spirit, and body.

The Lord experienced all the horror and regret wicked men feel for their crimes when they finally see the truth. He experienced the suffering of their victims whose righteous anger and natural resentment and disappointment must also be shed, and forgiveness given, in order for them **to find peace**. He overcame them all. He descended below them all. He comprehends it all. And **he knows how to bring peace** to them all. He knows how to love others whether they are the one who has given offense or the one who is a victim of the offense. . . .

In this extremity there was madness itself as he mirrored the evil which would destroy Him, and **learned how to come to peace with the Father** after killing the Son of God, and to love all those involved without restraint and without pretense even before they did these terrible deeds. His suffering, therefore, encompassed all that has happened, all that did happen, and all that would happen in the future.[38]

Each of us has done and will do things that we need to come to terms with, accept, forgive, and reconcile. This vision suggests that as we come to peace with what we have done as well as what others have done, we can be healed. It is important to note that when we find ourselves in situations where we cry out, "O God, where are you? How can you allow this to happen? Have You forsaken me?" that even our Lord had to come to peace with what His Father allowed to happen to Him. There should be no shame in the wrestle to come to peace with the Lord.

As we embrace and extend love through grace, charity, compassion, and forgiveness to ourselves, we will become much more inclined and capable of extending the same to others. How we judge others is how we will be judged. This may be, in part, because the faults and the criticisms we extend to others are often a reflection of how harshly we criticize and condemn our own selves. As we work on healing ourselves, we will become better equipped to forgive and love others, including the Lord.

Repentance. Reconciliation. Forgiveness. Charity. We can repent and accept the repentance of others. We can strive for reconciliation for the choices we have made that have hurt ourselves and others. We can accept the reconciliation

---

[38] T&C 161; emphasis in bold added. Consider that the waves of suffering that overcame the Lord are represented by the labor pains, or waves of contractions, a woman experiences as she gives birth.

extended by those who have harmed us.[39] We can forgive ourselves and accept the forgiveness of others. We can throw a cloak of charity upon ourselves and upon others.[40] In two different, yet similar, temple events, the Sermon on the Mount, and the Sermon at the Temple in Bountiful, the Lord encouraged His disciples to take on the challenge of healing through coming to a peace of mind, "Blessed are all the peacemakers, for they shall be called the children of God."[41] With the Lord's help, we can find peace of mind within ourselves, with others, and with God.[42]

Eternal Journey: We are eternal beings on an eternal journey of learning and growth. Joseph taught, "All spirit is matter but it is more fine or pure and can only be discerned by purer eyes. We can't see it but when our bodies are purified, we shall see that it is all matter."[43] If matter cannot be destroyed, then it is eternal. The scriptures teach that we lived in a state of existence before we were born into mortal bodies of flesh and blood on this earth and that we will continue to exist after this life has ended.[44] Beginning with Adam, prophets have taught,

---

[39] To accept reconciliation and forgiveness from someone who has harmed us does not mean that we put ourselves back into a situation where they can continue to harm us.

[40] Ehat and Cook (1980), *The Word of Joseph Smith*, p. 80, Salt Lake City: Bookcraft, Inc.

[41] NC—NT Matthew 3:12 and NC-BofM 3 Nephi 5:18.

[42] There are some great tools available today to help us on our healing journey of peace, a few of them are: prayer, meditation, mindfulness, professional counseling, studying and understanding the attributes of God and His gospel.

[43] Ehat and Cook (1980), *The Word of Joseph Smith*, p. 203, Salt Lake City: Bookcraft, Inc.

[44] See T&C 145—The Book of Abraham 6:1 and NC—BoM Alma 19:5-8.

"God is eternal. . . . He had no beginning, and can have no end. Eternity means that which is without beginning or end. . . the *soul* is eternal; and had no beginning; it can have no end."[45] The definition of the soul, according to Joseph, is the spirit and body together.[46]

Here, on this earth, we are souls currently participating in a cycle of learning and growth. We have been "moving from grace to grace" throughout eons of time.[47] These cycles can be described as a plan of progression, or Plan of Salvation. This is the plan whereby we become educated; the plan of coming to know God and the principles of godliness.[48] This eternal journey is not meant to be comprehended at once. Rather, it is designed to develop us line upon line, precept upon precept.[49] Eventually, we will have progressed to a point where we will "go no more out."[50] Joseph Smith compared this plan to climbing a ladder:

> When you climb up a ladder, you must begin at the bottom, and ascend step by step, until you arrive at the top; and so it is with the principles of the gospel — you must begin with the first, and go on until you learn all the principles of exaltation. But it will be a great while after you have passed through the veil before you will have learned them. It is not all to be comprehended in this world; it will be a great work to learn our salvation

---

[45] Ehat and Cook (1980), *The Word of Joseph Smith*, p. 33, Salt Lake City: Bookcraft, Inc.

[46] See T&C 86:2.

[47] See T&C 93:7.

[48] See T&C—A Glossary of Gospel Terms, "Grace" and "Plan of Salvation."

[49] See T&C 151:7.

[50] See NC-NT Revelation 1:18, NC—BoM Alma 5:6, 15:14, 16:37, 3 Nephi 13:6, and Helaman 2:7.

and exaltation even beyond the grave.[51]

The Apostle Peter summed up God's plan of progression in these words, "I ascend to the deep."[52] In other words, to become like the Gods necessarily requires that we must descend to a fallen world in order to learn by experience, to prove and to be proven, and to sacrifice. We began this life in sacrifice when we laid down any light and progression that we had previously attained to come down to this world.[53] Each time the choice is made to descend, any progress we have previously made is put at risk. By the very nature of choosing to descend, we put ourselves in peril.

And so, we find ourselves here, in this lone and dreary world, cast out of God's presence, walking through the valley of the shadow of death, at the bottom of Jacob's ladder.[54] Some individuals elect to take advantage of the opportunities which this world affords us to further their ascent toward God by obtaining more light and knowledge, others elect to rebel and descend farther away from it. The reality is that each of us has the capacity to do great good as well as the capacity to do great harm. While speaking with the Old Testament prophet, Enoch, God lamented, "And among all the workmanship of my hands, there has not been so great wickedness as among your

---

[51] Ehat and Cook (1980), *The Word of Joseph Smith*, p. 350, Salt Lake City: Bookcraft, Inc.

[52] See T&C 171—The Testimony of St. John 12:14. The deeper, or more "fallen" the world we descend to, the greater our ascension can be.

[53] Nibley, Hugh W. (1973) Treasures in the Heavens: Some Early Christian Insights into the Organizing of Worlds. *Dialogue: A Journal of Mormon Thought*, Vol. 8, No. 3/4 (Autumn/ Winter 1973), p. 79.

[54] See OC Genesis 9:20, Psalm 23:1, T&C—A Glossary of Gospel Terms, "Jacob's Ladder" and "Powers of Heaven."

brethren."[55] Understanding our great peril, and likewise understanding our great potential, can help us make sense of our eternal journey and give us hope to press forward and persevere knowing each day is a new day to begin again. We can be better today than we were yesterday.

As unique individuals, our lives are designed and woven in Wisdom, giving each of us the distinct experiences we need to face the lessons we have come down to this earth to learn.[56] No one else can learn our lessons for us. We are taught as much as we are willing to accept and act upon, "Going line upon line, precept upon precept, here a little and there a little, giving us consolation by holding forth that which is to come and confirming our hope."[57] As we act upon the light and truth we receive that is when belief begins to grow into faith. Faith, however, is not the end. As we act on our beliefs and continue to develop our faith, eventually it can become possible for us to obtain knowledge. Knowledge is what those who are redeemed from the fall through an encounter with the Lord acquire.

Our eternal journey is meant, little by little, to move us from belief to faith to knowledge, or from grace to grace. Every day is a new day wherein we get to choose for ourselves whether we will turn away from the lies and darkness of this world to embrace light and truth. The Lord does not leave us to wander to and fro alone. From the beginning of this creation, He has sent messengers from His presence to guide us. This world is such that pretenders have and always will exist among

---

[55] OC Genesis 4:17.
[56] See OC Proverbs 1:39, "Wisdom has built her house, she has hewn out her seven pillars."
[57] T&C 151:17.

us, giving us the opportunity to learn how to discern truth from error. It is up to each of us to choose between true messengers and false ones. Joseph Smith counseled,

> A man is saved no faster than he gets knowledge, for if he does not get knowledge, he will be brought into captivity by some evil power in the other world, as evil spirits will have more knowledge, and consequently more power than many men who are on the earth. Hence it needs revelation to assist us, and give us knowledge of the things of God.[58]

Once we have found true messengers, we then must not only listen to what they say, we must also act upon their teachings. As we learn to discern between truth and error, giving heed and diligence to the words of true messengers, our belief will grow into faith and our faith into a knowledge that saves.

It is God's work to bring to pass the immortality and eternal life of mankind.[59] Throughout our eternal journey, let us remember to have the kind of hope which is "far greater, more profound, more strongly felt, more firmly based than just

---

[58] See Hyrum Smith, April 8, 1844, Conference address, "Minutes and Discourses, 6–9 April 1844, as Reported by Thomas Bullock," p. 30-32, The Joseph Smith Papers, accessed February 12, 2002; https://www.josephsmithpapers.org/paper-summary/minutes-and-discourses-6-9-april-1844-as-reported-by-thomas-bullock/33. *After giving this talk and publishing my book on Hyrm Smith, *Hyrum Smith A Prophet Unsung*, the Joseph Smith Papers removed this document. The only place an original can be seen as of today is the LDS Church History Library, Historian's Office general Church minutes, 1839-1877; 1839-1845; Nauvoo, Illinois, 1844 April 6-9; Church History Library, https://catalog.churchofjesuschrist.org/assets/daa151c4-7bae-49d0-8cef-d281a70f1d32/0/0?lang=eng (accessed: January 2, 2024).
[59] See OC Genesis 1:7.

expectancy from vague desire."[60] Each of us should strive to have the type of hope that involves unshakable faith or confidence and comes from "many revelations and the spirit of prophecy and is based upon [witnesses of the Risen Lord] coming from beyond the veil to confirm the expectations."[61] This is the hope that causes a faith which is unshakable, "powerful, controlling, and causes a thing to come to pass because it is now your right to receive the thing promised because God has conferred that right upon you."[62] This hope is more than a wish, as it requires us to secure a promise from God, waiting for the time this promise will be fulfilled.[63] One who has received a promise from God has hope that the promise will eventually be fulfilled, "as sure as God's word cannot fail, one's hope is secure in Him."[64]

This is the hope that Ether was referring to when he cried unto the people from the morning even until the going down of the sun, exhorting them to believe in God unto repentance, crying out:

> [B]y faith all things are fulfilled. Wherefore, whoso believeth in God might with surety hope for a better world, yea, even a place at the right hand of God, which hope cometh of faith, maketh an anchor to the souls of men, which would make them sure and steadfast, always abounding in good works, being led to glorify God.[65]

---

[60] See T&C—A Glossary of Gospel Terms, "Hope."
[61] Ibid.
[62] Ibid.
[63] Ibid.
[64] Ibid.
[65] NC—BoM Ether 5:1.

With God,
all things are possible.
By faith,
all things are accomplished.

 The End

APPENDIX

My husband and I were asked to speak at a conference in Lexington, Kentucky in March 2022. He chose to speak on how we can see and understand God's pattern of calling true messengers in the storms that rage around us. Specifically, he focused on the concept of discerning true prophets from false ones. His talk is an excellent work and worth sharing on a broader scope. I asked him if I could include it in this book on gospel topics. I hope it enlightens your mind and lifts your eyes. I owe a deep debt of gratitude to Vern. He has patiently, gently, and persuasively led me along out of darkness and into ever increasing light. I consider myself his greatest convert to the gospel of Jesus Christ.

Whitney

Seeing God's Pattern in the Storm[1]

Vernon R. Horning
©March 2022

I grew up in a good LDS home in Minnesota where I was taught the gospel as restored through Joseph Smith. While serving as a missionary in California, I developed a love for the scriptures and grew closer to the Lord. I saw that the Heavens had been opened again with revelations restoring truth to the

---

[1] This talk was originally given at the Hear and Trust the Lord in the Storm conference held on March 25-27, 2022, in Lexington, Kentucky.

earth. I came to believe that Jesus Christ was doing a great work among the children of men and felt how blessed I was to be a member of His church. I loved teaching His gospel and sought earnestly to bring souls unto Him. I loved the Plan of Salvation and wanted to build His kingdom on the earth. I looked forward to hearing and studying the teachings and words of the Lord's living apostles and prophets. I was committed to not only keeping the commandments but also the counsel of these men. I was truly converted.

After my mission, I attended Brigham Young University in Provo, Utah to continue my education and with the hope that I would also find a wife. On my second day there I bumped into a beautiful girl named Whitney who also shared my love of the Lord. 33 years later we are still in love and have raised 4 wonderful children by striving to live the gospel in our home. Whitney and I loved the Church and found great wisdom and joy living its teachings and serving others. We saw blessings from living it. I was content and at peace and believed that we were living the fullness of the Gospel.

Several years ago, while serving as bishop for my LDS ward, I had a life changing set of events which started off innocent enough. I had been informed that my friend Keith was teaching false doctrine, he "was saying that Mormons were Gentiles." I went to his home and asked if he could help me understand what this was about. For the next three hours, he opened the scriptures and persuaded me to see that we are the Gentiles of the Book of Mormon. It was exhilarating to read from the scriptures and learn something new. I could not deny what the scriptures taught and the spirit of the Lord that was with us. Keith told me that he and another man from our ward,

Alan, got together on Sunday evenings to share insights from the scriptures. A few Sundays later I joined them and had more wonderful experiences, learning from the scriptures, principles and truths I had never seen before or only understood at a surface level. I was like a kid in a candy store. I was waking up to what the Fulness of the Gospel was really about: progressing from unbelief to belief, then to exercise faith, which must ultimately lead to knowledge. I discovered that the scriptures actually mean what they say- the purpose of this life is to come to know the Lord, literally. What I was learning through the scriptures and having the more mysterious passages opened up to me, made me determined to be a better follower of Christ.

I want to share some of the truths I have learned from my journey. I am still a student and by no means have a perfect understanding.

We are living in a day when the storms of this faithless world are growing. We see "iniquity shall abound, the love of many shall wax cold. But he that remains steadfast and is not overcome, the same shall be saved" (Matt 11:30 RE).

The definitions of things matter. When you change or limit a word, you corrupt its meaning. My further education required me to understand what the Lord meant by His words. I want to start today with the word **"Prophet."**

Prophets are men that are called by God's own voice. Once they have entered into His presence, He may call them to declare His message to the world. This is the pattern found throughout all of scripture. A prophet is one who has the spirit of prophecy.

Joseph Smith taught:

If any person should ask me if I were a prophet, I should not deny it, as that would give me the lie; for, according to John, the testimony of Jesus is the spirit of prophecy; therefore if I profess to be a witness or a teacher, and have not the spirit of prophecy, which is the testimony of Jesus, I must be a false witness; but if I be a true teacher and witness, I must possess the spirit of prophecy, and that constitutes a prophet; and any man who says he is a teacher or a preacher of righteousness, and denies the spirit of prophecy, is a liar, and the truth is not in him; and by this key, false teachers and imposters may be detected (DHC: 5:215-216). No man can be a minister of Jesus Christ except he has the testimony of Jesus; and this is the spirit of prophecy. Whenever salvation has been administered, it has been by testimony (DHC 3:389-390).

We see that the spirit of prophecy is the testimony of Jesus. Some churches teach that this is merely the testimony believers have about Him, but it is so much more. We need to get this right because one must have the testimony of Jesus to be a Prophet.

Joseph defined it when he said, "To obtain a promise from God for myself that I shall have Eternal life, that is the more sure word of prophycy . . . to be sealed with the Holy Spirit of promise, that is the testimony of Jesus" (JS, May 21, 1843, James Burgess Notebook).

The testimony of Jesus comes directly from Him. Prophets have a knowledge of God because they receive it by revelation and have received this heavenly gift. Receiving the Testimony of Jesus as taught by Joseph is more than having the Spirit of the Lord enter into your heart or merely believing in

Jesus. Imposters either overstate their connection to God, lie about it, or do not understand that it is essential for a prophetic call. They claim the honorary title of "Prophet" that comes with their church calling and the people who sustain them in it. They believe keys are bestowed to them by men and can be perpetually distributed throughout time. This is exemplified in the Catholic Church which believes that the papal keys have been passed from the apostle Peter down to the current Pope.

The next natural question we should ask is how do we obtain Eternal life? According to Joseph you must be sealed with the "Holy Spirit of Promise," which is the "more sure word of prophecy."

What do these phrases mean?

The Holy Spirit of Promise is the sealing word of God that must be confirmed or ratified by Him for it to become eternal. Joseph explained we can know this, if we receive an actual knowledge that the course of life which we pursue is according to the will of God. This is essentially necessary to enable us to have that confidence in God, without which no person can obtain Eternal life (LoF 6:2 RE). If one does not obtain this knowledge of a promise sealed by God, through His word — sealed by the Holy Spirit of Promise — then it will not last into the eternities. The only thing that will endure is that which is established by God and must come in mortality (Glossary of Gospel Terms: Holy Spirit of Promise).

The Lord taught the relationship of the Holy Spirit of Promise is connected to the Second Comforter when He said,

> Wherefore, I now send upon you another Comforter, even upon you my friends, that it may abide in your

hearts, even the Holy Spirit of Promise, which other Comforter is the same that I promised unto my disciples, as is recorded in the Testimony of John. This Comforter is the promise which I give unto you of eternal life, even the glory of the Celestial Kingdom, which glory is that of the church of the Firstborn (T&C 86:1 RE).

The Lord referenced the apostle John's testimony which states,

If you love me, keep my commandments. And I will ask the Father, and he shall give you another Comforter, that he may be with you for ever — even the Spirit of Truth, whom the world cannot receive because it sees him not, neither knows him. But you know him, for he dwells with you, and shall be in you. I will not leave you comfortless. I will come to you (John 9:8).

There has been some confusion among teachers of religion regarding the Holy Spirit of Promise and the second comforter. Some claim that it is just another name for the Holy Ghost which they associate with feelings of emotion. However, Joseph Smith, who was intimately connected with these things, clearly taught,

The other Comforter spoken of is a subject of great interest and perhaps understood by few of this generation. After a person has faith in Christ, repents of his sins, and is baptized for the remission of his sins, and receives the Holy Ghost (by the laying on of hands) which is the first Comforter, then let him continue to humble himself before God, hungering and thirsting after Righteousness, and living by every word of God, and the Lord will soon say unto him, Son thou shalt be exalted. When the

Lord has thoroughly proved him, and finds that the man is determined to serve him at all hazards, then the man will find his calling and Election made sure, then it will be his privilege to receive the other Comforter which the Lord hath promised the Saints, as is recorded in the testimony of St. John. . . . Now what is this other Comforter? It is no more nor less than the Lord Jesus Christ himself, and this is the sum and substance of the whole matter, that when any man obtains this last Comforter he will have the personage of Jesus Christ to attend him or appear unto him from time to time (TPJS, pp. 150-151).

The question that seems to be asked the most often by those who are taught this principle is "If this is essential for salvation, does it really need to happen to us while in the flesh?"

The Lord answered this way,

Truly I say unto you, it is not everyone that says unto me, Lord, Lord, that shall enter into the kingdom of Heaven, but he that does the will of my Father who is in Heaven. For the day soon comes that men shall come before me to judgment, to be judged according to their works. And many will say to me in that day, Lord, Lord, have we not prophesied in your name, and in your name have cast out devils, and in your name done many wonderful works? And then will I say unto them, You never knew me. Depart from me, you that work iniquity (Matt 7:21).

It should be noted that Joseph, in his inspired translation of the Bible, changed this statement from "I never knew you" to "you never knew me."

Jesus Christ taught that Eternal life comes by knowing

God, "And this is life eternal: that they might know you, the only true God, and Jesus Christ whom you have sent" (John 9:19 RE). This is why "A man is saved no faster than he gets knowledge" (HC 4:588).

Another question that is often asked is, "If this is correct and necessary, why do church leaders not teach it?"

The Lord's statement "you never knew me" was proceeded by His warning:

> [B]eware of false prophets that come to you in sheep's clothing, but inwardly they are ravening wolves. You shall know them by their fruits. . . . A good tree cannot bring forth evil fruit, neither a corrupt tree bring forth good fruit. Every tree that brings not forth good fruit is hewn down and cast into the fire. Wherefore, by their fruits you shall know them (Matt 3:46).

One of the tests in this life is to receive true messengers and reject false prophets.

There are several ways you can look at what the Lord means by "fruit." One way is to test a messenger's words. Do they "enlarge my soul and enlighten my understanding and are the words delicious to me?" (Alma 16:28 RE). Does your mind begin to expand? If so, "it is because it is light; and whatsoever is light is good, because it is discernible; therefore, ye must know that it is good" (Alma 16:29 RE). To figure out who is a true or false prophet requires that we be seekers of truth. "[B]lessed are all they that do hunger and thirst after righteousness, for they shall be filled with the holy ghost" (Matt 3:9 RE).

Coming to know correct doctrine requires study and

prayer until you have become familiar with the voice of God. For "the things of God are of deep import, and time, and experience, and careful and ponderous and solemn thoughts can only find them out" (T&C 138:18 RE). This requires a sacrifice of time, putting off the distractions of this world to read, listen, ponder, discuss, and pray. This stuff matters.

There are some natural obstacles to overcome to increase in light and truth. One is false traditions. "And that wicked one comes and takes away light and truth, through disobedience, from the children of men, and because of the tradition of their fathers" (T&C 93:11 RE). Usually when a true messenger is sent from the Lord to a people, what they have to say challenges their current cultural and religious beliefs and practices. False traditions fool man into thinking he's obedient when he is actually misled.

Joseph had this problem with the people in his day. "This generation," he said, "it has been like splitting hemlock knots with a corn dodger for a wedge, and a pumpkin for a beetle. Even the Saints are slow to understand. I have tried for a number of years to get the minds of the saints prepared to receive the things of God, but we frequently see some of them, after suffering all they have for the work of God will fly to pieces like glass, as soon as anything comes that is contrary to their traditions" (HC, 6:184–85).

Fear can stop or limit spiritual progression. It is the opposite of faith and hope. Those controlled by their fears will view Christ's way as a stumbling block and an offense. We ought to fear God more than we fear anything else including the influences of man. We ought to love God and fear Him because it's our relationship to Him, and Him alone, that matters.

Do the words of the messenger or prophet match scripture or contradict what the Lord has already revealed? Because God is the same yesterday, today, and for ever, and in him there is no variableness neither shadow of changing (Moroni 4:7 RE), true prophets will never contradict another true prophet, past, present or future. Their words are the Lords. This is what is meant when the Lord said "And though the heaven and the earth pass away, my word shall not pass away, but shall all be fulfilled, whether by my own voice or by the voice of my servants it is the same (T&C 54:7 RE).

False prophets are ones who believe that by the nature of their calling anything they say is the same as if God said it. They use this scripture to justify that anything they teach must be believed and obeyed. Their arrogance creates confusion and causes their members to all go "astray, save it be a few who are the humble followers of Christ. Nevertheless, they are led, that in many instances they do err because they are taught by the precepts of men" (2 Nephi 12:2 RE).

True Prophets restore eternal ordinances and correct corruptions to the gospel. They teach that in the beginning, Adam was set to watch over the ordinances, to reveal them from heaven to man, or to send angels to reveal them. Ordinances have been the same and are to remain the same forever and ever (JS, History of the Church, vol.4, p. 208.)

The real test of a messenger's fruit is demonstrated by the end result: what does the teaching accomplish? Do their words produce good fruit? If a messenger's fruit is good, then it has the potential to redeem the soul of the hearer by bringing them back into the presence of Christ. Jesus condemned the religious leaders in His day because they "shut up the kingdom of Heaven against men; for you neither go in yourselves, neither suffer them that are entering to go in" (Matt 10:27 RE). Jesus was pointing out that the church leaders were not true messengers because they had not entered in at the correct gate, did not know God, and were incapable of leading others to life and salvation. The Lord said of them "They are blind leaders of the blind, and if the blind lead the blind, both shall fall into the ditch" (Matt 8:9 RE).

This is why it matters whether or not leaders of religion actually have real experience with heaven and point others to the same source.

We must have correct, scriptural knowledge and use it in order to discern the fruit of anyone claiming to be a prophet.

The creation story begins with Adam and Eve standing in the presence of the Lord. After transgressing a law of God, they found themselves cast out of paradise.

> Adam called upon the name of the Lord, and Eve also, his wife; and they heard the voice of the Lord from the way toward the Garden of Eden speaking unto them, and they saw him not, for they were shut out from his presence. And he gave unto them commandment that they should worship the Lord their God and should offer the firstlings of their flocks for an offering unto the Lord. And Adam was obedient unto the commandments of the Lord.
>
> And after many days, an angel of the Lord appeared unto Adam, saying, Why do you offer sacrifices unto the Lord? And Adam said unto him, I know not but the Lord commanded me. And then the angel spoke,

saying, This thing is a similitude of the sacrifice of the Only Begotten of the Father who is full of grace and truth. Wherefore, you shall do all that you do in the name of the Son. And you shall repent and call upon God in the name of the Son for ever more.

And in that day the holy ghost fell upon Adam, which bore record of the Father and the Son, saying, I am the Only Begotten of the Father from the beginning, henceforth and for ever, that as you have fallen, you may be redeemed — and all mankind, even as many as choose. And in that day, Adam blessed God, and was filled, and began to prophesy concerning all the families of the earth, saying, Blessed be the name of God, for because of my transgression my eyes are opened, and in this life I shall have joy, and again, in my flesh I shall see God (Gen 3:2-4 RE).

Through the story of Adam and Eve we learn what the gospel is: it is to be obedient to the commandments of God, sacrifice, receive the ministry of angels, do everything in the name of the Son, repent and pray, and by so doing receive the holy ghost. Adam was promised that if he chose, he could see God in the flesh or in other words, be redeemed from the fall. This was at least fulfilled at Adam-Ondi-Ahman but most likely earlier than this event.

Adam was the first prophet. All true messengers follow the pattern established by the Lord through him and have likewise been redeemed and brought back into the presence of God.

The Brother of Jared followed this pattern. While praying to the Lord on the top of a mountain,

[T]he Lord shewed himself unto him and said, Because thou knowest these things, ye are redeemed from the Fall. Therefore, ye are brought back into my presence; therefore I shew myself unto you. Behold, I am he who was prepared from the foundation of the world to redeem my people. Behold, I am Jesus Christ. I am the Father and the Son. In me shall all mankind have life; and that eternally, even they who shall believe on my name. And they shall become my sons and my daughters (Ether 1:13 RE).

As a fallen and unredeemed people, we, like sheep, have gone astray — we have turned everyone to his own way (Isaiah 19:2 RE). Without divine intervention we would be lost. Apostasy is a falling away from God's revealed truth. There seems to be two forms apostasy takes. One is a deliberate casting away of the Gospel. To reject the way of a disciple of Christ and give completely to the natural man. To mock God and see no value in the holy scriptures.

The other form of apostasy can be harder to see. It affects the very religious. It always involves small changes that introduce incorrect teachings or modify ordinances. It includes innovations by men which grow and evolve over time. Changes may also be subtractive. Truths are lost, ordinances are reduced and simplified and finally discarded.

No one in apostasy ever thinks that they are in it. This is the great deception. They trust their leaders are inspired and led by God and incapable of leading their church astray. This is one reason the Lord warns us about being at ease in Zion. Self-assurance as to salvation by an institution allows the "Devil to cheateth their souls and leadeth them away carefully down to hell . . . He whispereth in their ears until he grasps them with his awful chains, from whence there is no deliverance" (2

Nephi 12:4 RE).

Those who are in apostasy reject, mock, or even become angry with true messengers. This was the reaction to Lehi after he delivered the Lord's warnings to the very religious people in Jerusalem:

> And it came to pass that the Jews did mock him because of the things which he testified of them, for he truly testified of their wickedness and their abominations. And he testified that the things which he saw and heard, and also the things which he read in the book, manifested plainly of the coming of a messiah and also the redemption of the world. And when the Jews heard these things they were angry with him (1 Nephi 1:5 RE).

Joseph Smith taught:

> The world always mistook false prophets for true ones, and those that were sent of God, they considered to be false prophets, and hence they killed, stoned, punished and imprisoned the true prophets, and these had to hide themselves 'in deserts and dens, and caves of the earth,' and though the most honorable men of the earth, they banished them from their society as vagabonds, whilst they cherished, honored and supported knaves, vagabonds, hypocrites, impostors, and the basest of men (TPJS, p. 206).

For people in apostasy to repent, it first has to be noticed, acknowledged and exposed. One sign of apostasy is that the heavens have gone quiet. I'm not talking about endless manifestos, declarations, proclamations, and policy changes, but real words from the Lord.

False prophets justify this silence by saying, "We don't

need much revelation. We need to pay more attention to the revelation we've already received" (Gordon B. Hinckley, *San Francisco Chronicle*, Sunday Interview, April 13, 1997). Or they say "The great reservoir of revelation for our dispensation—meaning the things that we need to know to govern our conduct in order to gain an eternal life—these things have already been given. And there will not be great added reservoirs of substantive revelation that will come before the Second Coming" (Bruce R. McConkie, 1979).

This is like saying that the reason for the almost 1800 years of God's lack of speaking to the earth during the great apostasy was because He had said everything He needed to say in the Bible.

In truth, the only reason the heavens go quiet is because the world lacks men who have the faith to become true prophets. Moroni said it best,

> For it is by faith that miracles are wrought, and it is by faith that angels appear and minister unto men. Wherefore, if these things have ceased, woe be unto the children of men, for it is because of unbelief, and all is vain. For no man can be saved, according to the words of Christ, save they shall have faith in his name. Wherefore, if these things have ceased, then has faith ceased also, and awful is the state of man, for they are as though there had been no redemption made (Moroni 7:7).

Damned leaders and damned people believe that keeping the creeds of their religion is all that is necessary in order to be saved. No man has ever been saved without a direct connection with heaven. All who have received salvation and the words of eternal life have followed the same pattern. The *Lectures on Faith* teach that,

> It is in vain for persons to fancy to themselves that they are heirs with those, or can be heirs with them, who have offered their all in sacrifice, and by this means obtained faith in God and favor with him so as to obtain eternal life, unless they in like manner offer unto him the same sacrifice, and through that offering obtain the knowledge that they are accepted of him (LoF 6:8 RE).

The truth is out there, but it was never meant to be easy to find. There is a reason the Lord said "Repent therefore and enter in at the strait gate; for wide is the gate and broad is the way that leads to destruction, and many there are who go in there at, because strait is the gate and narrow the way that leads unto life, and few there are that find it" (Matt 3:45 RE).

This is why the Lord sends prophets to people in apostasy. Prophets have a heavenly perspective and have been instructed how to call out and correct errors. Almost everyone believes that they have the full truth and do not need anything new. In order for a people to receive truth they must cast off a hard heart. They must give place for the word and at least consider that what they are hearing could be true. It would be better to be humble and open to the possibility that God wants to say more. Alma explained it this way,

> And therefore, he that will harden his heart, the same receiveth the lesser portion of the word. And he that will not harden his heart, to him is given the greater portion of the word, until it is given unto him to know the mysteries of God, until they know them in full. And they that will harden their hearts, to them is given

the lesser portion of the word until they know nothing concerning his mysteries; and then they are taken captive by the Devil and led by his will down to destruction. Now this is what is meant by the chains of hell (Alma 9:3 RE).

True prophets have the following in common:

1. They are called of God, which means they speak with Him face to face, and receive a message from Him which must be delivered exactly as it was given to him.

2. They call humanity to repentance and restore corrupted or lost ordinances.

3. They are overwhelmingly rejected, especially by their own people.

4. They teach the Lord's commandments in order that true faith which leads to salvation may be exercised.

5. They teach the correct character, perfections, and attributes of God.

6. They declare to the people that faith isn't the goal but the means to receive knowledge from heaven for themselves as well as personal revelation that they are approved of God. In other words, a true prophet wants to work themselves out of a job. Moses declared, "Would to God that all the Lord's people were prophets, and that the Lord would put his spirit upon them" (Numbers 7:19 RE).

When the Heavens begin a work with the children of men, they work through prophets. When Moses reestablished the direct connection between God and His chosen people, the Lord explained to them, "Hear now my words: If there is a prophet among you, I the Lord will make myself known unto him in a vision and will speak unto him in a dream" (Numbers

7:22 RE).

The night before he was killed, the Prophet Joseph Smith had a dream. I believe it contains insights concerning what was to become of the restoration. Joseph recounted,

> I was back in Kirtland, Ohio, and thought I would take a walk out by myself and view my old farm, which I found grown up with weeds and brambles, and altogether bearing evidence of neglect and want of culture. I went into the barn, which I found without floor or doors, with the weather boarding off, and was altogether in keeping with the farm.
>
> While I viewed the desolation around me, and was contemplating how it might be recovered from the curse upon it, there came rushing into the barn a company of furious men who commenced to pick a quarrel with me.
>
> The leader of the party ordered me to leave the barn and the farm, stating it was none of mine and that I must give up all hope of ever possessing it.
>
> I told him the farm was given me, and although I had not had any use of it for some time back, still, I had not sold it, and according to righteous principles it belonged to me.
>
> He then grew furious and began to rail upon me, and threaten me, and said it never did belong to me.
>
> I then told him that I did not think it worth contending about, that I had no desire to live upon it in its present state, and if he thought he had a better right, I would not quarrel with him about it, but leave. But my assurance that I would not trouble him at present did not seem to satisfy him, as he seemed determined to quarrel with me, and threatened me with destruction of my body.
>
> While he was thus engaged, pouring out his bitter

words upon me, a rabble rushed in and nearly filled the barn, drew out their knives, and began to quarrel among themselves for the premises, and for a moment forgot me, at which time I took the opportunity to walk out of the barn, about up to my ankles in mud.

When I was a little distance from the barn, I heard them screeching and screaming in a very distressed manner, as it appeared they had engaged in a general fight with their knives. While they were thus engaged, the dream or vision ended (T&C 153 RE).

Joseph did not leave an explanation regarding the dream's purpose or interpretation. But we do know that he viewed dreams as an important source of revelation as evidenced by the fact that he recorded his dreams and used them in his public sermons.

I believe we can see this as a foreseeing dream, rich in symbolism.

This is what I see in Joseph's dream:

The farm was symbolic of the Restoration as viewed in a future time. Its neglected state and disrepair suggest a condition of apostasy. Following the deaths of Joseph and Hyrum the church was left without a prophet. Even Emma understood this when she said, "without Joseph Smith there is no church" (William Clayton Journal, August of 1844). What had once been a living church, directed by the voice of God, rapidly fractured into many off shoots. Some were run by men who sincerely wanted to preserve what Joseph had started. But it did not take long for new doctrines to be added, ordinances to be corrupted, truths and principles to be lost.

While Joseph was viewing his desolate farm, the leader

of the angry men who ordered Joseph to leave rationalized his ownership of the church. This symbolizes those men who took leadership following the death of Joseph and believed that all they needed was authority from the members who sustained them rather than from God. Of the men who competed to replace Joseph, I know of none who claimed to have been caught up to heaven or where the Lord declared their prophetic call.

Nephi saw these false leaders in our day and said, "And they say unto the people, Hearken unto us and hear ye our precept, for behold, there is no God [or at least not speaking revelation] today, for the Lord and the Redeemer hath done his work, and he hath given his power unto men. Behold, hearken ye unto my precept" (2 Nephi 12: 1 RE).

The rabble that rushed into the barn were the competing parties of the various churches coming from Joseph's restoration. When the usurpers turned on each other and began fighting among themselves, they fulfilled these words,

> Woe unto them that turn aside the just for a thing of naught, and revile against that which is good and say that it is of no worth, for the day shall come that the Lord God will speedily visit the inhabitants of the earth. And in that day that they are fully ripe in iniquity, they shall perish. But behold, if the inhabitants of the earth shall repent of their wickedness and abominations, they shall not be destroyed, saith the Lord of Hosts. But behold, that great and abominable church, the whore of all the earth, must tumble to the earth, and great must be the fall thereof. For the kingdom of the Devil must shake,

and they which belong to it must needs be stirred up unto repentance, or the Devil will grasp them with his everlasting chains and they be stirred up to anger and perish. For behold, at that day shall he rage in the hearts of the children of men and stir them up to anger against that which is good (2 Nephi 12: 4 RE).

The role of Joseph Smith in relation to the restoration was to continue even after his death. The Lord declared, "Behold, verily I say unto you, I have reserved those things which I have entrusted unto you, my servant Joseph, for a wise purpose in me, and it shall be made known unto future generations. But this generation shall have my word through you" (JSH 12:1).

When the Gospel is conferred on mankind through a dispensation head like Joseph Smith or Moses, then those who live in that Dispensation are obligated to honor the ordinances laid down through that servant. This means no one that follows has the keys or rights to change anything. Especially in the absence of revelation. The Lord declared "The earth also is defiled under the inhabitants thereof, because they have transgressed the laws, changed the ordinance, broken the everlasting covenant" (Isaiah 9:3 RE). This is what happened to the farm progressing from condemnation, then to rejection, and finally to complete termination of all priestly claim.

Joseph would not want anything to do with any of the Restoration churches in their current state:

For it shall come to pass in that day that the churches which are built up, and not unto the Lord, when the one shall say unto the other, Behold, I, I am the Lord's — and the other shall say, I, I am the Lord's — and thus shall everyone say that hath built up churches and not unto the Lord. And they shall contend one with another, and their priests shall contend one with another, and they shall teach with their learning, and deny the holy ghost which giveth utterance (2 Nephi 12:1 RE).

The Lord knew that what He began through Joseph would become a leaky ruin of a farm. In order for the Lord to fulfill all of his words, we need to preserve the restoration.

The Lord has promised,

[B]lessed are those who hearken unto my precepts and lend an ear unto my counsel for they shall learn wisdom. For unto him that receiveth I will give more; and from them that shall say, We have enough — shall be taken away even that which they have. Cursed is he that putteth his trust in man, or maketh flesh his arm, or shall hearken unto the precepts of men, save their precepts shall be given by the power of the holy ghost. Woe be unto the gentiles, saith the Lord God of Hosts, for notwithstanding I shall lengthen out mine arm unto them from day to day, they will deny me. Nevertheless, I will be merciful unto them, saith the Lord God, if they will repent and come unto me, for mine arm is lengthened out all the day long, saith the Lord God of Hosts.

But behold, there shall be many at that day when I shall proceed to do a marvelous work among them, that I may remember my covenants which I have made unto the children of men, that I may set my hand again the second time to recover my people which are of the house of Israel, and also that I may remember the promises which I have made unto thee, Nephi, and also unto thy father, that I would remember your seed, and that the words of your seed should proceed forth out of my mouth unto your seed. And my words shall hiss forth unto the ends of the earth for a standard unto my people which are of the house of Israel (2 Nephi 12:6-8 RE).

The Lord has been merciful to the gentiles. The restoration of the Gospel from 1820 through 1844 was the Lord's first attempt to use the gentiles to reclaim the house of Israel. The rejection and murder of the Smith brothers required three and four generations to pass before the Lord would begin His work again. The required time has passed, and as prophesied, the Lord has now set His hand again the second time to recover His people which are of the house of Israel (2 Nephi 12:8 RE).

About the Author

Whitney N. Horning is a wife, mother and grandmother living in the beautiful state of Utah. She spent her early years running wild in the mountains, learning how to work hard on her grandpa's farm, and digging countless rocks out of her parents' yard. She graduated Cum Laude from Brigham Young University with a Bachelor of Arts degree from the college of Family, Home, and Social Science. BYU holds a special place in her heart—it is where she met her best friend and sweetheart. Nothing brings her more joy than being a mother and grandmother.

Made in the USA
Thornton, CO
12/25/24 11:21:16

f185a89c-fd94-4307-901b-6cd90bcca79fR01